GREAT EXPECTATIONS

AN ADAPTED CLASSIC

GREAT
EXPECTATIONS

CHARLES DICKENS

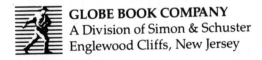

GLOBE BOOK COMPANY
A Division of Simon & Schuster
Englewood Cliffs, New Jersey

Cover design: Marek Antoniak
Cover illustration: Copie Rodriguez
Text illustrations: Ted Burwell

ISBN: 0-83590-258-7

Printed in the United States of America.
10   9

Globe Book Company
A Division of Simon & Schuster
Englewood Cliffs, New Jersey

ABOUT THE AUTHOR

In 1861 Charles Dickens earned both fame and success when he published *Great Expectations* in his magazine—a chapter at a time. The novel, along with *David Copperfield, A Tale of Two Cities,* and *Oliver Twist,* made him popular in England and in The United States.

His description of poverty captures some of the unhappiness he felt when his father went to debtor's prison. Dickens, at the age of 12, was forced to work in a shoe-polish factory. Early in his adulthood he chose newspaper work and eventually fiction-writing as an escape from the humiliation of his family's humble lifestyle.

Born the second child of a family of eight, Charles Dickens fathered ten children. His works reveal his concern for young people who struggle to overcome evil and suffering. His most famous young heroes, Oliver Twist, Tiny Tim, and Pip, denote the deep understanding and sympathy that make Charles Dickens one of the great novelists of all times.

PREFACE

Great Expectations is the story of a young man who learns the value of friends. Charles Dickens sets his novel in England during the mid-1800s when the Industrial Revolution was making far-reaching changes in people's lives. Pip, the main character, undergoes a rapid alteration from orphaned country boy to young London gentleman.

Pip leaves his hated job as a blacksmith after he is promised a mysterious fortune. As he makes friends in his new London home, he forgets the love he has enjoyed in his boyhood from Joe, the blacksmith, and Biddy, his teacher. Although he desires to be a gentleman, he becomes a self-centered snob.

When Pip learns the truth about his sudden rise to money, he also learns much about himself. He suffers heartache and loss before he is able to construct a sensible, pleasing life for himself.

Dickens fills this exciting story with memorable, unusual characters—a pair of convicts, a cheated bride who refused to remove her wedding dress, a law secretary who lives in a make-believe castle, and a tough lawyer with a tender heart. *Great Expectations* binds the reader firmly to the adventures of Pip, until the last twist of the story is unraveled.

Mary Ellen Snodgrass

former English Department Chairperson,
Hickory High School, Hickory, North Carolina

ADAPTER'S NOTE

This adaptation follows the original as faithfully as possible. No characters have been omitted, and no events important to the plot have been left out. To make the story briefer and more understandable to the reader, lengthy descriptions have been shortened, the vocabulary has been simplified, and colloquial or out-of-date expressions have been omitted.

CHARACTERS IN THE STORY

PIP, the hero, whose great expectations are realized

JOE, Pip's brother-in-law, the blacksmith, who is more of a hero than Pip

MRS. JOE, Pip's sister, who never spares the rod

BIDDY, a sweet and kind village girl

MISS HAVISHAM, who has let misfortune poison her mind and her life

ESTELLA, who is as cold as she is beautiful

Two convicts:

    ABEL MAGWITCH, also known as Provis

    COMPEYSON, a villain

Villagers among whom Pip grows up:

    UNCLE PUMBLECHOOK, who sells seeds

    MR. HUBBLE, the wheelwright

    MRS. HUBBLE, his wife

    ORLICK, whose business is making trouble

    MR. WOPSLE, a clerk turned actor

    TRABB, the tailor

    TRABB'S BOY

Greedy relatives of Miss Havisham:

    CAMILLA, GEORGIANA, COUSIN RAYMOND, SARAH POCKET

Pip's London friends and acquaintances:

    MATTHEW POCKET, Pip's tutor

    HERBERT POCKET, Pip's best friend

    BENTLEY DRUMMLE and **STARTOP**, Pip's fellow students at Mr. Pocket's

MR. JAGGERS, a lawyer who specializes in criminal cases

MOLLY, Mr. Jaggers's housekeeper

MR. WEMMICK, Mr. Jaggers's assistant

AGED PARENT, Wemmick's father

MISS SKIFFINS, a friend of the Wemmicks

CLARA, Herbert's girlfriend

MR. BARLEY, Clara's father

CONTENTS

Part 1

Presenting Pip, Who Has
Great Hopes for the Future

Part 2

Showing What His
Great Expectations Did for Pip

Part 3

Proving That What a Man Is, Not What He Has, Is All Important

Part 1

Presenting Pip, Who Has Great Hopes for the Future

1 *An Unwelcome Stranger*

My father's family name was Pirrip and my given name Philip, but when I was a little boy, all I could manage to call myself was Pip. By that I became known to everyone. I never saw either my father or my mother. But I used to visit their graves and read the names on their tombstones.

We, my sister Mrs. Joe Gargery, her husband, who was a blacksmith, and I lived in a marshy part of the country down by the river* within twenty miles of the sea. The first event I can remember most plainly happened on a cold afternoon toward evening when I was about seven. I was visiting the churchyard, as I often did, and reading on their tombstones the names of my father and mother, Philip and Georgiana Pirrip. In the distance were flat fields with cattle grazing on them, and beyond them the low dark line of the river. A cold wind was blowing in from the sea. For some reason I felt afraid and began to cry.

"Stop your noise," cried a terrible voice, as a man jumped up from among the graves. "Keep still, you little devil, or I'll cut your throat!"

He was a dreadful-looking man dressed in gray with a huge chain on his leg. He had an old rag tied around his head and worn-out shoes on his feet. He looked as though

* The river Thames in England.

he had been soaked in water and smothered in mud and torn by briars. He limped and shivered and glared and growled. His teeth chattered as he seized me by the chin.

"O! Don't cut my throat, sir," I begged in terror. "Please don't do it, sir."

"Tell me your name!" said the man. "Quick!"

"Pip, sir."

"Once more," said the man, staring at me. "Speak up!"

"Pip, sir."

"Show me where you live," said the man. "Point out the place."

I pointed to our village, a mile or so away from the churchyard where we were. The man, after looking at me for a moment, turned me upside down and emptied my pockets. There was nothing in them but a piece of bread. Then he turned me right side up and made me sit on a tombstone while he ate the bread eagerly.

"You young dog," he said, licking his lips, "what fat cheeks you have."

Maybe they were fat, though at that time I was small for my age and not very strong.

"Darn me if I couldn't eat them," said the man, with a shake of his head, "and if I haven't half a mind to do it."

I expressed the hope that he wouldn't and held tighter to the tombstone on which he had put me, partly to keep myself on it and partly to keep myself from crying.

"Now lookee here!" said the man. "Where's your mother?"

"There, sir," said I.

He jumped, started to run away, and then looked back over his shoulder.

"There, sir," I explained timidly, pointing to a tombstone. "Georgiana. That's my mother."

"Oh!" said he, coming back. "And that is your father beside your mother?"

"Yes, sir," said I. "Him too."

"Ha!" he said, then asked, "Who do you live with—supposin' you're allowed to live, which I haven't yet made up my mind about?"

"My sister, sir—Mrs. Joe Gargery—wife of Joe Gargery, the blacksmith, sir."

"Blacksmith, eh?" said he. And he looked down at his leg. After gazing at it and me several times he came closer to my tombstone. He took me by both arms and bent me back as far as he could hold me. His eyes looked down into mine and mine looked helplessly up into his.

"Now lookee here," he said. "The question is whether you're to be let live. You know what a file is?"

"Yes, sir."

"And you know what wittles* are?"

"Yes, sir."

After each question he bent me over a little more, so as to give me a greater feeling of helplessness and danger.

"You get me a file." He bent me over a little more. "And you get me wittles. You bring 'em both to me. Or I'll have your heart and liver out."

I was dreadfully frightened and so dizzy that I clung to him with both hands and said, "If you would please let me stand up, sir, perhaps I could listen better."

He dipped me back once more and then held me by the arms in an upright position on the top of the tombstone as he went on.

"You bring me tomorrow morning early that file and them wittles. You bring them to that old sea wall over there. You do that and don't you dare say a word to anyone about your having seen a person such as me. Then I'll let you live. You fail in any way, no matter how small, and your heart and your liver shall be tore out, roasted, and ate. Now, I ain't alone, as you may think I am. There's a young man

* Wittles: food.

hid with me. Compared to him, I'm an angel. That young man hears the words I speak. A boy couldn't hide himself from that young man. A boy might lock his door, might be tucked in bed, but that young man could creep in to him and tear him open. I am keeping that young man from hurting you at the present moment with great difficulty. Now what do you say?"

I said that I would get him the file, and I would get him whatever food I could, and I would come to him at the sea wall early in the morning.

"Say Lord strike you dead if you don't," said the man.

I said so and he took me down.

"Now," he went on, "you remember what you've undertook, and you remember that young man, and you get home."

"Goo—good night, sir," I managed to say.

He limped toward the low church wall, shivering with

the cold. He climbed over it like a man whose legs were numb and stiff and then turned around to look for me. When I saw him turning, I ran toward home as fast as I could. But soon I looked over my shoulder and saw him going on toward the river. The marshes were just a long black line then, and the river another line, not so broad and not so black. On the edge of the river I could just barely see the only two black things in all the scene that seemed to be standing upright. One of them was the beacon by which the sailors steered their boats up the river. The other was a gibbet* with some chains hanging on it which had once held a pirate. The man was limping toward this latter as if he were the pirate himself come to life and going back to hook himself up again. It gave me a terrible scare when I thought so. I looked all around for the horrible young man and could see no sign of him. But now I was frightened again and ran home without stopping.

* Gibbet: a structure on which people were hanged.

2 *True to His Word*

My sister, Mrs. Joe Gargery, was more than twenty years older than I. She had a hard and heavy hand, which she used on both her husband and me. She was not a good-looking woman. I had the idea that she must have used her heavy hand to make Joe Gargery marry her. Joe was a mild, good-natured, easy-going fellow. He had blonde curly hair and pale blue eyes. My sister, Mrs. Joe, had black hair and eyes and very red skin. She was tall and bony and almost always wore an apron tied behind her with two loops. It had a bib in front that was stuck full of pins and needles. She was always blaming Joe because she had to wear it so much.

Joe's forge was next to our house. When I got home from the churchyard that day, the forge was closed and Joe was sitting alone in the kitchen. "Mrs. Joe's been out a dozen times looking for you, Pip," he told me. "And she's out now."

"Is she?"

"Yes, Pip," said Joe: "and what's worse, she's got Tickler with her."

Tickler was a stick, worn smooth from hitting my tickled body.

"She sat down," said Joe, "and she got up and made a grab at Tickler and then ran out. That's what she did."

"Has she been gone long, Joe?"

"Well," said Joe, glancing at the clock, "she's been out this last spell about five minutes, Pip. Get behind the door."

I took the advice. My sister, throwing the door wide open and finding something behind it, pulled me out and put Tickler to good use. Then she threw me at Joe, who sat me down beside him in the chimney corner. Here he could protect me from further blows.

"Where have you been, you young monkey?" said Mrs. Joe, stamping her foot.

"I have only been to the churchyard," said I, crying and rubbing myself.

"Churchyard!" repeated my sister. "If it warn't for me you'd have been to the churchyard long ago and stayed there. Who brought you up?"

"You did," said I.

"And why did I do it, I should like to know?"

"I don't know," I sobbed.

"I don't!" said my sister. "I'd never do it again! I know that I've never had this apron of mine off since you were born. It's bad enough to be a blacksmith's wife without being your mother too."

My thoughts wandered away from that question. For the man out on the marshes with the chain on his leg, the mysterious young man he had talked about, the file, the food, and the dreadful promise I had made filled my mind.

As my sister started to work on the tea things, Joe and I sat silent as we always did when she was in that mood. She had her own way of cutting our bread and butter for us. First, with her left hand she held the loaf hard against her bib. Sometimes it got a pin or a needle in it, which we had to pull out of our mouths later on. Next, she took some butter—not too much—on a knife and spread it on the loaf, using both sides of the knife with a slapping sound. Then she sawed a thick round piece off the loaf, giving half of it to Joe and half to me.

This time, though I was hungry, I dared not eat my slice. I felt that I must save something for my dreadful new friend and the still more dreadful young man. I knew how strict Mrs. Joe's housekeeping was. I might find nothing in the pantry. Therefore, I decided to put my hunk of bread and butter down the leg of my pants.

I found this dreadfully hard to do. And Joe, without meaning to, made things ever harder. Usually at night he and I played a little game with our bread and butter. We would hold up the slices as we bit into them, showing each other what big bites we could take. Tonight Joe several times invited me, by showing me his rapidly disappearing slice, to play our game as usual. Each time he found me with my slice untouched. At last, deciding that I would have to do what I had planned, I took advantage of a moment when he looked away from me and got the bread and butter down my leg.

Joe meanwhile seemed to be worried by my lack of appetite and took a thoughtful bite out of his slice, which he didn't seem to enjoy. He was about to take another bite when he looked at me and saw that my bread and butter was gone. He stared at me so hard that he attracted my sister's attention.

"What's the matter now?" said she as she put down her cup.

"I say, you know," muttered Joe, shaking his head at me with disapproval. "Pip, old chap, you'll hurt yourself. It'll stick somewhere. You can't have chewed it, Pip."

"What's the matter now?" repeated my sister more sharply than before.

"If you can cough any of it up, Pip, I'd recommend it to you," said Joe. "Manners is manners, but still your health is your health."

By this time my sister was so angry she pounced on Joe and knocked his head against the wall behind him.

"Now perhaps you'll tell what's the matter," said she, out of breath.

Joe looked at her in a helpless way. "You know, Pip," he said seriously and speaking as if we two were alone, "you and me is always friends, and I'd be the last to tell on you. But such a great big bite as that!"

"Been swallowing his food whole, has he?" cried my sister. She made a dive at me and pulled me up by the hair, saying these awful words, "You come along and be dosed."

In those days tar water was considered a fine medicine, and Mrs. Joe always kept a supply of it on hand. Sometimes she gave me so much I felt as though I were going around smelling like a new fence. On this evening she gave me a pint of the mixture. Joe got off with half a pint. My sister thought he needed some because he had had a shock over my manners.

All through that evening my conscience troubled me because I was going to rob Mrs. Joe. It never occurred to me that I was going to rob Joe, for I never thought of anything as being his. Added to my feeling of guilt was the trouble I had keeping one hand on my bread and butter as I sat down or when I was ordered around the kitchen. Then, as the marsh winds made the fire glow, I thought I heard outside the voice of the man with the chain on his leg calling out that he couldn't starve until tomorrow but must be fed now. At other times I thought, What if the young man who wanted my heart and liver should come for them tonight? My hair stood on end with terror.

It was Christmas Eve, and I had to stir the pudding for next day. I tried it with the load on my leg sliding down to my ankle. Finally I slipped away to my attic bedroom and hid the bread and butter there. Then I went on with my stirring.

When my task was finished and it was time for me to go to bed, I heard the sound of guns in the distance.

"Ah!" said Joe. "There goes another convict."

"What does that mean, Joe?" said I.

Mrs. Joe said crossly, "Escaped! Escaped!"

"What's a convict?" I asked.

"There was one convict escaped last night," said Joe, "after sunset. And they fired a warning about him. And now I guess they are giving warning of another one. Seems like another one escaped."

"Who's firing?" said I.

"Drat that boy," interrupted my sister. "What a questioner he is is. Ask no questions and you'll be told no lies."

"Mrs. Joe," I kept on, "I should like to know—if you wouldn't much mind—where the firing comes from?"

"Lord bless the boy!" exclaimed my sister. "From the prison ship across the marshes.

"I wonder who's put into prison ships and why they're put there?" I went on with my questions, feeling that I had to find out.

It was too much for Mrs. Joe, who got up at once. "I tell you what, young fellow," she said. "I didn't bring you up to annoy people to death. People are put on prison ships because they murder and rob and do all sorts of bad things. Now get to bed."

I was never allowed a candle to light me to bed. As I went upstairs in the dark, I felt that I was on my own way to the prison ships. I had begun by asking questions. And I was going to rob Mrs. Joe. I was in terrible fear of the young man who wanted my heart and liver. I was in fear of the man with the iron chain.

When I slept at all that night I imagined myself drifting down the river in a strong spring tide to the prison ship. A pirate called out to me when I passed the gibbet that I had better come to shore and be hanged at once. I was afraid to sleep much for I knew that at first sign of dawn I must rob the pantry.

As soon as I could see a gray light outdoors, I got up and went downstairs. Every board on the way squeaked, calling after me, "Stop, thief!" and, "Get up, Mrs. Joe!" In the pantry I had no chance to pick and choose, for I had no time to spare. Because of the holiday season I found more food than usual there. I stole some bread, some cheese, about half a jar of mince meat, some brandy from a stone jug (some of which I poured into a bottle, filling up the jug with a brown liquid on one of the shelves), a meat bone with very little meat on it, and a beautiful round pork pie. I nearly went away without the pie, but when I climbed up to see what had been put away so carefully in a covered dish in the corner, I found it. I took it, hoping that my sister did not plan to have it eaten until later and so it would not be missed right away.

A door in the kitchen led to Joe's forge. I unlocked and unbolted it and got a file from among Joe's tools. Then I locked the door as I had found it and ran for the misty marshes.

It was a very damp morning. I had seen the mist on the outside of my little window as though a goblin had been crying there all night and using the window for a handkerchief. The mist was heavier yet when I got out on the marshes, so that instead of my running at everything, everything seemed to run at me. All this time I was getting to the river. I knew my way pretty straight to the sea wall, for I had often been there with Joe. However, confused by the mist, I found myself too far to the right and had to go back along the river bank. I had just crossed a ditch and scrambled up a slope when I saw the man sitting in front of me. His back was toward me. He had his arms folded and seemed to be asleep.

I thought he would be glad if I came to him with his breakfast in that unexpected manner. So I went up softly and touched him on the shoulder. He jumped up at once,

and it was not the same man but another man! Yet he was dressed in coarse gray too and had a big chain on his leg. He too was lame and hoarse and cold and everything that the other man had been. But he hadn't the same face and had a flat felt hat on. All this I saw in a minute, for I had only a minute to see it in. He swore and struck out at me. It was a weak blow that missed me and almost made him stumble. Then he ran into the mist and I lost him.

"It's the young man," I thought as my heart beat fast.

Soon after that I was at the sea wall, and there was the right man. He was limping back and forth as if he had never stopped all night, waiting for me. He was awfully cold. His eyes looked hungry too. When I handed him the file and he laid it down on the grass, it occurred to me that he would have tried to eat it if he hadn't seen my bundle. He did not turn me upside down to get what I had. This time he left me right side up while I opened the bottle and emptied my pockets.

"What's in the bottle, boy?" said he.

"Brandy," said I.

He was already cramming the mincemeat down his throat, but he stopped to take some of the liquor. He shivered all the time so hard he could hardly keep the neck of the bottle between his lips without biting it off.

"I think you have the chills," said I. "It's bad for you lying out here on the marshes."

"I'll eat my breakfast before they're the death of me," said he.

He was gobbling mincemeat, bread, cheese, and pork pie all at once. At the same time he was staring at the mist all around us. Often he even stopped eating to listen. Some sound that he might have imagined now gave him a fright. "You're not fooling me?" he asked. "You brought no one with you?"

"No, sir! No!"

"And giv' no one directions to follow you?"

"No!"

"Well," said he, "I believe you. You'd be a bad young dog indeed if you could help to catch a poor man hunted nearly to death as I am." He ran his ragged rough sleeve over his eyes.

Feeling sorry for him, I was brave enough to say, "I'm glad you enjoy it."

"Thankee, my boy, I do."

I had often watched a large dog of ours eating his food. This man ate his in the same way. He took sharp sudden bites, just like the dog. He snapped up every mouthful too soon and too fast. He looked sideways while he ate as if he thought there was danger in every direction of someone's coming to take the pie away.

"I am afraid you won't leave any of it for him," I said after a silence. "There is no more where that came from."

"Leave any for him? Who's *him*?" said my friend, stopping his crunching of the pie crust.

"The young man that you spoke of that was hid with you."

"Oh," he replied with a laugh. "Him? Yes, yes! He don't want no wittles."

"I thought he looked as if he did," said I.

The man stopped eating and stared at me with the greatest surprise.

"Looked? When?"

"Just now."

"Where?"

"Over there," said I, pointing. "I found him there asleep and thought it was you. Dressed like you, you know, only with a hat," I explained, "and—and—with the same reason for wanting to borrow a file. Didn't you hear the cannon last night?"

"Then there *was* firing," he said to himself.

"I wonder why you didn't hear it," I replied. "We heard it at home. That's further away and we were indoors besides."

"Why, see now!" said he. "When a man's alone on these marshes with a light head and a light stomach, when he's dying of cold and hunger, he hears guns firing and voices calling all night. He sees the soldiers with their red coats lighted up by torches closing in around him. He hears his number called. He hears the orders, 'Seize him, men,' and is laid hands on—even when there's nothing there." He had said all of this as though he had forgotten my being there. "But this man," he went on, coming back to me, "did you notice anything about him?"

"He had a badly bruised face," said I.

"Not here?" asked the man, striking his left cheek with the palm of his hand.

"Yes, there!"

"Where is he? Show me the way he went. I'll pull him down like a bloodhound. Curse this chain on my leg. Give me the file, boy."

I showed him where to find the man. He sat down on the wet grass, filing at the chain like a madman. He paid no more attention to me. His leg was bloody, but he paid no attention to that either. I was very much afraid of him again now that he was in this fierce hurry, and I was afraid of staying away from home any longer. I told him I must go, but he did not notice me. So I thought the best thing to do was to slip off. The last I saw of him his head was bent over his knees and he was working hard at the chain, swearing at it and his leg. The last I heard of him when I stopped in the mist to listen was his file still going.

3 *An Anxious Christmas*

I fully expected to find a policeman in the kitchen waiting to arrest me when I got home. But no one had even discovered the robbery as yet. Mrs. Joe was busy getting the house ready for the day's Christmas celebration. Joe was sitting on the kitchen doorstep out of her way.

"And where have you been?" was Mrs. Joe's Christmas greeting when I appeared.

I said I had been down to hear the carols. "Ah, well," remarked Mrs. Joe, "you might have done worse." No question of that, I thought.

"Perhaps if I warn't a blacksmith's wife and—what's more—a slave with her apron never off, I should have been to hear the carols," said Mrs. Joe.

Joe, who had dared to follow me into the kitchen, looked at her timidly. Then when she wasn't noticing him, he secretly crossed two fingers and held them up to me. It was our sign that Mrs. Joe was in a bad mood. She was that way so much that Joe and I would often, for weeks at a time, need to go around with our fingers crossed.

We were to have a fine dinner—a leg of pork with vegetables and a pair of roast chickens. A big mince pie had been made yesterday morning. That was why the mince-meat I had taken hadn't been missed. The pudding had already been put on to boil. We had practically no breakfast because of these big preparations. "I ain't," said Mrs. Joe, "going to have no preparing a meal and washing dishes now, with what's before me, I promise you."

So she handed out slices of bread to us, and we had our milk standing up. While we ate she put clean white curtains up and put a new flowered cover on the mantel over the fireplace. She even opened the little parlor across the hall and took off the covers on the furniture there. That room was never opened at any other time. Mrs. Joe was a very clean housekeeper, though to us dirt would have been less of a bother than her cleanliness.

Because my sister had so much work to do, Joe and I were going to church in her place. In his working clothes Joe was a strongly built, typical blacksmith. In his holiday attire he looked more like a well-off scarecrow than anything else. Nothing that he wore then fitted him or seemed to belong to him. This time, when the church bells rang, he came out looking miserable in his Sunday suit. As for me, whenever my sister took me to the tailor, she always had my clothes made much too tight for me.

Everybody who saw Joe and me going to church must have felt very sorry for us. Yet my suffering over my appearance was mild compared to my terror over what I had done that morning. Whenever Mrs. Joe had gone into the pantry, fear and remorse had gripped me. I wondered whether the church I was about to enter would be powerful enough to protect me from the terrible young man. I wondered whether I ought to confess to the minister what I had done.

Our guests at dinner that day were to be Mr. Wopsle, the clerk at church, Mr. Hubble, the wheelwright,* and

* Wheelwright: a man who kept the wheels on farmers' carts in good repair.

Mrs. Hubble, and Joe's Uncle Pumblechook, a wealthy business man from the nearest town, who drove his own carriage. The dinner hour was half past one. When Joe and I got home, we found the table set, Mrs. Joe dressed, and the dinner ready. And still no word was said about the robbery. Soon after our arrival, the company came. Mr. Wopsle came first. He had a large nose, a shining bald head, and a deep voice, which he was very proud of. In fact, he believed that he would have made a fine minister if he had had the chance. Next came the Hubbles, and last of all Uncle Pumblechook.

"Mrs. Joe," said Uncle Pumblechook—a large slow man with a mouth like a fish, dull, staring eyes, and light hair standing straight up—"I have brought you the season's good wishes. I have brought you a bottle of sherry wine. And I have brought you a bottle of port wine."

Every Christmas day he said exactly the same thing and brought the same present. Every Christmas day Mrs. Joe replied, "Oh, Uncle Pumblechook, this is very kind!"

We ate on these occasions in the kitchen and then went into the parlor for nuts and oranges and apples. My sister was always very lively and I was never allowed to speak. I was given the worst portions of chicken and pork. All of that I wouldn't have minded if they had let me alone. But they didn't.

It began the moment we sat down to dinner. Mr. Wopsle asked the blessing as though he were on the stage, ending with the hope that we would all be truly grateful. At that my sister stared at me and said in a low voice, "Do you hear that? Be grateful."

"Especially," said Mr. Pumblechook, "be grateful to those as brought you up."

Mrs. Hubble shook her head sadly and asked, "Why is it that the young are never grateful?"

Joe was even less important in his home when there was company. But he always helped and comforted me in any way he could. Today, there being plenty of gravy, he now spooned about half a pint into my plate.

"Think," said Mr. Pumblechook, turning to me at this point, "what you've got to be grateful for. Here you are, enjoying yourself with those older and better than you. Here you are, living in luxury."

Joe offered me more gravy, which I was afraid to take.

"He is a great deal of trouble to you, ma'am," said Mrs. Hubble, sorry for my sister.

"Trouble?" repeated my sister, "trouble?" Then she began to tell about all the sicknesses I had had and all the sleep she had lost taking care of me. She told about all the high places I had fallen from and all the low places I had fallen into. She told about all the times I had hurt myself and all the times she had wished me dead.

I felt awful listening to her, but those awful feelings were as nothing to what I suffered when I heard my sister ask, "Have a little brandy, Uncle?"

Oh, heavens! It had come at last. He would find that it was weak and I would be lost. I held tight to the leg of the table with both hands and awaited my fate. My sister came back with the stone bottle and poured Uncle Pumblechook's brandy out. He took it up, looked at it, put it down. I couldn't keep my eyes off him. All this time Mrs. Joe and Joe were clearing the table for the pie and pudding. As I watched him he sprang to his feet, turned around several times, and then rushed outdoors. Through the window we could see him coughing and spitting and making terrible faces.

I held on tight while Mrs. Joe and Joe ran out to him. I felt sure that I had murdered him. It was a relief when he finally came back, sank into his chair, and gasped, "Tar!"

I had filled up the bottle from the tar-water jug! I knew from experience that he would feel worse later. I held on to the table so hard I moved it forward.

"Tar!" cried my sister. "How could tar ever get into the brandy?"

Uncle Pumblechook acted as though nothing much had happened and asked for hot gin and water. My sister, who had begun to scare me by looking thoughtful, had to be busy getting gin, hot water, and sugar ready. I was saved, for the moment at least. Gradually I became calm enough to stop holding on the table and began eating my pudding. Mr. Pumblechook ate his pudding. Everyone ate the pudding. Mr. Pumblechook began to smile under the warm influence of the gin and water. I began to think I would live through the day, when my sister said to Joe, "Bring in clean plates."

I hung on to the table leg again, knowing what was coming. This time I would surely be done for.

"You must taste, to finish up with," said my sister, "a wonderful present from Uncle Pumblechook."

"Must they?" I thought to myself. "They'd better not have any hopes of it."

"It's a pie," said my sister; "a tasty pork pie."

Uncle Pumblechook, feeling pleased with himself said, "Well, Mrs. Joe, we'll do our best by it. Let us have a piece of this pie."

My sister went out to get it. I heard her steps going to the pantry. I saw Mr. Pumblechook holding up his knife. I saw Mr. Wopsle looking hungry. I heard Mr. Hubble remark that "A bit of pork pie would be better than anything," and I heard Joe say, "You shall have some, Pip." I have never been certain as to whether I actually yelled in terror or just thought I did. I felt that I could stand no more and that I must run away. I let go the leg of the table and ran for my life.

But I got no farther than the door, for there I ran head first into a group of soldiers, one of whom held out a pair of handcuffs to me, saying, "Here, look out. Come on!"

4 *The Convict's Revenge*

At the sight of a line of soldiers pounding the ends of their muskets on our doorstep, the dinner party got up from the table in confusion. Mrs. Joe, coming back into the kitchen empty-handed, stopped short and stared in the midst of saying, "Gracious goodness, what's happened to the pie?"

The sergeant and I were in the kitchen by then. It was he who had spoken to me. Now he looked at everyone, holding out the handcuffs in his right hand and keeping his left one on my shoulder.

"Excuse me, ladies and gentlemen," he said. "I am chasing someone, and I want the blacksmith."

"And what do you want with him?" answered my sister. She was angry at anyone's wanting Joe.

"Missis," answered the sergeant, "I have a little job to be done. You see, blacksmith," he went on, after picking Joe out as the one he wanted, "we have had an accident with these handcuffs. The lock of one of them doesn't work. We need them at once. Will you take a look at them?"

Joe did so and said he would have to light the fire in his forge for the job. It would take two hours.

"Will it?" said the sergeant. "Then go at it at once. It's all in His Majesty's service. And if my men can help in any way, they'll make themselves useful." With that they all came into the kitchen, piled their guns in the corner, and stood around.

All these things I watched in an agony of fear. But as time went on and the matter of the pie was at least postponed, I began to relax a little.

"Would you give me the time?" the sergeant asked Mr. Pumblechook.

"It's just half past two."

"That's not so bad," said the sergeant, thinking a bit. "Even if I have to wait here two hours, it will do. How far is it to the marshes? Not over a mile, I should think?"

"Just a mile," said Mrs. Joe.

"That'll do. We begin to close in on them about dusk or a little before that. That'll do."

"Convicts, sergeant?" asked Mr. Wopsle in a matter-of-fact way.

"Ay," replied the sergeant, "two of them. They're pretty well known to be still out on the marshes. They won't try to get away from them before dusk. Has anyone here seen anything of them?"

Everyone except me said no with confidence. Nobody thought of me.

"Well," said the sergeant, "they'll find themselves trapped in a circle sooner than they count on. Now, blacksmith, go ahead."

Joe had taken off his coat and had put on his leather apron and gone into the forge. Soon a fire was roaring, and he began to hammer away as we all looked on with much interest. Even my sister unbent a little. She poured a pitcher of beer for the soldiers and invited the sergeant to have a glass of brandy. But Mr. Pumblechook said sharply, "Give him wine. There's no tar in that." The sergeant said he preferred his drink without tar and so would take the wine. When it was given to him, he drank to the king's health and smacked his lips.

I watched them gathered around the forge in such good humor. They were so looking forward to the "villains" being taken. I couldn't help but think of my friend out on the marshes. As the blaze of the fire rose and sank and the red hot sparks dropped and died, the late afternoon outside almost seemed to me to have grown pale because of what was to happen to him. I pitied him with all my heart.

At last Joe's job was done and the clanking of irons stopped. As he put on his coat, he got up courage to suggest that some of us go down with the soldiers to watch the chase. Mr. Pumblechook and Mr. Hubble declined, but Mr. Wopsle said he would go if Joe would. Joe asked and got permission from my sister to take me along. I'm sure she would never have consented if she hadn't been so curious to know all about what happened. As it was, she merely said, "If you bring the boy back with his head blown to bits by a musket, don't expect me to put it together again."

The sergeant said goodby to the ladies and to Mr. Pumblechook. His men picked up their muskets and we started off. Mr. Wopsle and I received strict orders to keep to the rear and to say no word until we reached the marshes. When we were all out in the chilly air and were steadily moving forward, I whispered to Joe, "I hope we won't find them, Joe." And Joe whispered to me, "I'd give a shilling if they'd run away, Pip."

No one from the village joined us because the weather was cold and stormy, darkness was coming on, and everyone was celebrating the Christmas holiday. A few faces looked out the windows at us, but no one came out. We passed the signpost on the road and headed straight for the churchyard. Then the sergeant signaled me to stop while two or three of his men scattered among the graves and searched the church porch. They found nothing, however, so we went on toward the open marshes. Bitter cold sleet struck us as we walked eastward, and Joe took me on his back.

Soon we were at the dismal place where the others could never have guessed that I had been eight or nine hours ago and had seen both men hiding. For the first time with great dread I began to wonder whether my convict would think that it was I who had brought the soldiers there. He had asked me if I would deceive him. He had said that I would be a fierce young dog if I joined the hunt for him. Would he think that I had gone back on him?

It was no use asking myself this question now. There I was on Joe's back, and there were the soldiers in front of us spreading out in a wide line. We were following the route I had taken first, but now there was no mist. In the low red glow of sunset the gibbet, the sea wall, and the opposite shore of the river were plain to see, though all of a dark gray color.

With my heart thumping against Joe's broad shoulder, I looked for any sign of the convicts. I could see none. I could hear none. Once I got an awful scare when I thought I heard the file still going, but it was only a sheep bell. Except for sheep and cattle grazing around us there was no break in the black stillness of the marshes.

The soldiers were moving on in the direction of the sea wall, when all of a sudden we stopped. For there had reached us on the wings of the wind and rain a long shout. It was repeated. It was at a distance toward the east, but it was loud and clear. In fact, there seemed to be two or more shouts raised together, if one could judge from the confused sound.

The sergeant and his nearest men were speaking under their breath when Joe and I came up. Then the sergeant ordered that the sound should not be answered but that his men should head toward it in double quick time. So we started to the right, and we pounded away so fast that I had to hold on tight to keep my seat. Down banks and up banks and over gates we raced. As we came nearer to the shouting, we could tell that it was made by more than one voice. Sometimes it seemed to stop altogether, and then the soldiers ran faster than ever and we after them. After a while we were so close that we could hear one voice calling "Murder!" and another voice, "Convicts! Runaways! Guard! This way for the runaway convicts!" Then both voices would seem to be muffled in a struggle and then would break out again. By this time the soldiers were running like deer and Joe after them.

The sergeant ran in first when we had reached the voices. His men were right behind him with their guns cocked and leveled.

"Here are both men!" panted the sergeant, struggling at the bottom of a ditch. "Surrender, you two beasts! Separate!"

Water was splashing and mud was flying when some more men went down into the ditch to help the sergeant drag out my convict and the other one. Both were bleeding and panting and cursing. Of course, I knew them at once.

"Be sure you see," said my convict, wiping blood from his face with his ragged sleeve and shaking torn hair from his fingers, "that I took him. I gave him up to you. Be sure of that."

"It's not much to notice," said the sergeant. "It'll do you very little good, my man, since you're in the same fix yourself. Handcuffs there!"

"I don't expect it to do me any good. I don't want it to do me more good than it does now," said my convict. "I took him. He knows it. That's enough for me."

The other convict was a terrible sight. In addition to the bruise on his left cheek, which I had noticed before, his whole face seemed to be bruised and torn. He could not even get his breath to speak until they were both handcuffed. He had to lean on a soldier to keep himself from falling.

"Take notice, guard, he tried to murder me," were his first words.

"Tried to murder him?" said my convict scornfully. "I could have done it if I'd tried. I took him and giv' him up. That's what I done. I not only prevented him from getting off the marshes, but I dragged him this far on his back to the prison ship. He's a gentleman, this villain. It wasn't worth my while to murder him when I could do worse and drag him back."

The other one still gasped, "He tried—to—murder me."

"Lookee here," said my convict to the sergeant. "Single-handed I got clear of the prison ship; I made a dash and I done it. I could have got clear of this place. See my leg? There's no chain on it. But I discovered that he was here. Let *him* go free? Let *him* gain by the way I found to get away? Let *him* make use of me as he has done before? No, no, no. If I had died at the bottom of the ditch there, I'd have held him until you came."

The other man, who was evidently scared to death of my convict, replied, "He tried to murder me. I would have been a dead man if you hadn't come."

"He lies," said the other man fiercely. "He was born a liar and he'll die a liar. Look at his face. I dare him to look me in the eye. Can't you see what a villain he is? Do you see his wandering eyes? That's how he looked when we were tried together. He never looked at me." With those words he would have rushed at his enemy if the soldiers hadn't prevented him.

"Enough of this," said the sergeant. "Light those torches."

Then my convict looked around for the first time and saw me. I gazed at him eagerly and moved my hands and shook my head. I had been waiting for him to see me so that I could try to let him know his capture wasn't my fault. Now I wasn't at all sure he knew what I meant, for he gave me a look I did not understand, and it was all over with in a minute. But ever afterward I remembered his look. If he had looked at me for an hour or for a day, I could not have remembered him more plainly.

The soldiers now had torches lighted. Before we left, four of them standing in a circle fired twice into the air. Soon we saw other torches lighted at some distance behind us and others on the opposite bank of the river. "All right," said the sergeant. "March!"

We had not gone far when three cannon were fired ahead of us with a sound that seemed to burst something inside my ear. "You are expected on board," said the sergeant to my convict. "They know you are coming."

I had hold of Joe's hand now, and Joe carried one of the torches. Mr. Wopsle had wanted to go back, but Joe was resolved to stay until the finish, so we went on with the party. When I looked around I could see other lights coming after us. Everything else was black. We could not go fast because of our prisoners' lameness. And they were so tired that two or three times we had to halt while they rested.

After an hour or so of traveling we came to a landing place and a guard of soldiers. The sergeant made some kind of report, and then the other convict was sent with his guard to go on board first.

My convict never looked at me except that once. Before he was sent out to the ship, however, he turned to the sergeant and remarked, "I wish to say something about this escape. It may prevent some person's being under suspicion because of me. A man can't starve. At least I can't. I took some wittles over yonder at the village."

"You mean stole," said the sergeant.

"And I'll tell you where from. From the blacksmith's."

"Well, Pip," said Joe staring at me.

"It was some odds and ends of wittles, and a dram of liquor, and a pie."

"Have you happened to miss a pie, blacksmith?"

"My wife did at the very moment when you came in. Remember, Pip?"

"So," said my convict, looking at Joe and without the least glance at me. "You're the blacksmith, are you? Then I'm sorry to say I've eat your pie."

"God knows you're welcome to it," replied Joe. "We don't know what you've done, but we wouldn't have you starve to death for it. Would we, Pip?"

Something seemed to catch in the man's throat, and he turned his back. The boat was ready for him then, and we saw him put into it. By the light of the torches we saw the dark outline of the convict ship lying a little way from the shore. We saw the boat go up to it, and we saw him taken up the side and disappear. Then the torches were flung hissing into the water and went out as if it were all over with him.

I was sleepy before we were far away from the prison ship. Joe took me on his back again and carried me home. By the time we had arrived I was fast asleep. All I heard before my sister grabbed me and assisted me to bed was Joe telling everyone about the convict's confession, and everyone trying to decide how he could have got into the house to steal the pie.

When I got up in the morning I had decided never to confess my part in the whole affair. I did not feel any need to do so now that I had escaped all consequences of what I had done. My conscience did not trouble me because of Mrs. Joe's loss. But I loved Joe. I had an idea that I ought to tell him the whole truth, especially when I saw him looking for his file. Yet I didn't do so because I was afraid he might think bad of me if I did, and I would lose the confidence and love of my companion and friend. In a very short time no one in our house even mentioned what had happened that Christmas night.

5 The Difficulties of Learning

At the time when I stood in the churchyard reading the family tombstones, I knew just enough to be able to spell out the names on them. When I was old enough, I was to be apprenticed* to Joe. Until then, so that I wouldn't find life too easy, I helped around the forge and ran errands for the neighbors. The money I earned was dropped into a box on the kitchen shelf. I could never believe, however, that I would be allowed to use it for myself.

Mr. Wopsle's great aunt kept an evening school in the village. She was a sickly old woman who needed money badly. Every evening from six to seven, children came to be taught by her for two pence** a week. She lived in a small cottage and Mr. Wopsle had the room upstairs. We students used to hear him reading aloud in an excited way and bumping on the ceiling. He was supposed to examine us four times a year. What he did on those occasions, though, was to recite us long speeches from Shakespeare instead of finding out what we knew.

Mr. Wopsle's great-aunt, besides keeping school, had in the same room a little general store. She never knew what she had for sale or what the price of anything was.

*Apprenticed: to be placed legally with a craftsman to learn a trade.
**Pence: a unit of British money equal to about two U.S. cents when this story was written.

Her granddaughter Biddy, a girl of the same age as I was, ran the store. She was an orphan like me. Through the week her hair always needed brushing, her hands always needed washing, and her shoes mending. On Sundays she went to church very much dressed up, however.

More with Biddy's help than that of my teacher, I struggled through the alphabet. After that I went on to numbers. Eventually I began to learn to read and write and do some figuring, all in the simplest way possible. One night about a year after my experience with the convict, I was sitting in the chimney corner. With an alphabet ready to refer to, I mangaged in an hour to write this letter to Joe:

"mI deEr JO i opE U r krWitE wELL i opE i shAL Soon B able tO teacH U Jo theN We shALL B so glad And wHen i am pRenTiced* to you What Fun wE wiLl have. Pip."

Since Joe was sitting right beside me and we were alone, there was no real reason for me to write to him, though when I handed him the letter he was very much impressed by my learning. "I say, Pip, old chap!" he cried, opening his blue eyes wide, "what a scholar you are, ain't you?"

"I should like to be," said I, looking at the letter as he held it up. I feared that the writing ran up hill a bit.

"Why, here's a J," said Joe, "and an O as clear as anything. Here's a J and an O, Pip, and a J-O, Joe."

I had never heard Joe read anything more than this aloud. In church when I held our prayer book upside down he didn't seem even to notice it. Now I wanted to find out whether I ought to begin at the very beginning to teach him. "Read the rest of it, Joe," I said.

"The rest, Pip?"said Joe, looking at my letter carefully. "Why, there's J's and there's O's and a J-O, Pip."

*Prenticed: Pip means apprenticed, that is, legally bound to Joe to learn the trade of blacksmith.

I leaned over him and read him the whole letter.

"You *are* a scholar, Pip," said he when I finished.

"How do you spell Gargery, Joe?" I asked him, trying to show off a bit.

"I don't spell it," said Joe.

"But supposing you did?"

"It can't be supposed," said Joe. "Though I'm fond of reading, too. Give me a good book or a good newspaper and sit me down before a good fire. I ask nothing better. When you come to a J and a O and a J-O, you think how interesting reading is!"

I figured out from this that Joe's education had just started. "Didn't you ever go to school when you were as little as me?" I asked him.

"No, Pip.

"Why didn't you, Joe?"

"Well, Pip," said Joe, poking at the fire, "I'll tell you. My father liked to drink, and when he had had too much, he would beat my mother and me most unmerciful. So my mother and me we ran away from my father several times. Then my mother she'd go out to work. Then she'd say, 'Joe,' she'd say, 'now please God you shall have some schooling child.' And she'd send me to school. But my father couldn't stand being without us. So he'd come and make a row at whatever house we lived in. Then the people we were staying with would give us up to him. Then he'd take us home and beat us some more. Which you see, Pip, was a drawback to my learning."

"Certainly! Poor Joe!"

"Though mind you, Pip," said Joe, "my father was good in his heart. Don't you see?"

I didn't see, but I didn't say so.

"Well," he continued, "somebody must keep the pot boiling. So my father didn't object to my going to work. So I went to work at my present job. I worked hard, I assure

you, Pip. In time I was able to keep him, which I did until he died of a fit. My mother was in poor health and quite broken up when he died. It warn't long before she followed him, poor soul, and had her share of peace at last."

Joe's blue eyes turned a little watery. "It were lonesome then," he went on, "living alone, and I got acquainted with your sister. Now, Pip—" here he looked firmly at me as if he knew I was not going to agree with him—"your sister is a fine figure of a woman."

I could not help looking doubtful.

"Whatever family opinions or whatever the world's opinions on the subject may be, Pip, your sister is a fine figure of a woman."

I could think of nothing better to say than, "I am glad you think so, Joe."

"When I got acquainted with your sister there was much talk about her bringing you up. Very kind of her, too, all the folks said, and I said so too. As to you, if you could have seen how small and skinny you were then!"

Not exactly liking this, I said, "Never mind about me, Joe."

"But I did mind, Pip," he answered tenderly. "When I asked your sister to come to live here at the forge with me, I said, 'And bring the poor little child. There's room for him at the forge!' "

I started to cry and hugged Joe around the neck. He hugged me too. "Ever the best of friends, ain't us, Pip?" he asked. "Don't cry, old chap."

When this little interruption was over, Joe went on. "Well, you see, Pip, here we are now. When you try to teach me something, Mrs. Joe mustn't see too much of what we're up to. It must be done on the sly. I'll tell you why. Pip, your sister ain't very anxious for me to be a scholar for fear I might get to be too important around here."

"But—" I began.

"Why don't I put her in her place? That's what you are going to ask, Pip?"

"Yes, Joe."

"Well," he said peacefully, "your sister is a master-mind."

"What's that?" I asked.

"And I ain't a mastermind," Joe went on. "And last of all, Pip, I saw too much in my poor mother of a woman slaving and drudging and never getting no peace all her life. So I'm afraid of not doing right by a woman. I'd far rather be too good to her and be inconvenienced myself. But I wish it was only me that had to take it, Pip. I wish there was no Tickler for you, old chap. I wish I could take it all on myself."

Young as I was, I felt a new admiration for Joe from that time on. We were equals afterward as we had been before. But later at quiet times when I sat looking at him

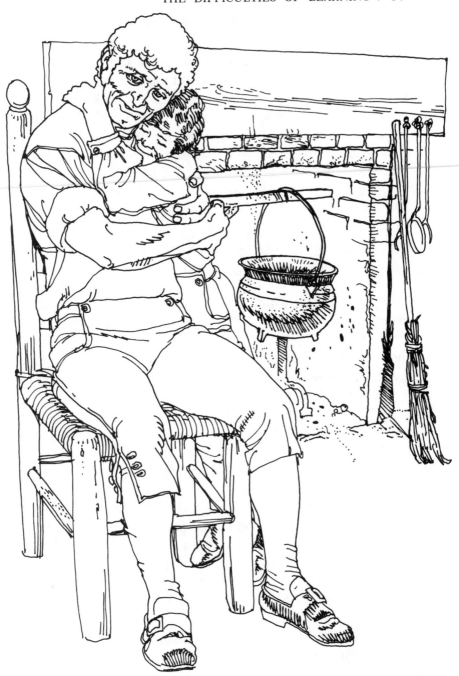

and thinking about him, I knew I was looking up to him in my heart.

"However," said Joe, rising to fix the fire, "here's the clock working up to strike eight and they ain't home yet. I hope nothing's happened to Uncle Pumblechook's horse."

Mrs. Joe sometimes went with Uncle Pumblechook on market days to help him buy things for his house. He had no wife and didn't trust his woman servant. This was market day, and Mrs. Joe was out on one of these trips.

Joe made a fire and swept the hearth. Then he went to the door to listen for the carriage wheels. It was a dry, cold night. The wind blew and the frost was white and hard. A man would die tonight lying out on the marshes, I thought.

"Here they come," said Joe.

We stirred up the fire so that they might see a bright window and took a final look at the kitchen to see that everything was in place. When we had finished, they arrived, wrapped up to the eyes. Mrs. Joe was soon down off the horse with Uncle Pumblechook right after her. We all gathered in the kitchen, bringing in so much cold air that it seemed to drive all the heat out of the fire.

"Now," said Mrs. Joe, unwrapping herself with haste and excitement, "if this boy ain't grateful tonight, he never will be."

I looked as grateful as any boy could who didn't know why he should look that way.

"Miss Havisham wants this boy to go and play at her house," said my sister. "And of course he's going. And he had better play there, or I'll fix him."

I had heard of Miss Havisham uptown. Everyone for miles around had heard of Miss Havisham as an immensely rich and grim lady. She lived all alone in a large and gloomy house.

"Well!" said Joe in surprise. "I wonder how she comes to know Pip."

"Stupid!" said my sister. "Who said she knew him?"

"Someone," Joe politely hinted, "mentioned that she wanted him to go and play there."

"And couldn't she ask Uncle Pumblechook if he knew of a boy to go and play there?" My sister asked this in disgust. "Uncle Pumblechook is a tenant of hers. Doesn't he go there regularly to pay his rent? And couldn't Uncle Pumblechook, who is always kind and thoughtful, mention this boy here?"

"Good!" cried Uncle Pumblechook. "Well expressed. Well, Joe, you understand the case."

"No, Joseph," said my sister. "You don't know all yet. You haven't thought that this boy's fortune may be made by his going to Miss Havisham's. And you don't know that Uncle Pumblechook has offered to take him into town to-night in his own carriage and keep him tonight and take him with his own hands to Miss Havisham's tomorrow morning. And here I stand talking," she broke off in sudden excitement, "with Uncle Pumblechook waiting and the horse catching cold and the boy dirty from the hair of his head to the sole of his foot!"

With that she grabbed me and soaped and rubbed and washed me until I was almost crazy. When my cleansing was completed, I was put into clean linen of the stiffest kind and buttoned into my tightest suit. Then I was delivered to Uncle Pumblechook, who said to me, as everyone always did, "Boy, be forever grateful to them as brought you up."

"Good-bye, Joe."

"God bless you, Pip."

I had never been away from him before. At first because of my feelings and because of my sister's soapsuds, I couldn't see the stars from the carriage. Gradually they twinkled at me one by one, though they didn't throw any light on the questions of why on earth I was going to play at Miss Havisham's and what on earth I was expected to play at.

6 A Strange Woman and a Beautiful Girl

When we arrived at Mr. Pumblechook's that night, I was sent straight to bed in his attic. The next morning he and I had breakfast at eight o'clock in a little room behind the shop where he sold corn and seeds. I thought he was very bad company. Besides putting as little butter as possible on my bread and watering my milk, he talked to me about nothing but arithmetic. When I said good morning to him, he replied, "How much is seven times nine, boy?" How could I answer a question like that taken by surprise in a strange place and on an empty stomach? I was hungry, but before I had swallowed a mouthful he made me add numbers together—and keep on adding them all through breakfast, while he sat back having a hot roll and bacon in comfort.

I was very glad when ten o'clock came and we started for Miss Havisham's. Still, I was not at all easy in my mind about what I had to do when I got there. When we arrived I found her house to be made of brick with a great many iron bars on it. Some of the windows had been walled up. There was a courtyard in front and that was locked. So we had to wait after ringing the bell until someone came to open it. While we waited I peeped in the gates and saw that at the side of the house there was a big brewery. No work was going on in it, however, and none seemed to have gone on for a long time.

A window was raised and a clear voice called out, "Who is there?" When she heard the name Pumblechook, the young girl who had asked the question came across the courtyard with keys in her hand.

"This," said Mr. Pumblechook, "is Pip."

"This is Pip, is it?" answered the young girl, who was very pretty and seemed very proud. "Come in, Pip."

Mr. Pumblechook was coming in also when she stopped him at the gate. "Miss Havisham doesn't wish to see you," she said, so firmly that Mr. Pumblechook, though somewhat upset, couldn't protest. He eyed me sharply—as if I had done anything to him!—and left me saying, "Boy, let your behavior here be a credit to them as brought you up."

The young girl locked the gate and we went across the courtyard. It was paved and clean, but the grass was growing in every crack. The brewery buildings were connected with it through high gates. Everything was empty and out of use. A wind which seemed colder to me here than outside the gates howled in and out of the open sides of the brewery.

The girl saw me looking around and said, "There is no beer brewed there now, boy. The whole place is idle and will stay that way until it falls apart." Though she called me "boy" so often, she was about my own age. She seemed much older than I, of course, being a girl and beautiful and sure of herself. She treated me as though she were twenty-one and a queen.

We went into the house by a side door. The first thing I noticed was that the halls were all dark and that she had left a candle burning there. She picked it up and we went through more halls and up a staircase all dark except for the candle. At last we came to the door of a room, and she said, "Go in, boy."

I answered more in shyness than politeness, "After you, miss."

To this she answered, "Don't be silly, boy. I am not going in." Then she walked away, taking the candle with her. I was half afraid, but I knocked on the door because that seemed to be the only thing to do. Someone inside told me to come in, and I did so. I found myself in a large room well lighted with candles. There was no daylight at all. It was a dressing room, I judged from the furniture, though I had no idea what some of the things in it were. Chief of all in the room was a table with a gilded mirror, which I recognized as a lady's dressing table. Sitting at it with her elbow resting on the table and her head leaning on her hand sat the strangest lady I had ever seen or ever shall see.

She was dressed in rich clothes—satins and lace and silks—all white. Her shoes were white. And she had a long white veil hanging from her hair. She had bridal flowers in her hair, but her hair was white. Jewels sparkled on her neck and on her hands, and some other jewels lay on the table. Dresses and half-packed trunks were scattered around her. She had not quite finished dressing, for she had only one shoe on. The other was still on the table. Her veil was only half arranged, and her watch and chain had not been put on. Her handkerchief and gloves, some flowers, and a prayer book lay together in a heap around the mirror.

I didn't see all these things in the first few minutes. But I saw that everything which ought to be white was now faded and yellow. I saw that the bride wearing the bridal dress was faded like the dress and the flowers. I saw that the figure wearing the dress had shrunk to skin and bone. I was frightened and would have cried out if I could.

"Who is it?" said the lady at the table.

"Pip, ma'am, Mr. Pumblechook's boy. Come to play."

"Come closer to me. Let me look at you."

When I stood near her I saw that her watch had stopped

at twenty minutes to nine and that a clock in the room had stopped at twenty minutes to nine.

"Look at me," said Miss Havisham. "You are not afraid of a woman who has never seen the sun since you were born?"

I'm sorry to say I was not afraid of telling a big lie in my answer "No."

"Do you know what I am touching here?" she said, laying her hands one on the other on her left side.

"Yes, ma'am, your heart."

"Broken!" she said with an eager look and a queer smile that was almost boastful. Afterward she kept her hands there for a little while and then slowly took them away as if they were heavy.

"I am tired," said Miss Havisham. "I want amusement. Play."

Nothing that she could have told me to do would have been much harder. Yet I was afraid of what my sister would do to me if I didn't follow instructions. For a moment I had an idea that I might run around the room, pretending to be Mr. Pumblechook's carriage. But I couldn't move. Miss Havisham and I stared at each other. Finally she asked, "Are you bad-tempered and stubborn?"

"No, ma'am. I am sorry for you and sorry I can't play now. If you complain about me, I'll get in trouble with my sister. I'd play if I could. But it's new here and so grand and so sad—" I stopped.

"So new to him," she said, "and so old to me. So strange to him, so familiar to me. So sad to both of us. Call Estella. You can do that. At the door."

It was hard for me to stand in the dark in a strange hallway and call out "Estella" to a scornful young girl— almost as hard as playing to order. But I did it, and she came at once.

Miss Havisham called her to come near. She picked up a jewel from the table and tried it against her neck and her pretty hair. "Your own, my dear, some day," she said. "You will use it well. Play cards with this boy."

"With this boy! Why, he is a common working boy!"

I thought I heard Miss Havisham answer, "Well, you can break his heart."

"What do you play, boy?" Estella asked me.

"Nothing but beggar my neighbor, miss."

"Beggar him," said Miss Havisham to Estella. So we sat down to cards.

It was then I began to understand that everything in the room had stopped, like the watch and the clock, a long time ago. I noticed that Miss Havisham put down the jewel on the exact spot from which she picked it up. As Estella dealt the cards, I looked at the shoe on the dressing table and saw that the stocking on Miss Havisham's foot where the shoe belonged was now yellow and ragged. Miss Havisham sat looking to me like a corpse while we played cards.

"This boy calls the knaves jacks," said Estella with disgust before we finished our first game. "What rough hands he has. And what thick shoes!"

I had never been ashamed of my hands before. Now I wondered about them. Estella looked down on me so much I began to feel the same way about myself.

"You aren't saying anything about her," Miss Havisham remarked to me, "no matter what bad things she says about you. What do you think of her?"

"I don't like to say," I answered.

"Whisper it in my ear," said Miss Havisham, bending.

"I think she is very proud," I replied in a whisper.

"Anything else?"

"I think she is very pretty."

"Anything else?"

"I think she is very insulting."

"Anything else?"

"I think I should like to go home."

"And never see her again, though she is so pretty?"

"I'm not sure I wouldn't like to see her again, but I'd like to go home now."

"You shall go soon," said Miss Havisham aloud. "Finish your game first."

I played the game to an end with Estella, and she won. She threw the cards down on the table when she had won them all as if she hated them because she had won them from me.

"When shall I have you here again?" said Miss Havisham. "Let me think."

I was beginning to remind her that today was Wednesday when she stopped me with her impatient movement of the fingers of her right hand. "There! there! I know nothing of the days of the week. I know nothing of the weeks of the year. Come again after six days. You hear?"

"Yes, ma'am."

"Estella, take him down. Let him have something to eat and let him look around while he eats. Go, Pip."

I followed the candle down as I had followed the candle up, and she put it in the place where we had found it. Until she opened the side entrance, I had imagined, without thinking about it, that it must be night time. The light of day was quite surprising to me and made me feel as if I had been in the candlelight of a strange room for hours.

"Wait here, you boy," said Estella as she disappeared and closed the door.

When I was alone in the courtyard, I looked at my rough hands and my common shoes. They had never bothered me before, but they bothered me now. I decided to ask Joe why he had taught me to call cards jack when they should be called knaves. I wished he had been brought up to be a gentleman and then I would have been one too.

She came back with some bread and some meat, handing them to me as if I were a dog. I was so hurt and angry that tears came to my eyes. The girl looked pleased that she had caused them. This made it possible for me to hold back and stare at her. Then she left me. But when she was gone, I got behind one of the brewery gates and cried bitterly.

My sister's bringing up had given me very tender feelings. I had known from babyhood that she was unjust to me. Often when I was alone I thought about the undeserved punishments she had given me. I think that was why I had grown up to be so shy and sensitive. Now when I had

finished crying, I came from behind the gate and ate the food. Then I looked around me.

It was indeed a deserted place. There were no horses in the stable, no pigs in the sty, no smells of grain and beer. At one spot there was a huge pile of empty barrels. Beyond the brewery there was a garden behind a wall low enough so that I could look over it. It was overgrown with weeds, but there was a path in the middle along which Estella was walking away from me. I saw her climb some iron stairs and disappear from my view as if she were going out into the sky. Soon I saw her coming back with the keys to let me out. She looked at me as if she were glad that my hands were so rough and my shoes so thick. She opened the gate, and as I went through she pushed at me. "Why don't you cry?" she asked.

"Because I don't want to."

"You do," she said. "You've been crying till you're half blind, and you are nearly crying now."

She pushed me out, laughing scornfully, and locked the gate. I went straight to Mr. Pumblechook's and was glad to find him out. So I set out on the four-mile walk home. On the way home I thought a lot about being a common working boy with rough hands and thick shoes. On the whole, I thought very little of myself.

When I reached home, my sister was very curious to know all about Miss Havisham's and asked a number of questions. But the more she asked me the less I wanted to tell her. I was sure she would not understand at all the way I felt about my experiences and the people I had met. The worst of it was that old Pumblechook, also filled with curiosity, came over in his carriage at tea time with his fishy eyes and mouth wide open for information. It was then I found out that he had never seen Miss Havisham. Whenever he paid his rent he was made to stand outside her door to talk to her.

Then it occurred to me for some reason I do not yet understand that they would believe anything I told them. I began to make up stories. I told them Miss Havisham was sitting in a black velvet coach when I arrived. I told them she and Estella and I had cake served on gold plates. I told them we waved swords and flags in the air and played with pistols. They believed everything and told all my tales to Joe when he came in from the forge. They were all sure Miss Havisham would "do something" for me—that she would "make my fortune."

After Mr. Pumblechook had driven off and when my sister was washing dishes, I went to Joe in the forge and told him I had made up everything. "It was terrible of me, Joe," said I.

"Awful!" cried Joe. "What made you do it?"

"I don't know, Joe," I said. Then I told him I was very unhappy and that there had been a beautiful young lady who said I was common. I wished I wasn't common and so the lies had come somehow, though I didn't know how.

"There's one thing you may be sure of, Pip," said Joe, "namely that lies is lies. Don't you tell no more of them. *That* ain't the way to get over being common, old chap. As to your being common, I don't believe it. And lookee here, Pip; if you can't get there by going straight, you'll never get there by going crooked. So don't lie any more, Pip, and you'll live well and die happy."

When I got up to my room and went to bed, I thought for a long time about how common Estella would consider Joe, a blacksmith; how thick his shoes and how rough his hands. I thought about how he and my sister were even then sitting in the kitchen and how Estella and Miss Havisham never did anything so common as sit in a kitchen.

That was an important day, for it made great changes in me. It was the first link in a long chain of experiences that altered my entire life.

7 The Past Returns

A morning or two later when I awoke, it occurred to me that I should get as much education as possible from Biddy. That, I thought, would be a step toward becoming less common.* Accordingly, when I got to Mr. Wopsle's great-aunt's that night, I told Biddy I had a special reason for getting ahead in life and would be obliged to her if she would teach me what she knew. She was the most good-natured of girls and promised to start at once. The pupils who were my companions at school spent most of their time eating apples and putting straws down each other's backs. Now and then a ragged book with the alphabet and numbers and figures in it was passed from hand to hand. But the boys were more interested in stepping on each other's toes than they were in learning. Once in the evening Biddy passed out Bibles to us. Then we were all supposed to read aloud together from them. None of us had the least idea what we were reading about, however. We were invited to practice writing, but the room where we met was so dark we couldn't see to do much.

It seemed to me I'd never learn to be anything else but common under those circumstances. Biddy started helping me by letting me read her list of prices for things in the store and giving me some letters to copy at home. It wasn't much, but it was at least a start.

There was a public house** in the village called the Three Jolly Bargemen where Joe sometimes liked to smoke

*Common: lacking refinement in manners.
**Public house: a saloon or bar.

his pipe. I had been given strict orders by my sister to call for him that evening on my way home from school. When I got there I found Joe in front of the big kitchen fire smoking with Mr. Wopsle and a stranger. "Hello, Pip, old chap," said Joe. The minute he heard my name the stranger turned his head and looked at me. He was a queer man whom I had never seen before. His head was bent over on one side and one of his eyes was half shut. He stared hard at me and nodded. So I nodded, and then he nodded again and made room for me beside him. I was used to sitting next to Joe, so I took a seat opposite the stranger. He nodded at me again when I had sat down and then rubbed his leg in what seemed to me a very odd way.

"You were saying," said the strange man, turning to Joe, "that you was a blacksmith."

"Yes, I said it, you know," said Joe.

"What'll you drink, Mr.—You didn't mention your name."

"Gargery," said Joe, and the stranger repeated it carefully after him.

"What will you drink, Mr. Gargery, at my expense, and what will the gentleman with you have?"

"Well," said Joe. "I ain't much in the habit of drinking at anyone's expense but my own. I don't want to be bad company, though. I'll have rum."

"Rum," said Mr. Wopsle.

"Three rums," said the stranger, calling out to the landlord.

"This other gentleman," said Joe, "is our clerk at church."

"Aha!" said the stranger quickly, winking at me. "The lonely church right out on the marshes with the graves around it?"

"That's it," said Joe.

The stranger grunted. He wore a broad-brimmed hat like a cap, which showed none of his hair. As he looked at the fire there was a sly expression on his face. "I am not familiar with this country, gentlemen," he said, "but it seems like a lonely place down by the river."

"Most marshes is lonely," said Joe.

"No doubt. Do you find any gypsies or tramps of any kind out there?"

"No," said Joe, "but there's a runaway convict now and then. They make things hard for everyone."

"Seems you have been out after them?" asked the stranger.

"Once," answered Joe. "Not that we wanted to catch them, you understand. We went as lookers on, me and Mr. Wopsle and Pip. Didn't us, Pip?"

The stranger stared at me again. "He's a likely young man, that one. What is it you call him?"

"Pip," said Joe. "It's kind of a name what he gave himself when he was a baby, and now is called by."

"Son of yours?"

"Well, no," said Joe. "He ain't."

"Nephew?" asked the strange man.

"No," said Joe, "he is not my nephew."

"What in blazes *is* he then?" asked the stranger.

Mr. Wopsle broke into the conversation here and explained in detail my relationship to Joe. All this time the stranger looked at nobody but me. He was silent until the rum and water was brought. Then he did something most peculiar. He said nothing, but went through entirely for my benefit a most unusual procedure. He stirred his rum and water as I watched. He stirred it and he tasted it—not with the spoon which had been brought to him but with a file!

He did this so that I was the only one who saw the file. And when he had done it he wiped the file and put it away in his pocket. I knew it was Joe's file, and I knew that he knew my convict the minute I saw it. I sat gazing at him in amazement. But after that he took little notice of me.

Since it was Saturday night, Joe dared to stay out a half

hour longer than usual. When his time was up, he prepared to leave.

"Stop half a minute, Mr. Gargery," said the stranger. "I think I have a bright new shilling* in my pocket. If I have, it's for the boy."

He found it among some change, folded it in a crumpled paper, and gave it to me. He said good night to all of us then and winked at me again.

On the way home I was so surprised about what had happened that I had nothing at all to say to Joe. My sister was not in a bad temper when we arrived. That gave Joe courage to tell her all about the shilling. "A bad one, I'm sure," said Mrs. Joe, "or he wouldn't have given it to the boy. Let's look at it."

I took it out of the paper and it wasn't a bad one. "But what's this?" said Mrs. Joe, picking up the paper. "Two one-pound* notes!"

Joe grabbed them up and ran back to the Jolly Barge-men to give them to their owner. I waited, feeling sure the man would be gone. Soon Joe came back. The man *was* gone. So my sister wrapped up the money and put it in a fancy teapot in the best parlor. There it stayed, giving me nightmares for weeks thereafter whenever I thought of it.

I slept very little that night because of worry about the strange man and about how common it was for me to be on good terms with convicts. I worried about the file, too. I had a feeling it would appear again when I least expected it. I fell asleep finally thinking about Miss Havisham's next Wednesday. In my sleep I saw the file coming at me out of a door without seeing who held it, and I screamed myself awake.

---

*Shilling: a British coin equal to about twenty-four U.S. cents when this story was written.
*Pound: a unit of British money equal to about U.S. $4.86 when this story was written.

8 The Greedy Relatives

At the time agreed on, I returned to Miss Havisham's. Estella let me in as before. She paid no attention to me except to say, "You are to come this way today." Then she led me to an entirely different part of the house. Here we were in a paved courtyard. Across it was a small separate house which looked as if it might have once belonged to the manager of the brewery. There was a clock on the outside wall of it. Like Miss Havisham's other time pieces, it had stopped at twenty minutes to nine.

We went through a door of this house and into a gloomy room at the back of it. Three ladies and one gentleman were there, and Estella told me to stand over by a window until I was wanted. All conversation stopped as we came in and then began again as I stood waiting. By the time I had listened five minutes, I had learned that these were Miss Havisham's relatives who were there to see what they could get out of her.

"Poor dear Miss Havisham," said one lady whom they called Camilla, "she's doing only herself harm living in this unnatural way."

"It is no way to get even with the one who did her such a terrible wrong," said the gentleman.

"Cousin Raymond," said another lady, whom they called Georgiana, "we shouldn't try to hurt our enemies. We should do good to our neighbors."

"Sarah Pocket," replied cousin Raymond, "isn't a man his own neighbor?"

They all laughed and seemed to think that a good idea. The third lady, who had not spoken as yet, said seriously, "Very true."

Then the ringing of a bell stopped the conversation and caused Estella, who had meanwhile come back, to say to me, "Now, boy!" When I turned around they all looked at me in disgust, and as I went out I heard Sarah Pocket say, "What next?" and Camilla said, "What a crazy idea!"

As we were going with our candle along a dark passage, Estella stopped and looked at me. "Am I pretty?" she asked.

"Yes, I think you are very pretty."

"Am I insulting?"

"Not so much as you were last time."

When I said that, she slapped my face as hard as she could, saying, "You rough little boy, what do you think of me now?"

"I shall not tell you."

"Because you're going to tell Miss Havisham. Is that it?" she asked.

"No," I said, "that's not it."

"Why don't you cry again?"

"Because I'll never cry for you again," said I. That was as big a lie as ever was said. I was crying inside for her then. How much she made me suffer afterward!

We went upstairs after this and on our way met a man trying to find his way down. He was a heavy gentleman with very dark hair and eyes and skin. He had a big head and big hands. He took my chin in his large hand and turned my face up to look at me in the candlelight. He was bald on the top of his head and had bushy black eyebrows that seemed to stand on end. His eyes were set deep in his head and were disagreeably sharp and suspicious. He wore a large black watch chain and looked as if he needed a shave. I could never then have guessed how much he was going to mean to me later on, but it happened that I looked him over very carefully.

"A neighborhood boy, eh?" he asked. "Why are you here?"

"Miss Havisham sent for me," I explained.

"Well, behave yourself," he said. "I've had a lot of experience with boys, and they're usually pretty bad. Behave yourself." With these words he let me go and went downstairs.

Everything in Miss Havisham's room was just the same. I stood near the door until she noticed me. "So," she said, "the days have gone by, haven't they? Are you ready to play?"

I was forced to answer, "I don't think I am, ma'am."

"Not even cards?" she asked me.

"Yes, ma'am, I could do that if you wanted me to."

"Since this house seems to you so old and sad, boy," said she impatiently, "and you are not willing to play, are you willing to work?"

I could answer that with a good heart, and I said I was quite willing to work.

"Then go into that room opposite this and wait until I come."

I crossed into the room she pointed to and found that the daylight was completely shut out of there too. It had a disagreeable, airless smell. Smoke for a fire which had recently been burned in the grate still filled the cold air like our marsh mist. Candles on the mantel gave the room a dim light. It was very large and had once been beautiful, but everything in it was covered with dust and mold and falling to pieces. The largest object there was a long table spread as if a feast had been in preparation when the house and the clocks all stopped together. A centerpiece covered with cobwebs was in the middle of the table. Spiders ran in and out of it. I could hear mice behind the wall boards.

I was looking at everything from a distance when Miss Havisham laid a hand upon my shoulder. Her other hand was leaning on a stick. She looked like a witch. "This," said she, pointing at the long table with her stick, "is where I will be laid when I am dead. They shall come and look at me here."

With some slight fear that she might get up on the table and die at once, I shrank away from her.

"What do you think that is?" said she, pointing again, "where the cobwebs are?"

"I can't guess what it is, ma'am."

"It's a huge cake. A bridal cake. Mine."

She glared all around the room and then said, leaning on me while her hand jerked my shoulder, "Come, come! Walk with me!"

I figured out from this that the work I was to do was

to walk Miss Havisham round and round the room. So I started at once while she leaned on my shoulder. She was not physically strong, and after a little time said, "Slower!" and after a little more, "Call Estella!" So I went out on the landing and roared her name as I had done before. When her light appeared, I went back to Miss Havisham and we started round and round the room.

With Estella came the three ladies and the man I had seen downstairs. To be polite I would have stopped walking, but Miss Havisham pushed my shoulder and we went on. I felt ashamed and was afraid they would think it was my fault.

"Dear Miss Havisham," said Sarah Pocket, "how well you look!"

"I do not," returned Miss Havisham. "I am skin and bones."

Camilla looked pleased when Miss Pocket was thus put in her place, and she said, "Poor dear soul! She could certainly not be expected to look well. The idea!"

"And how are you?" said Miss Havisham to Camilla.

"Thank you, Miss Havisham," she answered, "I am as well as can be expected."

"Why, what's the matter with you?" Miss Havisham asked sharply.

"Nothing worth mentioning," replied Camilla. "I don't want to make a show of my feelings, but I can't sleep at night for worrying about you.

"Then don't think of me," replied Miss Havisham.

"Easily said!" Camilla answered, trying not to cry. "Raymond will tell you how I worry in the night about those I love. If I weren't so sensitive and affectionate, I'd have better nerves. I wish it were so. But as to not thinking of you in the night—" she burst into tears.

I understood that the Raymond she referred to was the gentleman there and that he was Mr. Camilla. He came to her rescue at this point and said gently, "Camilla, my dear, we all know that your family worries are ruining your health."

"Oh, yes!" cried Camilla. "I know it's a weakness to be such a loving person, but I couldn't change my disposition." Here she started to cry again.

Miss Havisham and I had never stopped going around the room all this time.

"And there's my brother Matthew," said Camilla. "He never comes to see how Miss Havisham is. I can't understand him. I have been sick for days worrying about him too. And nobody thanks me for all I go through."

When Matthew was mentioned, Miss Havisham stopped me and herself and stood looking at the speaker. "Matthew will come and see me at last," said Miss Havisham, "when I am laid on that table. His place will be at my head. And yours, Camilla, will be there. And your husband's there. And Sarah Pocket's there. And Georgiana's there. You'll all know where to stand and gloat over me. Now go!"

At the mention of each name she had struck the table with her stick in a new place. Now she said, "Walk! Walk me!" and we went on again.

"I suppose there's nothing to do," exclaimed Camilla, "but get out! Imagine being told we'd gloat over our relatives! And being told to go!" Mr. Camilla led her out weeping. Each of the others tried to be the last one to go, but finally they got out.

While Estella was lighting them down, Miss Havisham still walked with her hand on my shoulder but more and more slowly. At last she stopped before the fire and muttered, "This is my birthday, Pip."

I was going to wish her many happy returns when she said, "I don't allow it to be mentioned. I don't permit those who were here just now or anyone else to speak of it. They come here on the day, but they dare not refer to it. Pip, on this day of the year before you were born, this pile of decay on the table was brought here. It and I have worn away together. The mice have gnawed at my wedding cake, and age and grief have gnawed at me."

She held the head of her stick against her heart as she stood looking at the table—she in her once white dress, all yellow and thin. The once white table cloth was all yellow and thin. Everything was in a state to crumble away at a touch. "When the ruin is complete," said she with a horrible look, "they will lay me dead in my bride's dress on the bride's table. This will be the finish of my curse upon him."

She stood looking at the table as if she were looking at her own figure lying there. I remained quiet. Estella returned and she too remained quiet. It seemed to me that we continued so a long time. In the heavy air of the room and in the heavy darkness in the corners of it, I had a frightening feeling that Estella and I might soon begin to decay.

At last Miss Havisham said, "Let me see you two play cards. Why haven't you begun?" With that we returned to her room and sat down as before. I was beggared as before. And again as before Miss Havisham watched all the time. She kept calling my attention to Estella's beauty and made me notice it more by trying jewels on her.

Estella, too, treated me as before, except that she did not talk to me. When we had played a half dozen games, a day was set for my return and I was taken down into the yard to be fed in the same doglike way. There, too, I was again left to wander about as I liked. This time I noticed a gate and through it walked into the garden and all around. Like everything else, this place was a neglected wilderness. When I had been all around I found myself in the corner that I had looked down at from the window where I had stood earlier that day. Feeling sure that the house was now empty, I looked in at another window and found myself, to my great surprise, staring at a pale young boy with red eyelids and light hair. In a minute he was out beside me. He had been studying when I had stared in at him. Now I saw that he had ink on his hands and face.

"Hello, young fellow," said he.

"Hello," I said in reply.

"Who let you in?" said he.

"Miss Estella."

"Who gave you permission to wander around?"

"Miss Estella."

"Come and fight," said the pale young man.

What could I do but follow him? His manner was so sure and I was so surprised that I followed where he led as though I were under a spell.

"Stop a minute, though," he said, turning around before he had gone very far. "I ought to give you a reason for fighting. There it is." In a most annoying way he pulled my hair and butted his head into my stomach. It hurt—especially when I had just eaten a meal, so I hit him back again, hard.

"Here," he said, dodging backwards and forwards. "We'll fight with regular rules." I was afraid of him when I saw how fast he could move around, but I was certain that his head did not belong in the pit of my stomach. So I followed him without a word to a hidden corner of the garden. When I assured him I was satisfied with the place he had chosen, he left me there for a minute and returned with a bottle of water and a sponge dipped in vinegar. "We can both use them," he said. Then he went to work pulling off not only his coat and vest but his shirt too in a businesslike and bloodthirsty way.

He didn't look very healthy. Still, these preparations quite frightened me. I judged he was about my own age, but he was much taller, and his elbows, knees, and wrists were large for his age. My heart failed me when I saw him looking me over as if picking out which one of my bones he would break. I was completely surprised when I gave out the first blow. There he was lying on his back with his nose bleeding and his face cut. He was on his feet at once, however, and began doubling up his fist again. My second great surprise was seeing him on his back again looking up at me with a black eye.

I had great respect for him. He seemed to have no strength, and he never once hit me hard and he was always knocked down. But he would be up again in a moment, sponging himself off and taking a drink of water. Then he would come at me as though he were really going to do for me at last. He got badly bruised, for I am sorry to say that the more I hit him the harder I hit him. He came back for more again and again until at last he got a bad fall, knocking his head against the wall. Then he threw up the sponge, saying to me, "That means you have won."

He seemed so brave and innocent that I didn't get much satisfaction out of my victory. I even thought I must be a sort of wild beast. However, I got dressed then and I said, "Can I help you?" and he said, "No thank you," and I said, "Good afternoon," and he said, "Same to you."

When I reached the courtyard I found Estella waiting with the keys. She didn't ask me where I had been or why I had kept her waiting. But her face was flushed as though something had happened to please her. Instead of going straight to the gate, she stepped back into the hallway and beckoned to me. "Come here! You may kiss me if you like."

I kissed her cheek. I would have gone through a great deal for the sake of kissing it. But I felt that the kiss was given to the rough common boy as a piece of money might have been and that it was worth nothing.

Because of the birthday visitors and the cards and the·fight, my stay had lasted a long time. When I got near home the light on the marshes was dim and Joe's furnace was throwing a path of fire across the road.

9 Dreams Ended

I worried about the pale young gentleman and my fight with him. The more I thought about him the more certain I was that something would be done to me. I had no idea what my punishment would be. But it was clear to me that village boys could not go about beating up young men in country estates. I stayed close to home for several days. There was blood from the young gentleman's nose on my trousers. I tried to wash it out late at night. I had cut my knuckles against his teeth. I made up all sorts of ways to explain my wounds if I were called to account by anyone.

When the day came for me to return to the scene of the fight, my terror reached its height. I imagined all sorts of dreadful things happening to me when I got there. However, go to Miss Havisham's I must and go I did. And nothing happened! No one referred to the fight in any way, and no pale young gentleman was to be seen. I found the same gate open and I explored the garden. I looked in the windows of the small house, but there was no one in it. Only in the corner where our fight had taken place could I see any sign that the young gentleman had really existed. There were traces of blood in that spot. I covered them with dirt.

On the broad landing between Miss Havisham's room and the room with the long table, I saw a wheelchair which had been put there since my last visit. The same day I started pushing Miss Havisham whenever she was tired of walking with her hand on my shoulder. Over and over again we would travel around her room, across the hall, and around the other room. Sometimes our trips would last three hours at a stretch. From that time on I went to Miss Havisham's every other day for at least eight or ten months to push her around in her chair.

As we began to get more used to each other, Miss Havisham asked me such questions as how much I had learned and what I was going to be. I told her I supposed I was going to be apprenticed to Joe. I told her I knew nothing and longed for more education, hoping she would offer to help me in some way. But she didn't; she even seemed to prefer my being ignorant. She gave me nothing but my daily dinner and did not offer to pay for my services.

Estella was always around and let me in and out. She never told me I might kiss her again. Sometimes she would be cold to me, sometimes friendly, and sometimes she told me that she hated me. Miss Havisham would often ask me in a whisper or when we were alone, "Does she grow prettier and prettier, Pip?" And when I said yes, she would enjoy it eagerly. When we played cards, Miss Havisham would look on and take special pleasure when Estella would hurt my feelings. Then she would hug Estella and say, "Break their hearts, my pride and hope. Break their hearts and have no mercy!"

What could I become in these strange surroundings? How could my character fail to be influenced by them? Is it any wonder that I was often in a daze when I came from the misty yellow room into the light of day?

I would have told Joe about the pale young gentleman if it had not been for the stories I made up after my first visit to Miss Havisham's. Now I felt sure he wouldn't believe me. Besides that, I still shrank from telling anyone about

Miss Havisham and Estella. It seemed I could talk to no one but Biddy about them. To her I told everything when I went to school at night at her aunt's. I didn't know then why she was so deeply interested in what I told her, though I think I know now.

Meanwhile, night after night that idiot Pumblechook and my sister would sit asking me questions and trying to guess what Miss Havisham would do for me some day in the way of making my fortune. Joe took no part in these discussions. I was old enough now to be apprenticed to him, but week after week nothing was done about it. For a long time we went on in this way, and it looked as though we would continue, when one day Miss Havisham stopped short as she and I were walking. "You are growing up, Pip," she remarked.

She said no more at that time but stopped and looked at me more than once in a thoughtful way. When we had finished our exercise the next day, she said, "Tell me the name again of that blacksmith of yours?"

"Joe Gargery, Ma'am."

"Is that the one you are to be apprenticed to?"

"Yes, Miss Havisham."

"You had better be apprenticed at once. Would Gargery come here with you and bring your indentures?"*

I told her he would consider it an honor to be asked.

"Then let him come soon and come along with you."

When I got home at night and told Joe and my sister, she was wildly angry and disappointed. She threw a candlestick at Joe, burst into tears, and then started cleaning the house to a terrible extent. Though it was ten o'clock at night, she made us stand shivering in the backyard until she had finished.

---

*Indentures: legal papers binding an apprentice to work for a master craftsman for a given period of time.

I hated to see Joe putting on his Sunday clothes to go with me to Miss Havisham's. Still, I couldn't tell him he looked better in his working suit when I knew he was getting dressed up just on my account. At breakfast my sister announced that she would go to town with us and stay at Mr. Pumblechook's while we were dealing with our "fine ladies," as she called them. We walked to town, my sister leading the way and leaving us when we got there.

Estella opened the gate as usual. She took no notice of either of us but led the way that I knew so well. I took Joe by the cuff and guided him into Miss Havisham's room. She was seated at her dressing table and looked round at us immediately.

"Oh," said she to Joe, "you are the husband of the sister of this boy?"

Joe stood speechless with his mouth open. In fact, he was so awed by Miss Havisham and her surroundings that all through our interview he talked to me instead of her.

"I mean ter say, Pip," said he, "as I certainly married your sister."

"Well!" said Miss Havisham. "And you have raised the boy with the purpose of making him your apprentice. Is that so, Mr. Gargery?"

"You know, Pip," said Joe, "as you and me were ever friends and it were looked forward to that we work together. Not but what, Pip, if you made objections things could be changed."

"Has the boy," said Miss Havisham, "ever made objections? Does he like the trade?"

"There weren't no objections, Pip, and it were the great wish of your heart," said Joe. I knew there was no use in my trying to get him to talk to Miss Havisham.

"Have you brought his indentures with you?" asked Miss Havisham.

"Well, Pip, you know," replied Joe, "you see me put

them in my hat and you know as they are here." He took them out and gave them, not to Miss Havisham, but to me. I was ashamed of the dear old good fellow when I saw Estella standing behind Miss Havisham's chair trying not to laugh. I took the indentures out of his hand and gave them to Miss Havisham.

"You expected," said Miss Havisham as she looked them over, "no premium* with the boy?"

"Joe," I protested, for he said nothing at all, "why don't you answer?"

"Pip," replied Joe, cutting me short as if he were hurt, "that question didn't need an answer between you and me. You know full well the answer is no, Pip. Why should I say it?"

Miss Havisham looked at him as if she understood him better than I would have thought possible. She took a little bag from the table beside her. "Pip has earned a premium here, and here it is. There are twenty-five guineas** in this bag. Give it to your master, Pip."

Even then, in his complete daze over the strange room and the strange woman, Joe continued to talk to me. "This is very generous, Pip," said he. "It is welcome, though no-wheres near that much money was ever looked for. And now, old chap," he went on, "may you and me do our duty by them as are so generous—may we do our duty—" There Joe could say no more.

"Good-bye, Pip," said Miss Havisham. "Let them out, Estella."

"Am I to come again, Miss Havisham?" I asked.

"No. Gargery is your master now. Gargery! One word!"

---

*Premium: a sum of money to be paid a master craftsman for teaching an apprentice the trade.

**Guinea: A British gold coin worth slightly more than five U.S. dollars when this story was written.

Calling him back as I went out of the door, I heard her say to Joe clearly, "The boy has been a good boy here and that is his reward. Of course, as an honest man yourself, you would not expect him to be anything else."

I don't know how Joe ever managed to get out of the door. When he did though, he started upstairs instead of down and I had to go after him. In another minute we were outside the gate and it was locked and Estella was gone. When we were out in the daylight again, Joe leaned against a wall and said to me, "Astonishing!" every now and then for so long I thought he was never going to come to his senses. At length and by degrees he was able to walk away with me. Somehow, though, our meeting with Miss Havisham must have sharpened his wits, for he acted in a very clever way when we got back to Mr. Pumblechook's.

"Well!" cried my sister then, speaking to both of us at once, "what's happened to you? I am surprised that you are willing to come back to such poor company as this."

"Miss Havisham," said Joe, "made it very particklar that we should give you her compliments."

"Much good they'll do me," said my sister, but still rather pleased.

"And she wished," continued Joe, "that the state of her health were such that it would have permitted—"

"Her to have the pleasure," I added.

"Of ladies' company," said Joe. And drew a long breath.

"Well!" cried my sister with a pleased glance at Pumblechook. "She might have had the politeness to send that message first, but it's better late than never; and what did she give this young one here?"

"She give him," said Joe, "nothing. What she giv' she giv' to his friends. And by his friends she said she meant his sister, Mrs. J. Gargery. Them was her words."

"And how much have you got?" asked my sister laughing. Actually laughing!

"What would present company say to ten pound?" asked Joe.

"They'd say," returned my sister, "not too much but pretty well."

"What would present company say," proceeded Joe, "to twenty pounds?"

"Handsome would be the word," replied my sister.

"Then to make an end of it," said Joe with delight, "it's five and twenty pound."

Pumblechook, the old cheat, acted as though he knew exactly what had been given. Now he took complete charge of me. "Now you see, Joseph and wife," he said, "I am one who likes to finish what he has begun. This boy must be bound over to Joe at once."

"Goodness knows, Uncle Pumblechook," said my sister, holding fast to the money, "we're deeply grateful to you."

"Never mind me," he answered. "A pleasure's a pleasure all the world over. We must have the boy bound as I promised." I knew that he had made no promises to anyone and had nothing to do with the money from Miss Havisham. Joe knew it too, but my sister believed everything he said. So over to the Town Hall we went and before a justice there I was bound over as an apprentice to Joe, with my papers duly signed and witnessed.

Afterward my sister was so excited by her twenty-five guineas that she decided we would all have dinner at the Blue Boar. Everyone had a good time at the party but me. Mr. Pumblechook sat at the head of the table and took all the credit for my good fortune. Mr. Wopsle recited poetry as usual. I fell asleep several times and they kept waking me up. Finally, when I got into my little bedroom, I remembered that I was really miserable. I felt sure I would never like Joe's trade. I had liked it once, but once was not now.

It is a miserable thing to be ashamed of one's home.

Home had never been a very pleasant place to me because of my sister's temper. But Joe had made it blessed and I had believed in the forge as the road to manhood and independence. Within a single year all this had changed. Now everything was rough and common. I would not have had Estella and Miss Havisham see it for anything.

How many of my ungrateful thoughts were my own fault, how many Miss Havisham's and my sister's is of no importance now. The change was made in me. The thing was done. Once it had seemed to me that when I at last rolled up my shirt sleeves and went into the forge as Joe's apprentice, I would be satisfied and happy. Now I felt as though I had a weight as heavy as the anvil on my heart. At least I'm glad to know I never breathed a word to Joe about how I felt. It is about the only thing I am glad to remember about those days. Only because Joe was so loyal to me I never ran away to become a soldier or sailor. Only because he was such a faithful, hard worker I became one too. And any good that came of our relationship came from Joe's peace of mind and contentment, not mine.

What I dreaded most was that I should some day lift my eyes and see Estella looking in one of the windows of the forge. I was filled with fears that she would sooner or later find me with black face and hands doing the toughest part of my work and that she would laugh at me and despise me. Often after dark when I was pulling the bellows for Joe, I would seem to see her face in the fire with her pretty hair flying in the wind and her eyes gazing at me with scorn. Then I would look toward the windows and imagine I saw her drawing her face away and would believe that she had come at last.

After that, when we went in to supper, the place and the meal would look commoner to me than usual. I would feel more ashamed of home than ever in my ungrateful heart.

10   *A Visit and a Tragedy*

When Biddy had taught me all she knew, I stopped attending school. I was getting too old for it anyway. Whatever I had learned I tried to pass on to Joe, but only, I fear, because I wanted him to be less ignorant for me to associate with. The old sea wall out on the marshes was our place of study every Sunday. Joe didn't remember anything from one week to the next. I never really taught him anything. Yet he would smoke his pipe in a learned fashion as though he were progressing greatly. Dear fellow, I hope he was.

It was pleasant and quiet out there with sails passing by us on the river. Whenever I watched the ships heading out to sea, I somehow thought of Miss Havisham and Estella. They and the strange house and their strange life seemed to have something to do with everything that was picturesque. One Sunday when Joe had been so dull that I had given him up for the day, I made up my mind to mention something I had been thinking about for quite a while.

"Joe," said I, "don't you think I ought to pay Miss Havisham a visit?"

"Well, Pip," said Joe slowly, thinking it over, "what fer?"

"What for, Joe? What is any visit made for?"

"There is some visits," said Joe, "that are forever open to question. As to visiting Miss Havisham, she might think you wanted or expected something of her."

"Don't you think I could say I didn't, Joe?"

"You might, old chap," said he. "And she might believe you. Or she mightn't. You see, Pip, when Miss Havisham done the generous thing by you, she called me back to say that was all!"

"Yes, Joe, I heard her."

"I mean to say, Pip, she might have meant make an end of things. Keep away!"

"But, Joe, here I have almost finished a year of my work, and since the day I was bound I've never thanked Miss Havisham or asked after her or shown I remembered her."

"That's true, Pip."

"What I want to say, Joe, is that work is rather slack now. If you would give me a half holiday tomorrow, I think I would go to town and pay a call on Miss Havisham. What do you think, Joe?"

In brief, Joe thought well of it if I thought well of it. But he was sure that I should never go again if I were not well received or asked to repeat my visit.

Joe kept a helper, a journeyman,* whose name was Orlick. He was a broad-shouldered, dark man with great strength who was never in a hurry and was always slouching around. He boarded out on the marshes with a man who had charge of the floodgates** there. On weekdays he would arrive at Joe's with his hands in his pockets and his lunch tied in a bundle around his neck. On Sundays he lay around watching the gates. He always walked with his eyes on the ground and acted as though he were angry when anyone spoke to him. He didn't like me. When I was very small, he used to tell me the Devil lived in a dark corner of the forge and every seven years made up the fire with a live

---

*Journeyman: a worker who has learned a trade but is not yet a master at it.

**Floodgates: gates used to keep water from flowing in and out with the tides.

boy. When I became Joe's apprentice, he probably thought I would one day take his place. Then he liked me still less. Not that he ever said or did anything openly. He was working with us the next day when I reminded Joe of my half holiday.

He said nothing at the moment but remarked a little later, "Now, master! Sure you're not going to favor only one of us? If young Pip has a holiday, do as much for old Orlick." He was only about twenty-five but always spoke of himself as ancient.

"Why, what'll you do with a holiday if you get it?" Joe asked. "Pip's going to town."

"Well, then, old Orlick he's going to town. Two can go to town!" he growled.

"Don't lose your temper," said Joe.

"Shall if I like," growled Orlick. "Now, master, no favoring anyone in this shop. Be a man."

Joe refused to talk until his helper was in a better mood. Orlick drew a red-hot bar of iron out of the furnace and acted as though he were going to hit me with it. Then he laid it on the anvil and hammered at it—as if it were I, I thought. Finally, when he had pounded it enough, he said, "Now, master."

"Are you all right now?" demanded Joe.

"I'm all right," said Orlick.

"Then, as you stick to your work as well as most men," said Joe, "let it be a half holiday for all."

My sister had been standing in the yard listening. Now she came to one of the windows of the forge. "It's like you, you fool!" said she to Joe. "Giving holidays to big, good-for-nothings like that. I wish I was his master."

"You'd be everybody's master if you dared," said Orlick with an evil grin.

"Let her alone," said Joe.

"I'd be a match for all stupid and bad people," said my

sister, working herself into a rage. "And you're the blackest-looking and the worst man between here and France."

"You're a foul, bad-tempered woman," growled the journeyman.

"Let her alone, will you?" said Joe.

"What did you say?" cried my sister, beginning to scream. "What did that fellow Orlick call me, Pip, with my husband standing by? Oh! Oh! Oh!" she continued, working herself up into a violent rage.

"Ah-h-h!" growled Orlick. "If you was my wife I'd hold you under a pump and choke your bad temper out of you."

"Just hear him!" cried my sister, clapping her hands together and screaming. "Hear the names he's calling me. That Orlick! With my husband standing there!" She began to tear her hair and try to get into the forge at Orlick, but the door was locked.

What could poor Joe do now but stand up to his helper? Without waiting even to take off their leather aprons, the men went at one another like two giants. But I've never seen anyone in that neighborhood who could hold out long against Joe. Orlick was very soon down in the coal dust and not anxious to get up. Then Joe picked up my sister, who had fainted by this time, and carried her into the house. At first when she came to she struggled and pulled at Joe's hair. Finally she calmed down. I went upstairs to dress.

When I came down I found Joe and Orlick sweeping up. A pot of beer had appeared from the Jolly Bargemen and they were sharing it peaceably. The storm was over.

I walked back and forth in front of Miss Havisham's gate before I could make up my mind to ring the bell. Miss Sarah Pocket answered. No Estella. "You're here again?" said Miss Pocket. "What do you want?" When I said that I had come only to see how Miss Havisham was, she seemed about to send me away. Then she thought better of it and let me in.

Everything was unchanged and Miss Havisham was alone. "Well!" said she, fixing her eyes on me. "I hope you want nothing. You'll get nothing!"

"No, indeed, Miss Havisham, I only wanted you to know that I am doing very well in my work and am always much obliged to you."

"There! There!" she said. "Come now and then. Come on your birthday. Oh!" she said suddenly turning toward me, "you are looking for Estella."

I had been looking for her. Now I said that I hoped she was well.

"She's abroad," said Miss Havisham, "being educated to be a lady. Out of your reach. Prettier than ever. Admired by all who see her. Do you feel you have lost her?"

She seemed to enjoy her words and laughed disagreeably. I was at a loss what to say. Then she sent me away. When the gates were closed behind me, I felt more than ever dissatisfied with my home and my trade and everything. That's all I got out of my visit.

As I was walking slowly on my way home, looking in shop windows and thinking about what I would buy if I were a gentleman, Mr. Wopsle came along. He insisted that I go to Mr. Pumblechook's with him and listen to him reading a play aloud, so I consented. It was a very dark night when it was over. I set out with Mr. Wopsle on my way home. Outside of town a heavy mist was falling wet and thick. As we walked along, we came upon a man standing in the damp. "Hello," we said, stopping. "Is that Orlick?"

"Ah," he said, "I was waiting for company home." We all walked on together. Presently I asked him if he had been spending his half holiday in town as I had been.

"Yes," said he," all of it. I come in right behind you. By the way, the guns is going again."

"From the prison ships?" said I.

"Yes. There's somebody escaped again. The guns have

been going since dark. You'll hear one soon."

We had not walked many feet when the well-remembered boom came toward us, deadened by the mist.

"A good night for getting away in," said Orlick. "It would be hard to find a jailbird tonight."

The subject called forth memories to me. I thought about them in silence. Orlick, with his hands in his pockets, slouched along at my side. It was very dark, very wet, very muddy, and so we splashed along. Orlick sometimes sang to himself. I thought he had been drinking, but he was not drunk.

When we got to the Three Jolly Bargemen we were surprised to find it in a state of confusion, though the hour was late. Doors were open and lights were on. Mr. Wopsle stopped in to ask what was the matter. "There's something wrong at your place, Pip," he said, running out at once, "Let's go."

"What is it?" I said, keeping up with him and with Orlick by my side.

"I don't quite understand. The house was entered while Joe was out—maybe by convicts. Somebody has been attacked and hurt."

We didn't stop running until we got into our kitchen. It was full of people. A doctor was there. So were Joe and a group of women in the middle of the room. They all drew back as I came in, and so I saw my sister lying without sense or movement on the bare boards. She had been knocked down by a blow on the back of the head. She was unconscious but not dead.

The next morning when the confusion died down, I found out more of what had happened. Joe had been at the Three Jolly Bargemen from a quarter after eight to a quarter before ten. While he was there, my sister had been seen standing at the kitchen door and had said good night to a farmer before nine. When Joe got home at five minutes to ten he found her on the floor and called for help. Nothing had been taken from any part of the house and nothing was upset in the kitchen. But there was one piece of evidence on the spot. She had been struck on the head and the spine with something blunt and heavy. And on the ground beside her when Joe picked her up was a convict's leg chain, which had been filed apart.

Joe, examining the chain with a smith's eye, declared it had been filed some time ago. It had not been worn by either of the two convicts who had escaped last night. I was sure the chain was my convict's—the one I had seen and heard him filing at on the marshes. I did not believe he had put it to this cruel use. I thought either Orlick or the strange man who had shown me the file that night at the Three Jolly Bargemen was guilty.

As to Orlick, he had gone to town exactly as he told Mr. Wopsle and me. He had been seen in town all evening and had come back with us. There was nothing against him but the quarrel, and my sister had quarreled with him and with everyone else ten thousand times. As to the strange man, if he had come back for his two bank notes, my sister was ready and willing to give them up. Besides, there had been no struggle. The attacker had come in so silently and suddenly she had been struck down before she looked around.

It was horrible to think that I had provided the weapon, though without intending to. Again I thought, as I had thought many times before, that I should tell Joe the whole story of my convict. But the secret was such an old one now, had become so much a part of me, that I couldn't do it. Besides, I feared that Joe would be either turned against me or would not believe me. So I kept silent.

The police were around the house for a week or so, but they could discover nothing. Long after they had gone, my sister lay very ill in bed. Her sight was affected so that she saw objects multiplied. Her hearing and her memory were

damaged and her speech could not be understood. When at last she could be helped downstairs, she tried to write for us what she couldn't say. But she wrote and spelled so badly we could often not guess what she meant. Her temper was greatly improved, however. Now she was patient and sweet.

We had no idea who would take care of her until something happened to solve our problem. Mr. Wopsle's great-aunt died and Biddy came to live with us. She was a blessing to Joe, for the dear fellow was badly broken up over what had happened to his wife. Every now and then he would say to me with tears in his eyes, "Such a fine figure of a woman as she once were, Pip." Biddy seemed to know at once how to take care of her, and Joe could get down to the Jolly Bargemen now and then for a change that did him good.

Biddy solved one problem for us soon after her arrival. Again and again my sister had written something that looked like an odd-shaped T and had called our attention to it as something she particularly wanted. I had shown her everything I could produce that began with a T, with no result. Then I thought perhaps what she had written looked like a hammer. When I called that word into her ear, she began to hammer on the table. Then I brought in all the hammers that we had, but she only shook her head. When she saw that Biddy was quick to understand her, she wrote the sign again. Biddy thought a moment and then ran into the forge and got Orlick. My sister had forgotten his name and could indicate him only by his hammer. When she saw him she seemed anxious to be on good terms with him and was pleased that he had come to see her. She showed every possible wish to be friends with him. After that a day seldom passed without her drawing the hammer and Orlick slouching in as if he knew no more than I did what to make of it.

11 An Understanding Friend

I now followed a regular routine in my life as an apprentice. It was a narrow life, including my work, the village, and the marshes. The only event in it was my paying another visit to Miss Havisham. Everything there was unchanged. Miss Sarah Pocket was still on duty at the gate. Miss Havisham spoke of Estella in the same way. I stayed only a few minutes. When I was about to go, she gave me a guinea and told me to come again on my next birthday. After that I went to see her every year. I tried to refuse the guinea the first time she offered it to me. She was very angry and asked me if I expected more. After that I took it without a word.

Everything in the dull old house was always the same. I felt as if the stopping of the clocks had made time in that mysterious place stand still. Daylight never entered the house, and my thoughts and feelings about it were strange and confused. Under its influence I continued in my heart to hate my trade and to be ashamed of home.

A change came about in Biddy, however. Her hair now was neat and her hands were always clean. She was not beautiful. She was common and could not be like Estella. But she was pleasant and wholesome and good natured. She had not been with us a year when I noticed one evening that her eyes were very thoughtful and very pretty. I was copying some passages from a book and saw her watching me. I stopped for a minute to talk to her. "Biddy," I said, "how do you manage to be such a wonderful housekeeper and still learn everything I learn and always keep up with me?" (I had been trying to educate myself at home.)

"I might as well ask you," said Biddy, "how *you* manage."

"No, I start to work every night when I come in from the forge. I never see you studying." I leaned back and watched her sewing. I began to think her a rather unusual girl. She knew all about my trade too—even the names of the tools. In short, whatever I knew Biddy knew. "You are the sort of person, Biddy," said I, "who makes the most of every opportunity. You never had a chance before you came here. See how you've improved yourself!"

Biddy looked at me for a moment and then went on with her sewing. "I was your first teacher though, wasn't I?" she asked.

"Biddy!" I exclaimed with surprise. "Why, you are crying!"

"No, I'm not," said she, looking up and laughing. "What put that idea in your head?"

I had seen a tear dropping on her sewing. I began to think of the hard work she had always done when she lived with Mr. Wopsle's great-aunt. I remembered the miserable little store and the noisy school. I remembered that even in those bad times Biddy had had possibilities. I had turned to her for help as a matter of course.

"Yes, Biddy," I continued, "you were my first teacher. In those days we never thought we'd ever be together in this kitchen."

"Ah, your poor sister," said Biddy, thinking as always of someone other than herself. "It's too bad that's true."

"Well," said I, "we must talk together more, as we used to. I must come to you more for advice. Let's have a quiet walk on the marshes next Sunday and a long talk."

My sister was never left alone now. That Sunday after-noon Joe took care of her while Biddy and I went out to-gether. It was summertime and lovely weather. When we had passed the village and the churchyard and were out on the marshes, we began to watch the ships sailing by. As usual they made me think of Miss Havisham and Estella. When we had sat down on the bank beside the river with the water rippling at our feet, I decided it was a good time to tell Biddy about my deepest thoughts. "Biddy," I said after making her promise not to tell, "I want to be a gentleman."

"Oh, I wouldn't if I was you," answered she. "I don't think it would be a good idea."

"Biddy," I said sternly, "I have a particular reason for wanting to be a gentleman."

"You know best, Pip. But don't you think you are hap-pier as you are?"

"Biddy!" I exclaimed impatiently, "I am not at all happy as I am. I'm disgusted with my trade and with my life. Don't be foolish."

"Was I foolish?" said Biddy, raising her eyebrows. "I didn't mean to be. I only want you to do well and be com-fortable."

"Well, then, understand once and for all, I can never be anything but miserable unless I can lead an entirely different sort of life."

"That's too bad," said Biddy, shaking her head sadly.

"If I could have settled down," I said, "and been even half as fond of the forge as I was when I was little, I know it would have been much better for me. You and Joe and I would have lacked nothing then. Joe and I would perhaps have been partners when I had finished my time. I might even have kept company with you when I was older. I would have been good enough for *you*, wouldn't I, Biddy?"

Biddy sighed as she looked at the ships sailing by. "Yes,

I'm not very particular." That didn't sound very flattering, but I knew she meant well.

"Instead of that," I said, "see how I am going on! I'm dissatisfied and uncomfortable. I wouldn't even have known I was rough and common if no one had told me so!"

Biddy turned and looked at me very attentively. "It was neither a very true nor a very polite thing to say," she remarked. "Who said it?"

I realized I had gone further than I had planned to. Now I had to go on, however, and answered, "The beautiful young girl at Miss Havisham's. She's more beautiful than anybody else ever was. I admire her dreadfully. I want to be a gentleman on her account."

"Do you want to be a gentleman to spite her or to win her admiration?" Biddy asked me quietly after a pause.

"I don't know," I answered sadly.

"Because if it's to spite her, I should think you could do that better by not caring about what she said. And if it's to win her admiration, I should think it wouldn't be worth winning."

Exactly what I had thought many times and thought now to be entirely sensible. But how could anyone expect a poor dazzled village lad to be sensible?

"That may be all quite true," said I to Biddy, "but I admire her dreadfully."

Biddy was the wisest of girls and she didn't try to reason anymore with me. She patted my shoulder in a comforting way while I cried a bit and felt that I was badly used by somebody or everybody, I can't say which.

"I am glad of one thing," said Biddy, "and that is, you have told me about it. And I'm glad you know I will never tell anybody else. I know what advice I'd like to give you, but you'd never take it. Perhaps it's too late for it now, anyway." So with a quiet sigh for me, Biddy rose and asked, "Shall we walk a little further or go home?"

"Biddy!" I cried, getting up, putting my arm around her neck, and giving her a kiss, "I shall always tell you everything."

"Until you're a gentleman," said Biddy.

"You know I never shall be, so that's always."

We walked a little further until the summer afternoon had passed into a beautiful evening. I began to think I was better off in these normal circumstances than I had been playing beggar my neighbor by candlelight and being despised by Estella. I thought it would be very good if I could get her out of my head and go to work determined to like what I had to do and stick to it and make the best of it. I had to admit to myself that if Estella were beside me instead of Biddy, I would be miserable. I said to myself, "Pip, what a fool you are!"

We talked as we walked, and all that Biddy said seemed right. *She* was never insulting or changeable. She would have been miserable if she made me unhappy. How could it be then that I did not like her much the better of the two?

"Biddy," I said as we were walking homeward, "if I could only make myself fall in love with you, *that* would be the thing for me."

"But you never will, you see," said Biddy.

It didn't seem so impossible to me that evening, but Biddy said it was, and in my heart I thought she was probably right. When we came near the floodgates, not far from the churchyard, we saw old Orlick slouching up to us. "Hello," he growled, "where are you two going?"

"Where should we be going but home?"

"Well then," said he, "I'll see you home."

Biddy was much against his going with us and said to me in a whisper, "Don't let him come. I don't like him." As I didn't like him either, I told him we thanked him, but we didn't want him. He received that piece of information with a yell of laughter but came slouching after us at a distance.

I was curious to know whether Biddy suspected him of attacking my sister. I asked her why she didn't like him.

"Oh," she replied, glancing back over her shoulder at him, "because I am afraid he likes me."

"Did he ever tell you he liked you?" I asked angrily.

"No," said Biddy, glancing over her shoulder again, "but he's always trying to attract my attention."

I was very angry about Orlick's daring to admire her. I felt that it was an outrage.

"But it makes no difference to you, you know," said Biddy calmly.

"No, Biddy, it makes no difference to me. Only I don't like it. I don't approve of it."

"Neither do I," said Biddy. "Though *that* makes no difference to you."

"Exactly," said I. "But I must tell you, Biddy, I would have a very low opinion of you if you gave him any encouragement."

I kept an eye on Orlick after that night and kept him away from Biddy. I would have had him sent away if my sister had not taken a sudden liking to him. He realized that and held it against me later.

And now I was more confused than ever about my life. Sometimes it was clear to me that Biddy was better than Estella and that I could be self-respecting and happy in the plain honest working life to which I had been born. Then I felt sure I would grow up to be Joe's partner and to keep company with Biddy. All in a moment, however, something would recall the Havisham days to me and I would change my mind and stick fast to my idea that Miss Havisham was going to make my fortune when I had worked out my apprenticeship.

If I *had* worked it out, I'm sure I would still have been undecided. My days with Joe were brought to a sudden end, however, as I shall tell about now.

12 *Great Expectations*

It was the fourth year of my apprenticeship, and it was a Saturday night. Mr. Wopsle and Joe and I were in a group of men gathered around the fire at the Three Jolly Bargemen. As we sat there listening to Mr. Wopsle read the paper aloud to us, a strange gentleman came in and spoke to our group. "I have reason to believe there is a blacksmith among you by the name of Joseph—or Joe—Gargery," he said. "Which one is he?"

"Here I am," said Joe as he stood up.

"You have an apprentice," continued the stranger, "commonly known as Pip. Is he here?"

"I am here!" I answered him.

He did not know me, but I recognized him the second I saw him as the gentleman I had met on the stairs the second time I visited Miss Havisham. I remembered in detail his large head, his dark complexion, his deep-set eyes, and his bushy black eyebrows. "I wish to have a private conference with you two," said he as he looked me over carefully. "It will take a little time. Perhaps we had better go to your home. I don't want to talk before all these people."

Amidst a wondering silence we three walked out. As we neared home, Joe, realizing it was an important occasion, went on ahead to open the front door. Our conference was

held in the best parlor. It began with the strange gentleman's sitting down at the table and looking over some papers
he carried. Then he began to talk. "My name," he said, "is
Jaggers, and I am a lawyer in London. I am very well known.
This business is not my idea and I advised against it. I am
merely a confidential agent of someone else. Now, Joseph
Gargery, I have brought you an offer to take this young
fellow, your apprentice, off your hands. You would be willing
to let him go, would you not? Without being paid for it?"

"Lord forbid that I should want money for not standing
in Pip's way," said Joe.

"Very well," said Jaggers. "Remember what you have
just said and please don't go against it later. Now I have
come here to tell you that this young gentleman has great
expectations."

Joe and I gasped and looked at each other.

"I have been told to tell him," said Mr. Jaggers, "that
he will someday come into a fortune. Further, it is the wish
of the one who owns it now that he be taken out of his
present way of life and be brought up a gentleman. That
he be brought up as a young fellow of great expectations."

My dream had come true! Miss Havisham was going
to make my fortune in a grand way!

"Now, Mr. Pip," the lawyer went on, "it is the request
of the person from whom I take my instructions that you
always keep the name of Pip. If you have any objections,
mention them now."

My heart was beating so fast that I could scarcely answer that I had no objections.

"I should think not! You are to understand secondly,
Mr. Pip, that the name of your benefactor is to remain a
deep secret until the person interested in you chooses to
tell it. That person will tell you by word of mouth when the
time comes. No one else can say where or when that will
happen. It may be years from now. You are meanwhile

positively forbidden to ask any questions about who your benefactor is or to make any reference to your benefactor in your communications with me. If you have any idea, keep it to yourself. You are not to ask why these conditions have been made. And you are bound to silence if you accept these conditions. I take my instructions from the person responsible for your great expectations. If you have any objections to these conditions, speak up!"

Once more I said that I had no objections.

"I should think not! Now, Mr. Pip, I have finished with rules and regulations." Though he called me Mr. Pip and seemed to want to make up to me, he treated me with some suspicion as though he knew something bad about me. "We come next to arrangements. You have more than expectations for the future. I have had placed with me a generous sum of money for your suitable education and your support. You will please consider me your guardian. Don't thank me. I am being paid for my services or I wouldn't give them. Your benefactor thinks you should start at once to get better educated for your higher position in life."

I said I had always longed for education.

"Never mind what you have always longed for, Mr. Pip. Keep to the subject. If you long for it now, that's enough. Are you ready to be placed at once under some able tutor?"

I said I was.

"Good. Now you are supposed to make a choice. Do you know of any tutor you would prefer?"

I had never heard of any tutor but Biddy and Mr. Wopsle's great-aunt. So I said no.

"There is a certain tutor who I think might suit the purpose," said Mr. Jaggers. "The gentleman I speak of is one Mr. Matthew Pocket."

I recognized the name at once. Miss Havisham's relative. The Matthew whom Mr. and Mrs. Camilla had spoken of. The Matthew whose place was to be at Miss Havisham's head when she lay dead in her bride's dress on the bride's table.

"You know the name?" said Mr. Jaggers looking sharply at me.

My answer was that I had heard of the name.

"Oh!" said he. "You have heard of it. But the question is, what do you say about it?"

I said that I was much obliged to him for his mention of Mr. Matthew Pocket and would gladly try that gentleman.

"Good. You had better try him in his own house. You can see first his son, who is in London. When will you come to London?"

I said that I supposed that I could come at once.

"Say, a week from today? You should have some new clothes, not working ones, to come in. You'll want some money. Shall I leave you twenty guineas?"

He counted them out and pushed them across the table to me. Then he looked at Joe. "Well, Joseph Gargery," he said, "you looked amazed."

"I am," said Joe in a very decided manner.

"It was understood that you wanted nothing for yourself, remember?"

"It were understood," said Joe. "And it ever will be."

"But what," said Mr. Jaggers, "if it is in my instructions to pay you for the loss of his services?"

Joe laid his hand on my shoulder with a touch as gentle as a woman's. I have often thought since about his combination of strength and gentleness. "Pip is hearty welcome," said Joe, "to go free from me to honor and fortune. But if you think as money can pay me for the loss of the little child—and ever the best of friends—"

Dear good Joe, whom I was so ready to leave and so ungrateful to! I can see him now with his powerful blacksmith's arm hiding his eyes, and his broad chest heaving, and his voice dying away. Dear faithful Joe. I can still feel the loving tremble of his hand on my arm.

But I encouraged him at the time to let me go. I was so excited by my future fortune I could not even think of the past. I begged Joe to be comforted. I said we had always been the best of friends and always would be. Joe mopped his eyes but said not another word.

Mr. Jaggers watched us as though he thought Joe the village idiot and I his keeper. "Now, Joseph Gargery," he said, "I warn you this is your last chance. If you want a present of money from me, speak out. If you mean to say—" Here to his great surprise, Joe started toward him as though he meant to strike him.

"I mean ter say," cried Joe, "that if you go on annoying me, come out and fight with me. That's what I mean ter say."

I drew Joe away, and he at once became peaceable. Mr. Jaggers had risen and backed toward the door. With no desire to return to the room again, he made his parting speech. "Well, Mr. Pip, as you are to be a gentleman, I think the sooner you leave here the better. Let our arrangement of a week from today stand. I shall meanwhile send you my address. You can take a hackneycoach at the stagecoach stand, and some straight to me. Understand that I am doing just what I am paid for. None of it is my idea.

Something came into my head which made me run after him as he was on his way back to the Jolly Bargemen. "I beg your pardon, Mr. Jaggers," I said. "I wish to keep to your directions, and so I thought I'd better ask you. Would there be any objections to my saying good-bye to anyone I know around here before I went away?"

"No," said he. "No objections."

"Not just someone in the village," I said, "someone in town."

"No," said he, looking as though he did not understand me, "no objections."

I thanked him and ran home again. Joe had already left the parlor and was sitting by the kitchen fire gazing at the burning coals. I sat down beside him, and nothing was said for a long time.

My sister was in the corner in her chair with Biddy beside her working at her sewing. The more I looked at the fire the less able I felt to look at Joe. The longer the silence lasted the more unable to speak I felt. At last I said, "Joe, have you told Biddy?"

"No, Pip," said Joe, still looking at the fire, "I left it to yourself, Pip."

"I would rather you told, Joe."

"Pip's a gentleman of fortune, then," said Joe, "and God bless him for it."

Biddy dropped her work and looked at me. Joe looked at me. I looked at both of them. After a pause, they heartily congratulated me. But there was a touch of sadness in their good wishes that made me a bit angry. I impressed Biddy with the fact that even my friends should say nothing about the one who was to make my fortune. It would all come out in time, I said. Meanwhile, nothing was to be known except that I had come into great expectations from a mysterious person. She and Joe said they would be very careful. Then they congratulated me again. They were so surprised at the idea of my becoming a gentleman that I didn't quite like it.

Biddy tried her best to give my sister some idea of what had happened. I believe those efforts failed entirely. She would in her good days have been so much impressed with the news!

I never could have believed it, but as Joe and Biddy became more at cheerful ease again I became quite gloomy. Of course, I could not have been dissatisfied with my fortune. Perhaps I was dissatisfied with myself.

"Saturday night," I said at supper. "Five more days and then the day before the day! They'll soon go."

"Yes, Pip, they'll soon go," said Joe.

"They'll soon go," said Biddy.

"I have been thinking, Joe. When I go to town on Monday and order my new clothes, I'll tell the tailor I'll come and put them on there, or I'll have them sent to Mr. Pumblechook's. It would be very disagreeable to be stared at by all the people here."

"The Hubbles might like to see you in your new things, Pip," said Joe, spreading his bread in the palm of his hand. He looked at my untasted supper as if he thought of the time when we used to compare slices. "So might Wopsle. And the Jolly Bargemen might take it as a compliment."

"That's just what I don't want, Joe. They would make such a rough and common business of it I couldn't stand it," I said.

"Have you thought about showing yourself to Mr. Gargery and your sister and me?" asked Biddy. "You'll do that at least, won't you?"

"Biddy," I said in some anger, "you're too quick. If you had waited another moment, you would have heard me say that I shall bring my clothes in a bundle one evening—most likely on the evening before I go away."

Biddy said no more. Generously forgiving her, I soon said an affectionate good night to her and Joe and went up to bed. I sat down and looked around the mean little room I would soon be parted from forever. It held memories for me, though, and even at this moment my affections were divided between it and the better rooms I was going to, as they had so often been divided between the forge and Miss Havisham and Biddy and Estella.

As I opened the window and stood looking out, I saw Joe come out and walk back and forth. Biddy brought him a pipe and lighted it for him. He never smoked so late, and it gave me an idea he needed comforting for some reason. Then Biddy and he stood at the door directly under me quietly talking. I knew they were discussing me, for I heard my name mentioned more than once in loving tones. I would not have listened even if I could have heard. I sat down on the bed thinking it very sad and strange that the first night of my good fortune should be the loneliest I had ever known. Looking toward the open window, I saw light puffs of smoke from Joe's pipe floating in. I imagined they were like a blessing from Joe—not forced on me or meant to impress me, but filling the air we shared together. Then I put my light out and got into bed. It was an uneasy bed now, and I never slept the old sound sleep in it anymore.

13 End of the Old Life

I felt much more cheerful the next morning. What bothered me most was the thought that six days had to pass before I left for London. I had a fear that something might happen to that city or that it might disappear in the meantime. Joe and Biddy were very sympathetic and pleasant when I spoke of our approaching separation and referred to it only when I did. After breakfast, Joe brought out my indentures, and we put them in the fire. Then I was entirely free. It felt strange to me to be going to church with Joe just as usual.

After our early dinner, I went out alone to have a final walk on the marshes. As I passed the church, I felt sorry for the poor souls who were fated to go there Sunday after Sunday and to die unknown. When I saw the graves in the churchyard, I felt even more shame than usual over my acquaintance with the wretched, shivering convict with the chain on his leg. I was comforted by the thought that it had all happened a long time ago. He had probably been taken a long way off and might even be dead by now.

No more of the marshes or the floodgates! I thought. London and greatness were calling me! No more work as a blacksmith! I made my way to the old sea wall and, lying down there, I fell asleep wondering whether Miss Havisham intended me for Estella.

When I awoke I was much surprised to find Joe sitting beside me smoking his pipe. He greeted me with a cheerful smile and said, "This being the last time, Pip, I thought I'd foller."

"I'm very glad you did. You may be sure, dear Joe, that I shall never forget you."

"I'm sure of that," said Joe in a comfortable tone. "Bless you, it were only necessary for me to think it over carefully to be sure of it. It took a bit of time though, the change come so all of a sudden."

Somehow I wasn't pleased with Joe's being so sure of me. I would have liked it better if he had praised me for promising to remember him. But I merely said that I had always wanted to be a gentleman and had often tried to imagine what I would do if I were one.

"Have you, though?" said Joe. "Astonishing!"

"It's too bad now, Joe," said I, "that you didn't learn a little more when we had our lessons here."

"Well, I don't know," said Joe. "I'm so awful slow. I'm only master of my own trade. It's no worse now that I'm slow than it's ever been."

What I had meant was that when I came into my property, it would have been easier to do things for Joe if he could have improved himself. Since he didn't understand me, I dropped the subject and decided to talk to Biddy about it.

When we had had tea that afternoon, I went walking with her in our little garden. I told her too that I would never forget her and wished to ask a favor of her. "It is," said I, "that you will help Joe on a little whenever it's possible."

"Help him how?" said Biddy, looking at me steadily.

"Well, Joe is a dear good fellow, the dearest that ever lived, but he is rather backward in some things, for instance, in his learning and in his manners."

Biddy would not look at me. "Won't his manners do, then?" she asked, picking up a leaf.

"My dear Biddy, they do very well here—"

"Oh! They *do* very well here," interrupted Biddy, looking closely at the leaf.

"Wait until I finish. They won't do when I come into my property and make it possible for him to live better."

"And don't you think he knows that?" asked Biddy.

That had never occurred to me and I was annoyed.

"Have you never thought that he might be proud?" she asked.

"Proud?" I replied with scorn.

"There are many different kinds of pride," said Biddy. "He may be too proud to let anyone take him out of a place where he is efficient and is looked on with respect. I think he has that kind of pride."

"Now, Biddy," said I, "I am very sorry to hear you talking like this. You are just envious over my rise in fortune and you can't help showing it."

"If you have the heart to think so," said Biddy, "say so over and over again."

"You mean if you have the heart to be so, Biddy," I said in a superior tone. "Don't put it off on me. You're showing a very bad side of your nature. I wanted you to help Joe improve after I'm gone. Now I won't ask you to."

"Whether you scold me or approve of me," said Biddy, "I'll always do the best I can. And whatever opinion of me you take away with you will make no difference in my memory of you. Yet a gentleman shouldn't be unjust," she said, turning away her head.

I walked down the path away from Biddy, and she went into the house. I wandered around until supper time. It seemed very sad and very strange to me that the second night of my bright fortunes should be as lonely and as unsatisfactory as the first.

Morning once more made me cheerful. I forgave Biddy, and we dropped the subject. Putting on the best clothes I had, I went into town as early as I could possibly hope to find the shop open and presented myself to Mr. Trabb, the tailor. He was having breakfast in the room behind his shop. He did not think it worthwhile to come out, but called me in to him. "How are you and what can I do for you?" he asked.

"Mr. Trabb," said I, "I don't want to sound as though I were boasting, but I have come into a fortune."

A change came over Mr. Trabb. "Lord bless my soul!" said he.

"I am going up to my guardian in London," said I, taking some guineas out of my pocket and looking at them in an offhand way. "And I want a fashionable suit of clothes to go in. I wish to pay for them with cash."

"My dear sir," said Mr. Trabb respectfully, "don't hurt me by mentioning that. May I congratulate you? Would you do me the favor of stepping into my shop?"

Mr. Trabb's helper was the boldest boy in the whole countryside. When I had entered, he was sweeping the shop, and he had tried his best to sweep all over me, in order, I think, to let me know he was as good as a blacksmith any day. Now he went on sweeping.

"Stop that noise," said Mr. Trabb, "or I'll knock your head off. Do me the favor to be seated, sir," he said to me. Then he commanded his boy sternly to show me various samples of materials. I selected one and then was measured for my suit. Mr. Trabb had my size already, but said that "under the existing circumstances" what he had wouldn't do at all. So he fussed over me until I felt that no suit could possibly pay him for his bother. Then he arranged to send my new clothes to Mr. Pumblechook's on Thursday evening. As I was about to leave, he said, "I know, sir, London gentleman cannot as a rule be expected to buy from small-

town tailors. But if you could give me a chance now and then, I would surely appreciate it." As I left I saw Trabb's boy just about overcome with surprise. It was my first experience of the power of money.

After this I bought hats and shoes and hose. I also went to the stage coach office and bought a seat for Saturday morning. Whenever I told that I had come into money, I was given respectful attention. When I had finished all my business, I went to Pumblechook's. He was waiting for me with great impatience at the door of his shop, as he had already heard the news. I found that he had prepared a feast for me. "My dear friend," he said taking me by both hands, "I wish you joy of your good fortune. It is well deserved."

This seemed to me like a sensible idea. "To think," said Mr. Pumblechook, "that I should have been responsible for getting you this great reward!"

I reminded him that nothing was ever to be said or hinted at in that connection.

"My dear young friend," said Mr. Pumblechook, "you can count on me for seeing to it that Joe remembers. Poor Joseph!" he said, tapping his head to indicate that Joe was not too smart. "But you must be hungry," he went on. "Here is a chicken and a tongue and wine. I had them sent in for you. Let us drink to your good fortune."

He shook hands with me again and helped me to food. "And your sister," he went on after we had eaten steadily for a while, "who had the honor of bringing you up. It's a sad thing to realize she may never understand what's happened. Let us not be blind to her bad temper, but it is to be hoped that she meant well."

"Let's drink her health," I said.

"Ah," cried Mr. Pumblechook, "that's like a noble-minded person. Ever forgiving and every friendly." When I told him that I wished to have my new clothes sent to his house, he was overjoyed at my having honored him so much.

He agreed with me that I should not let myself be stared at in the village. Nobody but him was worthy of my trust. Then he asked me tenderly if I remembered our doing arithmetic problems together and how he had always been my favorite and chosen friend. If I had taken ten times as many glasses of wine, I would have known that wasn't true. Still, I remembered thinking as I left that I had been mistaken in him and he was a sensible, good-hearted fellow after all.

I had very little baggage to take to London with me. I felt that practically nothing I owned was good enough. But I began packing that same afternoon, filled with the idea that I must lose no time. So Tuesday, Wednesday, and Thursday passed. On Friday I went to Mr. Pumblechook's to put on my new clothes for my visit to Miss Havisham. Mr. Pumblechook gave up his own room for me to dress in. My clothes were rather a disappointment, of course, as new clothes often are. But after I had had the suit on a half hour or so and had posed before Mr. Pumblechook's rather small mirror, it seemed to fit me better. Still, when I went out, I was very self-conscious, fearing that I might look something like Joe in his Sunday suit.

I went to Miss Havisham's by all the back ways and rang her bell with some difficulty because of my stiff new gloves. Sarah Pocket came to the gate and positively staggered when she saw me so changed. "You?" said she. "Good gracious! What do you want?"

"I am going to London, Miss Pocket," said I, "and I want to say good-bye to Miss Havisham."

Miss Havisham was taking her exercises in the room with the long table, leaning on her stick. At the sound of our entrance she stopped and turned. "Don't go, Sarah," she said. "Well, Pip?"

"I start for London tomorrow," I said, being careful of the way I expressed myself, "and I thought you wouldn't mind my bidding you good-bye."

"You look grand, Pip," she said, pointing at me with her stick as if she, my fairy godmother, were giving me a final gift.

"I have come into a fortune since I saw you last, Miss Havisham," I said softly. "I am so grateful for it, Miss Havisham!"

"Yes, yes," she said, looking at the envious Sarah with delight. "I have seen Mr. Jaggers. I have heard about it, Pip. So you go tomorrow?"

"Yes, Miss Havisham."

"And you are adopted by a rich person?"

"Yes, Miss Havisham."

"Not named?"

"No, Miss Havisham."

"And Mr. Jaggers is made your guardian?"

"Yes, Miss Havisham."

"Well," she went on, delighted by Sarah Pocket's plainly shown jealousy. "You have a promising career before you. Be good—deserve it—and follow Mr. Jaggers' instructions. Good-bye, Pip. You will always keep the name of Pip, you know."

"Yes, Miss Havisham."

"Good-bye, Pip."

She stretched out her hand, and I went down on my knees and put it to my lips. I had not planned the way I would say good-bye to her. At the moment it came natural to me to do this. She looked at Sarah Pocket with triumph in her queer eyes. So I left my fairy godmother, standing with both hands on her stick in the middle of the dimly lighted room, beside the rotten bridal cake that was hidden by cobwebs.

Sarah Pocket let me out as if I were a ghost. To the last she could not get over my appearance. I went back to Mr. Pumblechook's and took off my new clothes, which I made into a bundle. I felt much more at ease going home in my old suit, to tell the truth.

And now these six days, which were to have gone by so slowly, were over as though all at once, and the morrow was near. As the days had gone by, I had begun to appreciate the company of Joe and Biddy more and more. On this last evening I dressed up in my new clothes to their delight, and sat in my glory until bedtime. We had a special hot supper for the occasion, though we were none of us in very good spirits.

I was to leave our village at five in the morning and had told Joe that I wished to walk away all alone. I'm afraid that was because I was ashamed to be seen with him, though I pretended it wasn't. When I went up to my little room that last night, I was sorry about my decision and had a strong desire to go down again and beg Joe to go with me. I didn't do it.

All night there were coaches in my restless sleep going to wrong places instead of to London. At dawn I got up and, partly dressed, sat at the window to take a last look out, and there fell asleep. Biddy was up early to get my breakfast. When I smelled the smoke of the kitchen fire, I started up with the terrible idea that it must be late in the afternoon. Then I couldn't make up my mind to go downstairs. I stayed there until Biddy called up to me that I was late.

It was a hurried breakfast with no taste in it. I got up from the meal, saying brightly, as if it had only just occurred to me, "Well I suppose I must be off!" I kissed my sister, who was laughing and nodding in her usual chair, and kissed Biddy and threw my arms around Joe's neck. Then I picked up my little bag and walked out. I looked back once to wave my hat. Dear old Joe waved at me and Biddy put her hand over her eyes.

I walked away at a good pace, thinking it was easier to go than I supposed it would be. I whistled and made nothing of it. But the village was very peaceful and quiet. Mists were rising as if to show me the world. I had been so young and so little in the village, and all beyond was so unknown and so big that in a moment I broke into tears. I put my finger on the signpost at the end of the village and said, "Good-bye, dear friend." After I had cried I was better off, more sorry, more aware of my own ingratitude, more gentle. If I had cried before, I would have had Joe with me then.

I was so changed by those tears and by more that I shed as I walked along that I wondered when I was on the coach whether I shouldn't get off and walk back. Then I could have had another evening at home and a better good-bye. But we got farther and farther away as I thought about it until it was too late and too far to go back. The mists had risen now and the world lay before me.

Part 2

Showing What His Great Expectations Did For Pip

14 *First London Experience*

The journey to London took about five hours. It was a little past noon when I arrived there and at once started out for Mr. Jaggers's. After noticing that his office was on a gloomy street, I entered and asked if he was in. "He is not," answered his clerk. "He is in court at present. Am I speaking to Mr. Pip?"

I said that he was.

"Mr. Jaggers left word for you to wait in his room. He couldn't say how long he would be, as he has a case in court. His time is so valuable that he won't be any longer than he can help."

Mr. Jaggers' room was lighted by a skylight only and was a most dismal place. There were not so many papers around as I would have expected. But odd objects that I would not have expected were there—an old rusty pistol, a sword, some strange-looking boxes, and two dreadful casts of faces on a shelf. Mr. Jaggers' own high-backed chair was of a deadly black with rows of brass nails around it like a coffin. I could imagine him sitting back in it. The room was so small that clients must have been in the habit of backing against the walls. The one opposite his chair was greasy with the marks of shoulders.

I was at once affected by the gloomy atmosphere of the place. Even the clerk, like Mr. Jaggers, acted as though he knew something to someone else's disadvantage. I wondered about all the things in the room and how they came there. I wondered especially about the two terrible faces. Perhaps the hot city air made things seem more dark and unnatural to me. After a while I got up and went out walking. I came soon to a grim stone building which someone told me was Newgate Prison.* The road around it was covered with straw to deaden the noise of passing wagons. From this and from the number of people standing around I concluded that trials were going on. While I stood there, a very dirty and partially drunk prison guard told me that if I would like to step in and watch a trial he would get me a good seat for half a crown.** When I said no, he took me into a yard and showed me where the gallows were and where people were publicly whipped and where criminals came out of a door to be hanged. Four of them, he said, would be killed in a row day after tomorrow. This was horrible and gave me a sickening idea of London. I got rid of him with a shilling.

Mr. Jaggers had not come back when I returned, so I strolled out again. Then I noticed all the other people waiting around for him. Two strange-looking men I heard say that "Jaggers would do it if it was to be done". One woman crying loudly was told that "Jaggers is for him. What more could you have?" I was impressed with their confidence in my guardian.

At last I saw him coming across the road toward me. All the others who were waiting saw him at the same time and made a rush at him. Putting his hand on my shoulder and walking me at his side without saying anything to me,

*Newgate Prison: one of the oldest and most famous of London prisons.
**Crown: a British coin worth about U.S. $1.22 at the time this story was written.

he dealt with them one by one. Some he said he would go on helping; some he talked to about trials he was conducting for them; some he drove away harshly. All of them he reminded to pay his clerk Wemmick or he would do nothing for them. Finally he took me into his own room, and while he had his lunch standing up, he told me what arrangements had been made for me.

I was to go to Barnard's Inn to young Mr. Pocket's rooms. A bed had been sent in for me to sleep on. I was to stay there until Monday. Then I was to go with my host to his father's house on a visit to see how I liked it there. Also I was told what my very generous allowance was to be and whom I was to deal with for clothes and any other things I would want. "You will find your credit good, Mr. Pip," said my guardian. "But in this way I shall be able to check your bills and see that you are not spending too much. Of course you'll go wrong somewhere, but that's no fault of mine."

He told me that his clerk, Wemmick, would show me the way to my rooms if I liked. As we went out into the street, we found a new crowd of people standing around. Wemmick made a path for us through them, saying, "It's no use. He won't say a word to one of you." We finally got away from them.

I found Mr. Wemmick to be a little, withered man, with a square wooden face. I thought that he must be a bachelor because his shirt needed mending. He had glittering eyes—small, sharp, and black—and thin lips. I judged that he was between forty and fifty years old.

"So you were never in London before," said Mr. Wemmick to me. "I was new here once, too. It's hard to realize it now."

"You are well acquainted with it?" I asked.

"Why, yes," said Mr. Wemmick.

"Is it a very wicked place?" I asked, more for the sake of saying something than for information.

"You may be cheated, robbed, and murdered in London. But there are plenty of people anywhere who'll do that for you."

"If there is bad feeling between you and them," said I, to soften it a little.

"Oh! I don't know about bad feeling," said Mr. Wemmick. "They'll do it if they can gain anything by it."

He wore his hat on the back of his head and looked straight before him as if there were nothing in the street worth looking at. His mouth was such a slit in his face that he seemed to be smiling when he wasn't smiling at all.

"Do you know where Mr. Matthew Pocket lives?" I asked him.

"Yes," said he nodding in the direction. "At Hammersmith, west of London, about five mile from here."

"Do you know him?"

"Why, you are a great questioner," said Mr. Wemmick. "Yes. I know him. I know him."

He showed so little enthusiasm for Mr. Pocket that I felt a bit discouraged. I felt no more cheerful when we arrived at Barnard's Inn. I had expected it to be a hotel. Instead of that, it was a group of shabby buildings squeezed together in a corner. We entered through a gate and found ourselves in a little square that looked like a burying ground. It had, I thought, the most dismal trees and sparrows and cats I had ever seen. There were about half a dozen houses around this square. *To Let* signs glared at me from empty rooms. The air was filled with bad smells.

I was so disappointed at this first sign of my great expectations that I looked in dismay at Mr. Wemmick. "Ah," said he, not understanding my expression, "the quietness of this must remind you of the country. It does me, too."

He led me up a flight of rickety stairs to a set of rooms on the top floor. *Mr. Pocket, Junior,* was painted on the door, and there was a sign saying, "Return shortly."

"He hardly thought you'd come so soon," Mr. Wemmick explained. "You don't want me anymore?"

"No, thank you," said I.

"As I keep the cash, we shall most likely meet pretty often. Good day."

When we had shaken hands and he was gone, I stood looking out of the dirty window. I said to myself London was decidedly overrated. Mr. Pocket, Junior's, idea of shortly was not mine. I had been there for half an hour and had written my name with my finger several times in the dirt of every pane of the window before I heard footsteps. Gradually there appeared up the stairs the hat, head, necktie, waistcoat, trousers, and shoes of someone about my own age. He had a paper bag under each arm and a box of strawberries in one hand and was out of breath. "Mr. Pip?" said he.

"Mr. Pocket?" said I.

"Dear me!" he exclaimed. "I am very sorry. I knew there was a coach from your part of the country at noon, and I thought you would come by that one. The fact is, I have been out on your account. I thought, coming from the country you might like a little fruit after dinner. I went to Covent Garden Market to get it fresh."

Looking at him, I felt as if my eyes would fall out of my head. I began to think this was a dream.

"Dear me!" said Mr. Pocket, Junior. "This door sticks so!"

I held the fruit while he wrestled with the door. It opened so suddenly at last that he staggered back on me and I staggered back on the door opposite and we both laughed. Still, I felt as though this must be a dream.

"Come in," said Mr. Pocket, Junior. "It's a bit bare, but I hope you'll be able to make out until Monday. My father thought it would be nicer for you to stay with me than with him and look around until tomorrow. I'll be glad to show you the city. We'll have our meals sent in from the coffee-house here—at your expense, Mr. Jaggers says. This place is by no means luxurious because I have to earn my own living. My father hasn't anything to give me, and I wouldn't be willing to take it if he had. This is our sitting room—just some chairs and tables and carpets they could spare from home. This is my little bedroom, and this is your bedroom. The furniture's hired for the occasion. If you want anything else, I'll go and get it. It's quiet here and we'll be alone together, but I don't think we'll fight. But I beg your pardon. You're holding the fruit all this time. Let me take the bags from you."

As I stood opposite him, I saw a startled look come into his eyes too. "Lord bless me!" he said. "You're the boy who prowled around Miss Havisham's!"

"And you," said I, "are the pale young gentleman I fought with!"

15 *Miss Havisham's Past*

The pale young gentleman and I stood looking at each other until we burst out laughing. "The idea of its being you," said he. "The idea of its being *you*." said I. "Well," he said, stretching out his hand, "our fight is a thing of the past now, I hope, and it will be generous of you if you'll forgive me for having knocked you about so."

I judged from this that he had forgotten which of us was the winner, but I said nothing to that effect and we shook hands warmly.

"You hadn't come into your good fortune at that time," he said. "I heard it had happened very lately. *I* was rather on the lookout for good fortune in those days."

"Really?"

"Yes. Miss Havisham had sent for me to see if she could take a liking to me. But she couldn't—at any rate, she didn't."

I thought it polite to remark that I was surprised to hear that.

"Bad taste on her part," said Herbert, laughing, "but a fact. Yes, she sent for me on a trial visit, and if it had come out successfully, I suppose I would have been provided for. Perhaps I would someday have been engaged to Estella."

"How did you bear your disappointment?" I asked.

"Ah," he said, "I didn't mind too much. Estella's hard and proud and changeable. She's been brought up by Miss Havisham to get revenge on all men."

"What relation is she to Miss Havisham?"

"None," said he. "Only adopted."

"Why should she get revenge on all men? What revenge?"

"Lord, Mr. Pip!" said he. "Don't you know?"

"No," said I.

"Dear me! It's quite a story. I'll save it until dinner time. Now let me ask *you* something. How did you happen to be there that day?"

I told him, and he listened carefully until I had finished. "Mr. Jaggers is your guardian, I understand," he went on. "You know he is Miss Havisham's lawyer and has her confidence when no one else has."

I felt that this was coming to dangerous ground. I told him carefully that I had seen Mr. Jaggers in Miss Havisham's house on the day of our fight but never at any other time. I believed he did not remember seeing me there.

"He was so obliging as to suggest my father as your tutor. Of course he knew about him from Miss Havisham. My father is Miss Havisham's cousin. They are not friendly, though, because my father will not try to get on her right side."

Herbert Pocket had a frank and easy way with him. I felt then and knew surely later that he could never do anything secret or mean. He was still pale and did not seem strong. He was not handsome but was good-natured and cheerful. He wore his rather old clothes with more style than I did my new ones. As he was so friendly, I told him about my fortunes, emphasizing the fact that I was forbidden to ask who my benefactor was. I also told him that as I had been brought up to be a blacksmith in a small place, I knew very little about good manners. I said I would appreciate it if he would give me a hint whenever he saw me doing anything wrong.

"With pleasure," said he, "though I predict you'll need

very few hints. Do me the favor of calling me by my first name, Herbert."

I thanked him and said I would if he would call me Philip.

"I don't take to that name," said he, smiling. "We're going to be so friendly and you have been a black-smith—would you mind if I called you Handel? There's a charming piece of music by Handel* called *The Harmo-nious Blacksmith.*"

"I don't mind anything you suggest," I answered, "though I don't understand you."

"Then, my dear Handel," said Herbert as the waiter from the coffeehouse came in with our food, "here is our dinner. I must ask you to sit at the head of the table, since you have furnished the meal."

I wouldn't hear to that, so he sat there and I faced him. It was a nice little dinner and seemed even better to me because we two boys were independent, there were no older people, and London was all around us. It seemed like a picnic to me, eating that wonderful meal with a waiter bending over us, in the bare, inconvenient little room.

We had made some progress with the food when I reminded Herbert of his promise to tell me about Miss Havisham.

"I'll start at once," said he. "Let me tell you first, Handel, that in London it is not the custom to put the knife in the mouth—for fear of accidents—and that the fork should not be put further in than necessary.

"Also, the spoon is not generally used overhand, but under. This has two advantages. You get at your mouth better, and you save exercise with your right elbow."

He offered these friendly suggestions in such a lively way that we both laughed and I was not embarrassed.

---

*Handel: a famous German composer.

"Now," he went on, "about Miss Havisham. You should know first that she was a spoiled child. Her mother died when she was a baby, and her father gave her everything. He was a country gentleman down in your part of the world and was a brewer. I don't know why, but that business is everywhere considered most suitable for a gentleman. Well, Mr. Havisham was very rich and very proud. So was his daughter."

"Miss Havisham was an only child?" I guessed.

"Stop a minute. I'm coming to that. No. She had a half brother. Her father married again privately—his cook, I rather think. In the course of time *she* died. When she was dead, he told his daughter for the first time what he had done, and then the son became part of the family, living in the house you know. As the son grew up, he turned out to be extravagant, undutiful, fast—altogether bad. His father finally disinherited him. But the old man weakened when he was dying and left his son well off, though not nearly so rich as Miss Havisham. Take another glass of wine and excuse my mentioning that society does not expect one to turn one's glass bottom up with the rim on one's nose."

I had been so interested in his story I had not noticed what I was doing. I thanked him again as he went on.

"Miss Havisham was now an heiress and was considered a great match. Her half brother was in funds for a while but in no time had spent his money. He had a deep and lasting grudge against his half sister because he thought she had influenced her father against him. Now I come to the cruel part of my story, merely breaking off, Handel, to remind you that a dinner napkin will not go into a drinking glass.

"There now appeared upon the scene a certain man, who made love to Miss Havisham. I never saw him, for this happened twenty-five years before you and I were born. I have heard my father say that he was an attractive man and a man for the purpose. My father insists that he was not a gentleman. No man who is not a true gentleman at heart is ever a true gentleman in manner. Well, this man pursued Miss Havisham and said that he loved her. She had not been interested in anyone up to this time, but now fell deeply in love. He took advantage of her love so completely that he got large sums of money from her. Finally he persuaded her to buy out her brother's share in the brewery at an enormous price, saying that when he was her husband he must hold and manage it all. Mr. Jaggers was not her lawyer at that time. Anyway, she was too proud and too much in love to be advised by anyone. Her relations—all but my father—were poor and envious and looking out for themselves. My father warned her that she was doing too much for this man and placing herself too much in his power. She ordered him out of her house in a rage, and my father has never seen her since."

I thought of her having said, "Matthew will come and see me at last when I am laid on that table," and I asked Herbert whether his father had turned entirely against her.

"It's not that," said he, "but she accused him in front of her intended husband with being disappointed in his hope of getting something from her for himself. If he went back now, it would look true to him—and even to her. To get to the end of my story. The marriage day was fixed, the wedding dresses were bought, the wedding trip was planned, and the guests were invited. The day came, but not the bridegroom. He wrote a letter—"

"Which she received," I interrupted, "when she was dressing for her marriage? At twenty minutes to nine?"

"At the hour and minute," said Herbert, nodding, "at which she afterward stopped all the clocks. I can't tell you what was in the letter except that it most heartlessly broke off the marriage. She was taken violently ill then, and when she recovered, ordered that the place be left as it still is.

And she has never since looked upon the light of day."

"Is that all the story?" I asked, after thinking it over.

"All that I know of it. Even that much I pieced out for myself. My father always avoids the subject. Miss Havisham, when she invited me to stay there, told me no more than was absolutely necessary. But I've forgotten one thing.

The man whom she trusted was supposed all along to have operated with her half brother. It was a plot between them, and they shared the profits."

"I wonder why he didn't marry her and get all the profits," said I.

"He may have been married already. The dreadful shame she felt over that may have been a part of her half brother's scheme. I don't know that. I'm just guessing."

"What became of the two men?" I asked, again after much thought.

"They became worse and worse and were finally completely ruined. I don't know whether they're still alive."

"You said just now that Estella was not related to Miss Havisham but adopted by her. Adopted when?"

"There has always been an Estella ever since I have heard of a Miss Havisham. That's all I know. And now, Handel," said he, ending the story, "we have reached an understanding. All I know about Miss Havisham you know. So there can be no competition between us. And you can trust me to keep the terms of your fortune. I'll never ask or mention where it might have come from."

He said this with so much tact that I was sure the subject would be closed from that time on. Yet I felt from the way he spoke that he, too, thought I owed my good fortune to Miss Havisham. I realized that he had brought up the subject so that we could get things clear at the start. We were very gay and sociable after that. I asked him what his business was. "An insurer of ships," said he. "I work in an accounting house in the city."

In a way I was impressed by the sound of it, though I had again the feeling that Herbert Pocket would never be successful or rich. Then he told me some of his dreams of one day working his way up to own a fleet of cargo ships for trade in sugar, tobacco, and rum. I felt sure they were only dreams. At present, I figured out from what he said, he wasn't even earning his living while he was learning to be an accountant. He had the barest necessities of life and was plainly very poor.

We got on together fine. In the evening we went out walking through the streets and went to the theater. The next day we attended church at Westminster Abbey* and in the afternoon walked around the parks. I wondered who were blacksmiths for all the horses there and wished that Joe were one of them. I began to feel as though I had been home with Joe and Biddy months ago. My old life seemed many miles away. Yet even in the London streets crowded with people and brightly lighted, something would make me think of the life I had given up so easily, and I would feel guilty.

On Monday morning Herbert took me to the counting office where he worked. It was in a back room on the second floor of a grimy building. I waited around until noon, when we had lunch, went back to our rooms to get my suitcase, and then took a coach for Hammersmith, and Herbert's home. We arrived there about two o'clock in the afternoon and went at once to a little garden overlooking the river, where Mr. Pocket's children were playing about. There we met Mrs. Pocket, an absentminded woman, who sat reading and paying very little attention to what was going on. There also I discovered to my great surprise that there were seven little Pockets of all ages, with two nursemaids to take care of them. Then Mr. Pocket came out to be introduced to me. With such a family, I wasn't surprised to see that he looked always puzzled and untidy, as though he didn't quite see how to manage anything.

---

*Westminster Abbey: London's most famous church—kings and queens are crowned there.

16   *In and Around London*

Mr. Pocket was a young-looking man in spite of his gray hair, and his manner was quite informal. "I really am not," he said to me with a smile like his son's, "anyone to be afraid of even if I am to be your teacher." He and his family accepted me in the most friendly fashion. Before long I found out, and might as well mention here before I go on with my adventures, that Mrs. Pocket was the daughter of a knight. She had been brought up with the idea that she must marry a man with a title. So she had grown up to be entirely helpless and useless, with no knowledge at all of housekeeping. When they were both very young, however, she had met Mr. Pocket and they had married without her father's knowing it. They had been forgiven, though everyone thereafter looked upon Mrs. Pocket with pity because she had not married a man with a title. Since her father had no money at all to leave his daughter, life had never been easy for the Pockets.

Mr. Pocket took me into the house and showed me my room. It was very pleasant and furnished so well that I could use it as a sitting room. He then introduced me to two other boys who had rooms near mine and who were also his pupils. One of them, Bentley Drummle, whom Mrs. Pocket considered a person of importance because he might one day be a baron,* was a large, stout boy. The other, Startop, was smaller and looked younger.

Both Mr. and Mrs. Pocket seemed so completely helpless, I wondered who took charge of the big house and all its occupants. Before long I found out it was the servants. It was an easy way to live, I suppose, but it must have been very expensive. For the servants had even better things to eat and drink than their employers and entertained numerous guests in the servants' quarters. It was an odd arrangement.

By degrees I learned, chiefly from Herbert, that Mr. Pocket had been educated at Harrow and at Cambridge, where he had won honors. If he hadn't married when he was so young, he would probably have had a brilliant career. As it was, he made his living by teaching young boys like me and by doing some writing and editorial work.

After dinner that night, which seemed as confusing to me as everything else in that household, we went rowing on the river. Both Drummle and Startop owned a boat, and I decided to get one at once. I was pretty good at most of the sports that country boys enjoy, but didn't feel that I had style enough for rowing on the Thames. I hired a man to teach me and was anything but pleased when he said that I had the arm of a blacksmith!

It took me two or three days to go back and forth to London to buy what I needed and to get settled in my room. Then Mr. Pocket and I had a long talk. He knew more about the life that had been planned for me than I knew myself. Mr. Jaggers had told him that I was not to be educated for any profession. I was just to learn enough "to hold my own" with the average wealthy young man. He advised my visiting certain places in London. He said that he would guide me in my studies but hoped that I would do as much as I

*Baron: a title given to a man of social importance in England.

could for myself. I liked and trusted him. Throughout, he showed great interest in me, and I responded by doing the best I could. He was serious and honest and good.

When we had made plans for my education and I had started to work, it occurred to me that it would be a good idea if I kept my room at Barnard's Inn. Then I would often have an agreeable change in my living arrangements and my manners would improve in Herbert's company. Mr. Pocket did not object to my idea but said that I would have to ask my guardian. So off I went to see him.

"If I could buy the furniture that's now hired for me," I told Mr. Jaggers, "and one or two other little things, I would be quite at home there."

"Go to it!" said Mr. Jaggers with a short laugh. "I told you you'd get ahead. Well, how much do you want?"

I said I didn't know how much.

"Come on!" said Mr. Jaggers. "How much? Fifty pounds?"

"Oh, not nearly so much."

"Five pounds?" said Mr. Jaggers.

This was such a comedown that my face fell. "Oh! more than that!" I said.

"More than that, eh?" Mr. Jaggers lay in wait for me with his hands in his pockets and his eyes on the wall behind me. "How much more?" Twice five; will that do? Three times five; will that do? Four times five; will that do?"

I said I thought that would be a quite generous amount.

"Wemmick!" said Mr. Jaggers, opening his office door. "Take Mr. Pip's written order and pay him twenty pounds."

This systematic way of doing business made a strong impression on me and not an agreeable one. Mr. Jaggers never laughed. He stood now with his large head bent down and his eyebrows joined together. Wemmick, on the other hand, was brisk and talkative. I told him that I hardly knew what to make of Mr. Jaggers' manner. "Tell him that and he'll take it as a compliment," he answered me. "He don't mean that you should know what to make of it. Oh, it's not personal. It's professional."

Wemmick was eating lunch at his desk, crunching on a dry hard biscuit. He threw pieces of it now and then into his slit of a mouth as though he were posting them, like letters in a mailbox. "It always seems to me," said he, "as if he had set a trap for a man and was watching it. Suddenly—click—you're caught!"

I said I supposed he was very successful in his profession.

"Deep," said Wemmick, "as Australia. If there was anything deeper, he'd be it."

Then, I said, I supposed he had a fine business, and Wemmick said, "Won-der-ful."

"Tell me," said I, thinking of the two horrible heads that had upset me so the first day I arrived in London, "who is represented by the two heads in Mr. Jaggers' office?"

We went into it, and Wemmick got them down and blew the dust off them. "These are two famous heads, clients of ours. This one murdered his master and didn't plan it badly at all."

"Is it like him?" I asked, shivering as I looked at the brutal face.

"Like him? It's himself, you know. The cast was made in Newgate Prison directly after he was taken down from the gallows."

"Did the other creature come to the same end?" I asked. "He has the same look."

"You're right," said Wemmick. "It's a typical look. Yes, he came to the same end. It's quite the usual thing around here. He forged wills, this one did. Maybe he even put the ones who made the wills permanently to sleep. You were a gentlemanly rogue," he said to the head, patting it lovingly, "and you said you could write Greek. What a liar you were."

He put both heads back on the shelf and then went on in a friendly manner. "If at any time you have nothing better to do, I'd like to have you come over to my home in Walworth to see me. I should consider it an honor. I have not much to show you, but you might like to look over two or three odd things—like my garden and my summer-house, too."

I said I would be delighted to accept his hospitality.

"Thank you," said he. "Then I'll take it for granted you'll come when it's convenient for you. Have you dined with Mr. Jaggers yet?"

"Not yet."

"Well," said he, "he'll give you wine, and good wine. And now I'll tell you something. When you go to dine with Mr. Jaggers look at his housekeeper."

"Will I see something very unusual?"

"Well," said Wemmick, "you'll see a wild beast tamed. Not so very unusual, you'll tell me. I reply, that depends on the original wildness of the beast and the amount of taming. It won't lower your opinion of Mr. Jaggers' powers. Keep your eye on it."

Filled with interest and curiosity, I told him I would do so. As I was about to leave, he asked me if I would like to spend five minutes watching Mr. Jaggers "at it". I said that I would. We went then to a crowded police court, where someone who looked like the murderers whose heads I had seen was being tried. My guardian was cross-examining a witness and scaring her, the judge, and everyone else to death. If anybody said a word that he didn't approve of, he demanded that it be "taken down." If anyone wouldn't admit anything, he said, "I'll have it out with you." And if anyone admitted anything, he said, "Now I have got you." Thieves and police officers alike shrank from him when he turned to look at them. I couldn't make out what side he was on. When I stole out on tiptoes, he was violently criticizing the judge for the way the trial was being carried on.

17 *Two Dinners*

Bentley Drummle was a bad-tempered fellow. He even took up a book as if its writer had done him some injury. He made friends in the same spirit. He was heavy in figure, in movement, and in understanding. He was idle, proud, stingy, and suspicious. He came of rich people who had brought him up to be just what he was. Then, when he was of age, and they realized what a blockhead he had grown to be, they had sent him to Mr. Pocket, to make him over.

Startop had been spoiled by a weak mother and kept at home when he should have been at school. He loved and admired his mother greatly and was probably much like her in his gentleness and kindness. It was natural that I should take to him much more than I did to Bentley.

Herbert was my intimate companion and friend. I gave him a half share in my boat, which was the reason for his often coming to Hammersmith. And my owning a half share in his rooms took me up to London. We used to walk between the two places at all hours. I still have an affection for the road we traveled, even though it has changed much.

When I had been at the Pockets' a month or two, Mr. and Mrs. Camilla turned up. Camilla was Mr. Pocket's sister. Georgiana, whom I had seen at Miss Havisham's, turned up too. She was a cousin, a single woman with a bad digestion and a sour nature. These people hated me as only envious, disappointed people can hate. Of course they tried to hide their feelings for me and win my favor. They treated Mr. Pocket with patience as though he were a foolish child.

These are the surroundings in which I was educated. I soon began to spend money in reckless amounts, but I never neglected my books because I had sense enough to realize how much I needed to learn. With the help of Mr. Pocket and Herbert I got on fast.

I hadn't seen Mr. Wemmick for several weeks when I wrote to suggest that I accept his invitation to dine and go home with him on a certain evening. I met him at the office at six, and we decided to walk to his home in Walworth. "I'll tell you what I have for supper, Mr. Pip," said he. "I have stewed steak, which I prepared at home, and a cold roast chicken, which I bought already cooked. You don't object to an aged parent, I hope?"

I thought he was still speaking of the chicken until he added, "Because I have got an aged parent at my place."

Of course I answered that politely.

"So you haven't dined with Mr. Jaggers yet," he continued as we walked along. "He told me so this afternoon when he heard you were coming to my home. I expect you'll have an invitation tomorrow. He's going to ask your pals too. Three of 'em, ain't there?"

Although I was not used to considering Drummle one of my friends, I answered yes.

"You'll have good things to eat— not much variety, but good. There's another queer thing in his house," proceeded Wemmick as though he was continuing our earlier talk about Mr. Jaggers' housekeeper. "He never has a door or window fastened at night."

"Is he never robbed?"

"Never!" replied Wemmick. "He announces to everyone, 'I want to see the man who'll rob *me*.' I've heard him say it even to safecrackers in our office. Not a man of them would be brave enough to try it for love or money."

"They're afraid of him?"

"Afraid of him! They certainly are! He's clever though, in spite of his daring. He keeps no silver in the house. Every spoon is cheap metal."

"So they wouldn't get much," I said, "even if they—"

"Ah! But *he* would have much," said Wemmick, interrupting me. "He'd have their lives. And if he hasn't any silver, he has other valuables. His watch is gold and worth a hundred pounds if it's worth a penny. And look at his watch chain. Mr. Pip, there are about seven hundred thieves in this town who know all about that watch. There's not a man, woman, or child among them who doesn't know every link in that chain. Yet they'd drop it as if it were red-hot if they were persuaded even to touch it."

When we reached Walworth, I found it to be a dull place with narrow lanes and small gardens. Wemmick's house was a little wooden cottage. The top of it was cut out and painted like a fort and mounted with guns. "My own doing," said Wemmick. "Looks pretty, don't it?"

I praised it highly. It was the smallest house I've ever seen, with a door almost too small to get in.

"That's a real flagstaff, you see," said Wemmick, "and on Sundays I run up a real flag. And look here. After I have crossed the bridge, I hoist it up so no one can get over."

The bridge was a plank, and it crossed a ditch about four feet wide and two deep. But it was a pleasure to see the pride with which he raised it up and fastened it.

"At nine o'clock every night," said Wemmick, "I fire the gun. See, there it is."

I saw that it was mounted on a lattice work and covered by canvas.

"Then at the back of my house," he went on, "out of sight, there's a pig and chickens and rabbits. I grow cucumbers there too. So you see, if you can imagine that this place is really a fort, as I like to pretend it is, it would have plenty of provisions for a long time if it were besieged."

Then he led me to a little arbor about a dozen yards off, approached by a winding path. Here our punch was cooling in a tiny lake with an island in the middle. When you started a windmill and took a cork out of a pipe, a fountain sprayed water enough to wet the back of your hand.

"I am my own engineer, carpenter, plumber, gardener, and jack-of-all-trades," said Mr. Wemmick when I had complimented him. "It's a good thing, you know. It pleases the Aged. You wouldn't mind being introduced to the Aged at once, would you?"

We went inside the castle. There we found sitting by the fire a very old man, clean, cheerful, and well cared for, but extremely deaf. "Well, aged parent," said Mr. Wemmick, shaking hands will him, "how are you?"

"All right, John, all right!" replied the old man.

"Here's Mr. Pip, aged parent," said Wemmick, "and I wish you could hear his name. Nod away at him, Mr. Pip. That's what he likes. Nod away at him, like winking."

"This is a fine place of my son's, sir," cried the old man, while I nodded as hard as I possibly could. "This spot and the beautiful things on it should be kept as a park by the nation after my son dies."

"You're proud of it, ain't you, Aged?" said Wemmick with his hard face really softened. "There's a nod for you. And there's another. If you're not tired, Mr. Pip, nod once more. It pleases him so."

I kept at it and he was in great spirits. We left him preparing to feed the chickens and sat down to our punch. Wemmick told me as he smoked his pipe that it had taken a good many years to put the property to its present shape.

"I hope Mr. Jaggers admires it?" I asked.

"Never seen it," said Wemmick. "Never heard of it. Never seen the Aged. Never heard of him. No, the office is one thing and private life another. When I go to the office, I leave the castle behind me, and when I come into the castle, I leave the office behind me. If you don't mind, I'd be pleased if you'd do the same."

Of course I said I would. The punch being nice, we sat there drinking and talking until it was almost nine o'clock. "Getting near gun fire," said Wemmick, laying down his pipe. "It's the Aged's treat."

Going into the castle again, we found the Aged heating a poker in preparation for the nightly ceremony. Wemmick stood with his watch in his hand, until it was time to take the red-hot poker and go up on the fort. Finally he went out, and the gun went off with a bang that shook the house and made every glass and teacup rattle. Then the Aged cried out joyously, "He's fired! I heard him!" and I nodded until I positively couldn't see him.

There was a neat little girl who looked after the Aged during the day and waited on us at supper. Then the bridge was lowered for her and she went away for the night. The supper was excellent, and I liked my little bedroom in the tower. I was completely pleased with the way I was entertained. Wemmick was up early the next morning. I saw him doing a bit of gardening and nodding at the Aged pleasantly. Our breakfast was as good as the supper, and at half past eight we started back to the office. By degrees Wemmick got drier and harder as we went along, and his mouth tightened again. At last, when we got to his place of business, he looked as though the castle and the drawbridge and the arbor and the lake and the fountain and the Aged had all been blown away by his gun.

When we went into the office, my guardian was in his room and called me in to invite my friends and me to dinner. "No style and no dinner dress," he said. "Come tomorrow. Come here and I'll take you home with me."

We were there at six the next evening. There were people waiting around as usual when we went out into the street. And as we walked along Jaggers was recognized again and again, but he took no notice of anyone.

His house was in Soho. It was a large place badly in need of paint and with dirty windows. We all followed him into a bare, gloomy hall and up a staircase into a series of three dark brown rooms. The table was set for dinner. He told us that the whole house was his, but he seldom used any more of it. There was no silver on the table, of course, and there was a serving table beside his chair with a variety of bottles on it and dishes of fruit for dessert. Everything was where he could reach it and serve it himself.

A bookcase in the room was full of books about criminal law, trials, and such things. A table in the corner had papers on it and a shaded lamp. It all looked businesslike as though he had brought the office home with him.

As he had scarcely seen my three companions until now, he stood looking at them. To my surprise he seemed chiefly interested in Drummle. "Pip," said he, "I don't know one from the other. Who's the spider?"

"The spider?" said I.

"The sprawling, sulky fellow with the bad skin?"

"That's Bentley Drummle," I answered.

"I like the look of that fellow," said he, paying attention

to no one else but immediately starting to talk to Bentley.

Then the housekeeper came in with the first course. She looked to be about forty years old, though she might have been older. She was tall and graceful. She was very pale and had dull eyes and a great deal of hair, like a witch. Her lips were parted as though she found breathing difficult, and there was a look of nervousness on her face. She set a dish she was carrying on the table and then disappeared.

We had a very fine meal of fish and mutton and chicken. There were all the wines and sauces we could possibly want. Our host passed everything to us himself, even clean knives and forks for each course. There was no other servant but the housekeeper. I watched her particularly because Wemmick had told me to and because of her strange appearance. She kept her eyes on my guardian. Whenever she was in the room she acted as if she dreaded his calling her back when she had left.

Dinner was a gay affair. My guardian seemed to be letting us choose subjects of conversation though I had a feeling he was leading us all on to show our weakest sides. I found myself bragging about spending money and about my great expectations. Drummle, in his ill-natured and suspicious way, pretended that he was braver and stronger than all of us. We started stretching out our arms and showing our muscles to prove he was wrong.

When the housekeeper began clearing the table, my guardian seemed to pay no attention to her but to continue his interest in Drummle. Suddenly, he put his large hand on hers like a trap as she stretched it across the table. His action was so unexpected that we all stopped in the middle of what we were saying.

"If you talk of strength," said Mr. Jaggers, "I'll show you a wrist. Molly, let them see your wrist."

The hand which he held was on the table, but she put

the other one behind her back. "Master," she said in a low, pleading voice, "don't."

"I'll show you a wrist," he repeated. "Molly, let them see your wrist. Let them see both your wrists."

He turned the wrist of the hand he help up on the table. She put her other one beside it. It was much disfigured—deeply scarred across and across. She looked at each of us in succession as we gazed at her hands.

"Very few men have as powerful wrists as this woman has," said Mr. Jaggers coldly. "It's remarkable what a grip she has. I have noticed many hands, but I never saw stronger ones, man's or woman's."

She continued to look at each of us in succession as he said these words. When he had stopped, she looked at him again. "That will do, Molly," he said. "You have been admired and can go." She left the room as quietly as she had entered.

As the evening went on, I suppose we all drank a little too much and talked too much. And Drummle never missed a chance to show his meanness. He told us he would never lend anyone a cent of money, though we knew he had borrowed from Startop only that week. When we reminded him of it, he picked up a glass and would have thrown it at Startop if our host hadn't stopped him.

At nine-thirty Mr. Jaggers pulled out his gold watch and, looking at it, told us he was sorry but it was time for the party to be over. Drummle stalked off by himself, refusing Startop's invitation to walk with him. Herbert and I were staying in town that night. I could not see why my guardian had taken such a liking to Drummle. "I like that Spider, Pip," he said to me as I left. "Don't have too much to do with him, though. But I like him."

About a month after that the Spider's time with Mr. Pocket was up, and, to the great relief of all of us, he left for home.

18 Unwelcome Memories

My dear Mr. Pip,

"I write this by request of Mr. Gargery for to let you know that he is going to London in company with Mr. Wopsle and would be glad to see you. He would call at Barnard's Inn Tuesday morning at nine. Send word if that's not agreeable to you. Your poor sister is much the same as when you left. We talk of you in the kitchen every night and wonder what you are saying and doing. If our writing you is taking too much of a liberty, excuse it for love of the poor old days. No more, dear Pip, from

Your ever obliging and affectionate
Biddy.

P.S. I hope you'll see him even though you are a gentleman now. You always had a good heart, and he is a wonderful, wonderful man.

I received this letter in the mail Monday morning. So the appointment was for the next day. Let me admit that I didn't look forward to Joe's coming with pleasure. If I could have kept him away by paying money, I would have done so. I was relieved that he was not coming to Hammersmith, where Bentley Drummle would have to meet him. Even though I despised Bentley, I was ashamed to have him see Joe. I didn't mind Herbert or his father doing so.

By now our rooms at Barnard's Inn had been expensively furnished by me. I even had a boy to wait on me—the son of my washerwoman—whom I had dressed up in a blue coat, a yellow vest, and cream-colored trousers. I ordered this child to be on duty Tuesday morning. Herbert suggested things for breakfast that he thought Joe would like, and we both got up early to make the sitting room and the breakfast table as attractive as possible. As the time approached, I would have liked to run away. Soon I heard Joe's clumsy footsteps on the stairs. He stopped outside the door to read my name. Then Pepper, my boy, announced, "Mr. Gargery!"

"Joe! how are you, Joe?"

"Pip! how *air* you, Pip?"

With his good honest face glowing and shining, he put his hat down on the floor and caught both my hands in his.

"I am glad to see you, Joe. Give me your hat."

But Joe wouldn't part with it and held on to it while he talked with me.

"You are that growed up," said Joe. "You're gentlefolk now—an honor to your king and country."

"And you, Joe, look wonderfully well."

"Thank God," said Joe, "I'm equal to most. And your sister, she's no worse than she were. And Biddy, she's ever right and ready. And friends are all the same—except Wopsle. He's left the church and gone into playacting. Which is why he is in London now along with me."

Here Joe handed me a playbill of a small city theater announcing the first appearance that very week of a "celebrated actor from the country whose unusual performance in Shakespeare had been a sensation in local theaters."

Just then Herbert came in and I presented him to Joe. "Your servant, sir," said Joe, "and I hope you two gentleman can keep your healths in this stuffy place. It may be a very good inn according to London opinions, but I wouldn't keep a pig in it myself, not if I wanted him to grow fat and strong."

Having made this not very flattering speech about our home, Joe accepted our invitation to sit down at the table. He put his hat on the corner of the mantel piece, from which it fell off every now and then, and he rushed to pick it up and put it back.

"When did you come to town, Mr. Gargery?" asked Herbert, pouring our tea.

"Were it yesterday afternoon?" said Joe. "No, it were not. Yes, it were. It were yesterday afternoon."

"Have you seen anything of London yet?"

"Why yes, sir," said Joe, "me and Wopsle have been looking around."

All through the meal he sat up stiff and awkward. He had moved his chair so far away from the table that he dropped more food than he ate and pretended that he hadn't dropped it. He stared straight ahead of him and coughed with embarrassment. I was glad when Herbert left us to go to work.

I had neither the good sense nor the good feeling to know that this was all my fault. If I had been more at ease with Joe, Joe would have been more at ease with me. I felt impatient and bad tempered with him, I let him see that I was ashamed of him, and he heaped coals of fire on my head.

"Us two being now alone, sir—" began Joe.

"Joe," I interrupted crossly, "how can you call me sir?"

Joe looked at me with something like reproach. "Us two being now alone," he went on, "and me intending to stay not many minutes more, I will mention now what led me to come here. For I would not have had the honor to eat in the home of two gentlemen if I hadn't wanted to do something for you."

This time I had nothing to say.

"Well, sir," continued Joe, "this is how it were. I were at the Bargemen 'tother night when up come Pumblechook. He do often rub me the wrong way by giving out around town that you and he were always best friends."

"Nonsense. It was you, Joe."

"Which I fully believe it were, Pip, though it doesn't matter now, sir. Well, he come to the Bargemen and his words were, 'Joseph, Miss Havisham she wish to speak to you.'"

"Yes, Joe? Go on please."

"Next day, sir, having cleaned myself up, I go and see her. 'You hear from Mr. Pip?' she asks. Having had a letter from you, I were able to say, 'I do.' 'Would you tell him then,' said she, 'that Estella has come home and would be glad to see him.'"

My face grew red. I hope it was partly because I was ashamed of having been so mean to Joe when he had come to do me a favor.

"Biddy," continued Joe, "hung back a little when I asked her to write the message to you. Biddy say, 'I know he will be glad to hear it from you. It's now holiday time. You want to see him. Go.' I have now finished, sir," said Joe, rising from his chair. "And, Pip, I wish you to be ever well and happy."

"But you're not going now, Joe?"

"Yes, I am," said Joe.

"But you're coming back for dinner, Joe?"

"No, I am not."

Our eyes met, and all the "sir" melted out of his manly heart as he gave me his hand.

"Pip, dear old chap, life is made up of many parts welded together. One man's a blacksmith and one's a goldsmith, and one's a coppersmith. Separations between friends must come and must be met as they come. If there's been any fault at all today, it's mine. You and me are not two people to be together in London—or anywhere else but in private. It ain't that I'm proud. I just want always to be right. And I'm wrong in these clothes and wrong away from the forge and the kitchen and the marshes. You won't find half so much wrong about me if you'll think of me in the forge with the hammer in my hand. You won't find half so much wrong if you ever come to see me and put your head in at the forge window and see Joe the blacksmith there at his anvil sticking to the old work. I'm awful dull, but I hope I've beat out the truth for you in these words. And so God bless you, dear old Pip, old chap, God bless you!"

I was right when I thought there was a simple dignity about him. He touched me gently on the forehead and went out. As soon as I could think what to do, I hurried after him. But he was gone.

It was clear to me that I must go to our town next day. At first, when I thought of Joe's visit, it was my firm idea that I must stay at Joe's. But when I had bought a coach ticket and had been down to Mr. Pocket's and back, I began to change my mind and invent reasons why I should stay at the Blue Boar. I would be a bother at Joe's. I was not expected, and my bed would not be ready. I would be too far from Miss Havisham's. She might not like it. So I cheated myself with excuses.

Having decided that I must go to the Blue Boar, I wondered whether I should take my boy with me. It was fun to think of the impression he would make on Trabb's boy and all the other people who had known me in my earlier days. Miss Havisham might hear of him, however, and might disapprove. I decided to leave him behind. I had planned to take the afternoon coach. It was winter now, and I would not arrive until two or three hours after dark. At that time it was customary to carry convicts down to the docks by stagecoach. I had often seen them, and so was not surprised when Herbert, coming down to see me off, told me there were two convicts going down with me. I had an old, old reason for shivering whenever I heard the word convict.

"You don't mind them, Handel?" said Herbert.

"Oh, no!"

"I thought you acted as though you didn't like them."

"I can't pretend that I like them. But I don't mind them."

"See! there they are," said Herbert, "coming out of the bar. What a disgusting sight!"

I suppose they had been treating their guard, for all three came out wiping their mouths. The two convicts were handcuffed together and had chains on their legs—leg chains of a pattern I also knew well. One was taller and stouter than the other. I knew his half-closed eye at one glance. There stood the man whom I had seen at the Three Jolly Bargemen on a Saturday night, who had stirred his drink with a file!

He did not recognize me at all. He looked across at me and at my watch chain and then said something to the other convict. They both laughed and then looked away. The big numbers on their backs, their rough appearance, their chains, the way everyone tried not to look at them made them a most disagreeable sight. And as it happened, the convict I had recognized sat behind me with his breath blowing on my hair.

"Good-bye, Handel!" Herbert called out as we started. How lucky that he had found another name for me!

I can't describe how I felt about the convict's breathing on me. I shrank away from him as far as possible. The weather was miserably raw and the two cursed the cold. It made us all dull before we had gone far, and we dozed and shivered and were silent. I went to sleep asking myself whether I ought to give back a couple of pounds to this creature before we left the coach and how I could best

manage it. I must have slept longer than I thought, because when I wakened, I could feel marshland in the cold damp wind that blew at us. The convicts, bending forward for warmth, were closer to me than before. The very first words I heard from them were the words of my own thoughts— "Two one-pound notes."

"How did he get 'em?" said the convict I had never seen.

"How should I know?" replied the other. "He had 'em stowed away somewhere. Giv' him by friends, I expect."

"I wish I had 'em here," said his companion. "I'd sell all the friends I ever had for one and think it a good bargain. Well? So he says—"

"So he says—it was all said and done in half a minute behind a pile of timber on the dock—'you're going to be discharged'. I was. Would I find that boy that fed him and kept his secret and give him them two one-pound notes? Yes I would. And I did."

"More fool you," growled the other. "I'd have spent 'em on wittles and drinks. He must have been a green one. Mean to say he didn't even know you?"

"Not a bit. Different gangs and different ship. He was tried again for prison breaking and made a lifer."

After hearing this, I would surely have gotten out into the darkness of the highway if I hadn't felt sure the man didn't know who I was. Of course, I was not only so much older but in such different circumstances that it was not at all likely he would recognize me. Still, our happening to be together on the coach was so strange that I feared something else might occur to make him recognize me. So I decided to get out as soon as we reached the town. The convicts went their way on the coach. I knew where they would be taken down to the river. I could see in my imagination the boat with its convict crew waiting for them and the wicked ship lying out on the black water.

I don't know what I was afraid of, but I was completely terrified. As I walked to the hotel I was trembling. Probably the terrors of my childhood had come back to me. The coffeeshop of the Blue Boar was empty. I had ordered my dinner and sat down to it before the waiter knew me. At once he asked if he should send for Mr. Pumblechook.

"No," said I. "Certainly not."

He looked surprised and as soon as possible put a dirty old copy of a local newspaper on my table. I picked it up and read this paragraph:

"Our readers will be interested to learn something about the rise in fortunes of a certain young man of this neighborhood. His earliest helper, companion, and friend is a highly respected man connected with the corn and seed trade and with offices on High Street. It is good to know that someone in our town was the founder of the young man's fortunes."

I have a feeling that if I had gone to the North Pole, I would have met someone even there who would have told me that Pumblechook was the cause of my good fortune.

19 *A Strange Reunion*

I was up and out early in the morning—too early to go to Miss Havisham's. I walked around the town for a while, thinking of my benefactor and dreaming of all the plans she might have for me. She had adopted Estella. She had as good as adopted me. It surely must be her plan to bring us together. She intended me to restore the lonely house, let sunshine into the dark rooms, and set the clocks going. I was to be the young knight of romance who would marry the princess. Estella was my inspiration for everything. I loved her. Her influence on me had been all-powerful right from the start. Yet even this romantic morning I was not deceived about her. I loved her with no reason to love her. I knew she would not bring me peace or happiness.

I rang the bell at the same time I used to arrive at the house in the old days. I tried to get my breath and slow up the beating of my heart. Footsteps approached the gate, the gate opened, and there stood—Orlick! "Yes," he said, "here I am. There have been changes around here."

"How did you get here?"

"I come here on my legs."

"Are you here for good?"

"I ain't here for bad, young master, I suppose."

I was not so sure of that. I asked him how long it had

been since he left the forge. "One day is so like another here," he answered, "that I don't know without figuring it out."

"There never used to be a porter here," I said, as I followed him into a little room looking out on the courtyard, which was evidently his.

"No," said he, "not until the news went around that there was no protection from thieves and convicts here. Then I was recommended as a man who could give another man as good as he brought. It's easier than being a blacksmith."

I caught sight of a gun on the wall.

"That's loaded, that is," said he as I left him.

I went down the long hallway I had walked so often in the past. At the end of it was Sarah Pocket, who looked at me as sourly as usual and greeted me coldly. Then I climbed the stairs to Miss Havisham's room and knocked on her door.

"Pip's knock," I heard her say. "Come in, Pip."

She was in her chair near the old table with her two hands crossed on her stick and her eyes on the fire. Sitting near her, with the white shoe that had never been worn in her hand, was an elegant lady whom I had never seen.

"How do you do, Pip?" said Miss Havisham. "So you kiss my hand as if I were a queen, eh? Well?"

"I heard, Miss Havisham," said I, rather puzzled by her actions, "that you wished me to come to see you. So I came at once."

The lady beside her lifted up her eyes and looked at me with amusement. Then I saw it was Estella. She was much changed, much more beautiful. She had made much more progress in every way than I had. I imagined as I looked at her that I had become the rough and common boy again.

"Do you find her much changed, Pip?" asked Miss

Havisham. "Doesn't she seem like the old Estella? She was proud and insulting and you wanted to go away from her. Don't you remember?"

I said with confusion that that was long ago when I didn't know any better. Estella smiled and said that she probably had been very disagreeable then.

"Is he changed?" Miss Havisham asked her. "Less rough and common?"

Estella looked at me carefully and laughed as she put the shoe down. She still treated me as a boy, but yet she led me on. She had just come from France and was going to London, she said. She seemed as proud and willful as ever, but I thought these qualities unimportant compared to her beauty. Seeing her again, I could understand all my longings for wealth and importance and all my shame of home and Joe. She was part of my inmost life and thoughts.

I was to stay there all day, return to the hotel that night, and go to London the next day. When we had talked for a while, Miss Havisham sent us out to walk in the garden. As we went out through the gate I had used when I had my fight with Herbert, I was trembling with my worship of her. She was decidedly not worshipping me. When we came to the scene of our struggle she said, "I must have been a queer little creature to hide and see that fight that day. But I did, and I enjoyed it very much."

"You rewarded me very much."

"Did I? I know I had no liking then for the boy you fought with. I thought he was a pest."

"He and I are good friends now."

"Are you? Since your change in fortune, you must have changed your companions," said Estella.

"Naturally," said I.

"And very necessarily," she added in a proud tone.

"What was fit company for you once would be quite unfit for you now."

If I had had any intentions up to now of going to see Joe, I changed my mind at this.

"You had no idea of your approaching good fortune in those times?"

"Not the least."

I showed her where I had seen her walking that first day. "Did I?" she said with a cold and careless look. I reminded her where she had come out of the house and given me my dinner and she said, "I don't remember." "Not remember that you made me cry?" said I. "No," said she and shook her head. I believe that her not remembering and not minding in the least made me cry again in my heart.

"You must know," said Estella, "that I have no heart—if that has anything to do with my memory. I have no sympathy, no softness, no sentiment."

What was it that impressed me as she stood and looked attentively at me? Whom did she remind me of? I looked again, but the suggestion of someone else like her was gone. What was it?

"I am serious," said Estella. "If we are to be together much, you had better believe it at once. I have never loved anybody."

We walked into the brewery, and she remembered being up on the high gallery and seeing me standing scared below. As I watched her white hand point upward, again the strange suggestion of someone else I knew came over me. What was it?

"What is the matter?" asked Estella. "Are you scared again?"

"I would be if I believed what you said just now," I answered.

"Then you don't? Very well." Her beautiful dress had trailed on the ground. She held it up with one hand and put the other one lightly on my shoulder as we walked around the old garden. For me, it was as if it were all in flower now that I was with her. We were about the same age, but I felt as though she was so far above me in every way I could never reach her. I was miserable in spite of my belief that our benefactor had chosen us for each other.

At last we went back into the house, and there I heard with surprise that my guardian had come down to see Miss Havisham on business and would stay to dinner. Miss Havisham was in her chair now and waiting for me to push her as in the old days. It was like pushing the chair itself back into the past as we began our slow walk around the ruins of the bridal feast. But now Estella made everything bright and beautiful.

The time flew by and Estella left us to dress for dinner. She looked back over her shoulder before going out, and Miss Havisham blew a kiss at her with dreadful seriousness. When we two were left alone, she said to me in a whisper, "Is she beautiful? Do you admire her?"

"Everyone who sees her must, Miss Havisham."

She put an arm around my neck and pulled my head down close to hers. "Love her, love her, love her!" she cried. "If she is good to you, love her. If she hurts you, love her. If she tears your heart to pieces, love her!"

I have never seen such violent feeling shown by anyone.

"Hear me, Pip. I adopted her to be loved. I educated her to be loved. I made her what she is so that she would be loved. Love her!"

She said the word so often there could be no doubt that she meant to say it. But it sounded on her lips more like a curse.

"I'll tell you," said she, "what real love is. It is blind devotion and complete loss of pride. It is trust and belief against the whole world. It is giving your whole heart and soul to the one who goes against you—as I did!"

She cried out wildly and rose up in her chair. I caught

her around the waist and pulled her down to calm her. Then, turning around, I saw that my guardian had entered the room. Miss Havisham saw him at the same moment. Like everyone else she was afraid of him. She tried at once to be calm and stammered that he was as always on time.

"On time as ever?" he repeated. "Shall I give you a ride, Miss Havisham? And so you are here, Pip?"

I told him Miss Havisham had asked me to come and see Estella. To which he replied, "Ah! Very fine young lady!" Then he put one hand in his trousers pocket as though that pocket were full of secrets.

"Jaggers," said Miss Havisham, "go down with Pip to your dinner."

We went down the dark stairs together. On the way he asked me how often I had seen Miss Havisham eat and drink. I thought a minute and then said, "Never."

"And never will, Pip. She does not let herself be seen doing either one. She wanders around in the night and eats then."

"May I ask you a question, sir?" said I.

"You may, and I may refuse to answer it."

"Estella's name, is it Havisham or—"

"It is Havisham."

This brought us to the dinner table, where Estella and Sarah Pocket were waiting for us. We had a very fine meal served by a servant girl whom I had never seen there before. All through our meal Mr. Jaggers was more silent than I had ever seen him. He scarcely looked at Estella, though she looked at him often with curiosity, and, I thought, distrust. He seemed to me to act as though he knew so much about everyone there it would be safer if he said nothing.

After dinner Miss Pocket excused herself and we went back to Miss Havisham's room, where we four played whist. Miss Havisham had put some of her loveliest jewels on Estella. Even my guardian raised his eyebrows a bit when he looked at her. On the whole, he treated all three of us as though we were problems he had solved long ago.

Before we left at nine o'clock, it was planned that when Estella came to London, I would meet her at the coach. My guardian had the next room to mine at the Blue Boar. Far into the night Miss Havisham's words, "Love her, love her, love her!" sounded in my ears. Hundreds of times I said into my pillow, "I love her!" Then I was filled with gratitude that she was intended for me, a blacksmith's boy. But when would she begin to be interested in me? When could I make her know she had a heart?

I thought those were high and worthy feelings. But I never thought there was anything low or mean about my keeping away from Joe because Estella would look down on him. Only yesterday Joe had brought tears to my eyes. God forgive me, they had soon dried.

The next morning I told my guardian what I knew of Orlick. We agreed that he was not the right sort of man to fill a position of trust at Miss Havisham's. "I'll go around at once and pay our friend off," he said. I was a little frightened by his haste and suggested delay in the matter. I even hinted that he might be difficult to deal with. "Oh, no, he won't," said my guardian. "I should like to see him argue the question with *me.*"

I had been all the time in dread of Pumblechook's discovering me in town. In order to avoid passing his shop, I made a loop out into the country and came out on the road again far beyond him. It was interesting to be in the quiet old town. It was agreeable for me to be recognized by the storekeepers in what I thought was my important position. I would have been proud of myself if it had not been for Trabb's boy. When he caught sight of me he first pretended to be frightened. Then he strutted along beside me, imitating my walk so perfectly that he had a number of bystanders laughing. I was angry beyond words.

I got back to London that day safe, but not sound. My heart was gone. As soon as I arrived I sent a cod fish and a barrel of oysters to Joe to make up for my neglect of him and then went on to Barnard's Inn. Herbert was as always glad to see me. I had much to talk over with him and sent my boy—who was often more of a bother than a help—to the theater so that we could be alone.

When I told about my love for Estella, Herbert was not surprised. "I've always known it, Handel," he said. "When you told me your own story, you told me plainly that you began adoring her the first time you saw her, when you were very young indeed."

"She has come home a most beautiful and elegant creature," I said, "but she is thousands of miles away from me yet. I was a blacksmith's boy only yesterday. And what am I today? I feel unsafe and uncertain. All my hopes are dependent on one person."

Herbert cheered me up by saying that Mr. Jaggers would have had nothing to do with my affair if he hadn't been sure of what he was doing. "You'll be twenty-one soon, and then you'll know where you stand."

I would have felt better for his cheerful opinions if he had not ended our talk about Estella by warning me in the kindest way possible against her. "Think of her bringing up. Think of Miss Havisham," he said. "Think of what she herself is now. She may lead you into misery. Your inheritance cannot depend on your marrying her, for your guardian has never referred to her directly or indirectly in any way."

"I know all of that, Herbert," I said, "but I cannot think of giving her up, no matter what she does to me."

That ending the matter, Herbert changed the subject by telling me he too was in love.

"Her name is Clara," he said. "She lives in London, and the foolish idea of my family is that she is somewhat beneath me. Her father was a purser* on a passenger ship."

"What is he now?" I asked.

"He's an invalid," said Herbert. "I have never seen him because he has always stayed up in his room ever since I've known Clara. But I've heard him all the time. He makes terrible noises—roars and pounds on the floor."

"Don't you expect to see him?" said I.

"Oh, yes, I'm always expecting to see him," said he, "because I never hear him without being sure the floor will give way and he'll come tumbling down."

He told me that he expected to marry the young lady as soon as he had made some money. "But you can't marry, you know," said he "while you're looking around."

That night we went to the theater to see Mr. Wopsle act the part of Hamlet.** It was a bad enough performance. He thought it a great success—or so he told us when we invited him home to supper after the play.

I went to bed unhappy after all and thought miserably about Estella. I dreamed that I had no expectations and that I had to give my hand in marriage to Herbert's Clara or play Hamlet before twenty thousand people without knowing twenty words of it.

---

*Purser: an officer on a ship who takes care of the accounts.

**Hamlet: the hero of a play by Shakespeare called *Hamlet*.

20 *The Shadow of the Prison*

One day when I was busy with my books at Mr. Pocket's, I received a note in the mail which excited me very much. Though I had never seen the handwriting before, I knew at once whose it was. It had no usual beginning like Dear Mr. Pip or dear anything, but said as follows:

> I am to come to London day after tomorrow by the noon-time coach. I believe it was settled that you should meet me? At any rate, Miss Havisham expects you to. That is why I'm writing you. She sends you her regards.
>
> Yours,
> Estella

If there had been time, I would probably have ordered several suits of clothes for the occasion. As it was, I had to be content with those I had. My appetite disappeared at once, and I knew no peace or rest until the day arrived. When it did come, I was worse than ever, and went to meet the coach before it had left the Blue Boar in our town. I was just starting my long wait when Wemmick came along. I inquired after the Castle and the Aged. "Both fine, thank you," said Wemmick, "particularly the Aged. He'll be eighty-two next birthday. I have a notion to fire off the cannon eighty-two times, if it will hold out that long and the neighborhood don't object. Where do you think I'm going now?"

"To the office," said I.

"Next thing to it," answered Wemmick. "To Newgate Prison to have a word with some of our cases there. Would you like to have a look at the place?"

I had so much time to spare that the suggestion came as a relief. Before I left, I went into the office to make sure again of the earliest possible moment the coach could come, and then we set out. We were at Newgate in a few minutes. At that time jails were much neglected. It was visiting time when we arrived and a man was going around selling beer to the prisoners. It was a noisy, ugly, and heartbreaking scene. Wemmick walked among the prisoners like a gardener among his plants, greeting first one and then the other, and remarking about how well they looked. He was very popular. He consulted with several of them agreeably, once or twice telling them they didn't have money enough to pay Mr. Jaggers for defending them. Apparently my guardian could do wonders in court—but wouldn't do them unless the rewards were high. I was impressed with his cleverness. To tell the truth, I wished, and not for the first time, that I had some other guardian—one not quite so clever.

Mr. Wemmick and I parted at his office, and I went back to await the stage coach. There I spent my time thinking how strange it was that I should have been always so much connected with prisons and crime. In my childhood on the lonely marshes the first knowledge of them came to me. Two occasions since then I had been reminded of them. Now, through Mr. Wemmick and Mr. Jaggers, they were with me again. Then I thought of the beautiful, proud, young Estella. The contrast between the jail and her horrified me. I wished that I had not gone with Wemmick on this day of all days. I did not want the smell of a prison on me when I met her. Soon I saw her face at the coach window and her hand waving to me. Again the strange feeling I had

had about her before came over me. Where had I seen someone like her?

In her traveling dress trimmed with fur, Estella looked
to me more beautiful than ever. Her manner was more
pleasant than it had been. I felt that Miss Havisham was
probably responsible for the change. We stood in the inn
yard while I collected her luggage. "I am going to Richmond
in Surrey," she told me, "ten miles from here. I am to have
a carriage and you are to take me. Take my purse and pay
my expenses out of it. These are our instructions. We are
not free to follow our own ideas, you and I." I looked for
some hidden meaning in her words, but there seemed to
be none.

"Will you rest here while I get a carriage?" I asked.

"Yes, I am to rest here and drink some tea and you are
to take care of me."

The place where we ate was far from attractive. Yet
because Estella was with me, it seemed wonderful. I thought
I could be happy there with her for life.

"Where are you going in Richmond?" I asked her.

"I am going to live at great expense with a lady there
who will take me around and introduce me and show
me off."

"I suppose you will be glad of the change and the
admiration?"

"Yes, I suppose so," she answered carelessly, as though
she were speaking of someone else.

"How are you getting along with Mr. Pocket?" she
went on.

"I live quite pleasantly there. At least—"

"At least?" asked Estella.

"As pleasantly as I could anywhere away from you."

"You silly boy," said Estella calmly, "how can you talk
such nonsense? Your friend Mr. Matthew Pocket is, I believe, better than the rest of his family. He's above such

evils as jealousy and spite, I have heard. Is that the case?"

"I am sure I have every reason to say so."

"You have no reason to say so about her other relatives," said Estella. "They are constantly reporting bad things about you to Miss Havisham. They watch you, tell untruths about you, and write letters about you. You can't imagine how much they hate you."

Here Estella burst out laughing, to my amazement. "I'm laughing because they fail of their purpose so badly," she explained. "Ah, these people and the tortures they suffer with Miss Havisham!" She laughed again so hard that I thought her very strange. It did not seem to me there was anything that funny in the situation. She saw the thought in my mind and anwered it. "It is not easy for even you," said Estella, "to know what satisfaction it gives me to see these people defeated. You were not brought up from a baby in that strange house. I was. You haven't watched them for years plot against you and try to get you out of their way while they pretended to pity you and be kind to you. I have." It was no laughing matter with Estella now. I would not have wanted her to look that way about me for all my expectations.

"Two things I can tell you," she said. "You may feel sure that these people will never in a hundred years harm you with Miss Havisham. Second, I'm grateful to you that they are being so busy and so mean for nothing. And here's my hand on it."

So she gave it to me playfully. I held it and put it to my lips. "You foolish boy," said Estella, "will you never take warning, or are you kissing my hand in the same spirit in which I once let you kiss my cheek?"

"What spirit was that?" said I.

"I must think a moment. It was a spirit of scorn for the relatives plotting to get Miss Havisham's money."

"If I say yes, may I kiss your cheek again?"

I leaned down, and her calm face was like a statue's. "Now," she said, moving away the instant I had touched her, "you are to see that I have some tea, and you are to take me to Richmond."

I suffered because she spoke as though we were together only because we had been forced to be. Whatever her tone, it gave me no hope or trust in the future. So we had our tea and then drove away. On the way we passed the walls of the prison. "What place is that?" Estella asked me.

I acted at first as though I did not recognize it and then told her. As she looked at it and murmured, "Miserable people!" I would not have told her for anything that I had just been there. "Mr. Jaggers," I said then, "has a reputation for knowing more of the secrets in that dismal place than any man in London."

"He knows more of the secrets of every place, I think," said Estella in a low voice.

"You are used to seeing him often, I suppose?"

"I have seen him at irregular intervals ever since I can remember. But I know him no better than I did before I could talk. How do you get on with him?"

"Once I got used to his suspicious manner," I said, "I've done very well."

"Are you intimate with him?"

"I have dined at his house."

"I imagine," said Estella shivering, "that it must be a strange place."

"It *is* a strange place."

I shouldn't have discussed my guardian so freely with her. Yet I was about to go on to describe our dinner. Suddenly, however, the strange feeling I had had so often about her came over me. When it had passed she had changed the subject. We talked about the parts of London we were going through, and she told me the city was almost new to her. She had never left Miss Havisham's until she had gone to France. When I asked her if my guardian would have charge of her while she was in Richmond, she answered, "God forbid!" and no more.

When we passed through Hammersmith, I showed her where Mr. Pocket lived. I pointed out that it was not far from Richmond. I said I hoped I would see her sometimes.

"Oh, yes, you are to see me. You are to come when you wish. The family with whom I am to stay have already been told about you."

I asked whether it was a large household she was entering.

"No, there are only two, mother and daughter. The mother is important socially, though she doesn't object to adding to her income."

"I am surprised that Miss Havisham could part with you again so soon."

"It is part of her plans for me, Pip," she said with a sigh, as if she were tired. "I am to write to her constantly and see her regularly. I am to report how I get on—I and the jewels, for they are nearly all mine now."

It was the first time she had ever called me by my name. Of course she did so purposely, knowing I would treasure it.

We arrived in Richmond all too soon. The house was a dignified old one, where hoops and powder and embroidered coats and swords had held sway in the earlier days. A bell sounded in the moonlight, and two maids came out to receive Estella. She gave me her hand and a smile and said good night as she went in. I stood looking at the house, thinking how happy I would be if I lived there with her and knowing that I never was happy with her but always miserable.

With a bad heartache I got into the carriage to be taken back to Hammersmith.

21 *The Funeral*

As I grew accustomed to my expectations, I began to notice their effect on me and on those around me. I knew that they had not improved me. I was always uneasy about my treatment of Joe. My conscience was not comfortable about Biddy. When I woke up in the night, I used to think I would have been better if I had never seen Miss Havisham. Then I would have been satisfied to be partners with Joe in the honest old forge. Many a time in the evening when I sat alone looking at the fire, I thought, after all, there were no fires like the forge fire and the kitchen fire at home.

How much Estella was responsible for my restlessness I couldn't say. I realized, however, that I was being of no use to anybody, particularly Herbert. My extravagance had led his easy nature into expenses he could not afford. I had done him only wrong by crowding his rooms with elaborate furniture and letting him be waited on by my boy. I had begun to be heavily in debt, and Herbert had followed my example. We had joined a useless and expensive club. Bentley Drummle, who now owned his own carriage, was one of its members.

Meanwhile Herbert was finding no work to do that would enable him to make a good living. He was still "looking around" but finding nothing. Our debts mounted until we were in constant fear of the people to whom we owed money.

One evening when we had settled down to go over our debts and see what we could do about them, a letter arrived for me. It was signed Trabb, the Undertaker, and it told me that my sister, Mrs. J. Gargery, had died, and my attendance at the funeral was requested.

It was the first time that death had touched me, and I was greatly affected by it. Day and night I thought of my sister in her chair by the fire. I could not imagine the place without her. And though she had seldom been in my thoughts lately, now the sound of her voice and the look of her face and figure were with me constantly. No matter what my life had been like, I could not have remembered my sister with much tenderness. Still, I felt a shock of regret at her death. Under its influence, I was seized with a violent rage against the person who had attacked her. I would have pursued Orlick or anyone else who would be proved guilty to any lengths to get revenge.

I wrote my sympathies to Joe and told him I would come to the funeral. I went down early in the morning and walked over to the forge. It was fine summer weather. As I went along, I thought of the times when I had been a little helpless creature and my sister had not been easy on me. Now I was forgiving toward her because I wondered how harshly people would judge *my* life after I was gone.

At last I came in sight of the house and saw that Trabb had taken possession. All the children of the village and most of the women were gathered around outdoors. The windows of the house and the forge were closed. Inside, Mr. Trabb was busy pinning mourning veils and bands on the hats of anyone who entered. Poor dear Joe, wrapped up in a black coat, was sitting in a corner of the room by himself. As chief mourner he had been put there by Trabb. When I bent down and said to him, "Dear Joe, how are you?" he said, "Pip, old chap, you knowed her when she was a fine figure of a—" and clasped my hand and said no more.

Biddy, looking very neat and attractive in her black dress, went quietly here and there and was very helpful. When I had spoken to her, I sat down near Joe. At one end of the room a table was set with refreshments for the mourners. Pumblechook was standing there stuffing himself and trying to attract my attention. The moment he succeeded he came over to make a fuss over me. The Hubbles were there too. We were all going to follow my sister's body to the church.

"I mean ter say, Pip," Joe whispered to me as we were being lined up two by two in the parlor, "as I would have preferred to carry her to the church myself along of three or four friendly ones wot come to do it with willing hearts and arms. But it was thought that the neighbors would look down on such as lacking proper respect."

"Handkerchiefs all!" cried Mr. Trabb now in a business-like voice. "We are ready!" So we all put handkerchiefs up to our faces and filed out two by two—Joe and I, Biddy and Mr. Pumblechook, Mr. and Mrs. Hubble. The body of my poor sister was brought around by the kitchen door, and we started out.

Soon the marshes lay clear before us with the sails of the ships on the river just beyond. We went into the church-yard close to the graves of my parents, Philip Pirrip and Georgiana, his wife. There my sister was laid quietly in the earth while the larks sang high above and the light wind made beautiful shadows of clouds and trees.

Pumblechook came home with us after the service, telling me he wished my sister could have known the great honor I had done her by rising in the world. The Hubbles came too, to drink wine and talk things over. After they had all gone and when Trabb and his men had left too, the house seemed more normal. Soon afterwards, Biddy, Joe, and I had a cold dinner together. But we dined in the best parlor, not the old kitchen, and Joe was so careful about his table manners that we were not at ease. After dinner when I made him get his pipe, and when we sat down on the big stone outside the forge, we got on better. I noticed that after the funeral he had changed his clothes and looked natural, like the man he was.

He was very much pleased by my asking if I might sleep in my own little room. I was pleased too, for I felt that I had been very generous in making the request. When the shadows of evening were falling, I found an opportunity to go into the garden with Biddy for a little talk. "Biddy," said I, "I think you might have written to me about all the sadness here."

"Do you, Mr. Pip?" said Biddy. "I would have written if I had thought I should have."

"*I* think you should have."

"Do you, Mr. Pip?"

She was so quiet and had such a pretty way with her, I did not want to hurt her feelings. "I suppose it will be difficult for you to remain here now, Biddy dear?"

"Oh! I can't do that, Mr. Pip!" said Biddy sadly. "I am going tomorrow to stay with Mrs. Hubble. I hope we'll be able to take care of Mr. Gargery until he gets used to being alone."

"How are you going to live? If you want any mon—"

"How am I going to live?" repeated Biddy. "I'll tell you, Mr. Pip. I am going to try to get a position as the teacher in the new school nearly finished here. I have been recommended by the neighbors. I can teach myself while I teach the others. You know, I learned a good deal from you and have had time since to improve myself."

"I think you would improve under any circumstances."

We walked on. "I have not heard the details of my sister's death, Biddy."

"There's not much to tell. She had been in one of her bad spells for four days. Then she came out of it in the evening, just at tea time, and said quite plainly, 'Joe.' It was the first time she had said even a word for a long while. I ran to the forge and got Mr. Gargery. She made signs to me that she wanted him to sit down close to her and wanted me to put her arms around his neck. When I did so she laid her head down on his shoulder quite content. Soon she said, 'Joe,' again and once 'pardon' and once 'Pip.' She never lifted her head up again. Just an hour later we laid her down on her own bed because she was gone."

Biddy cried. Tears in my own eyes dimmed the sight of the garden growing dark and the stars coming out.

"Nothing was ever discovered, Biddy?"

"Nothing."

"Do you know what has become of Orlick?"

"I think he is working in the quarries."

"Of course you have seen him then? Why are you looking at that dark tree in the lane?"

"I saw him there the night she died. I have seen him there since we have been walking here. It is no use," she said, putting her hand on my arm as I was about to run after him. "He was there only a minute and is gone now."

It made me very angry to learn that she was still being pursued by the fellow. I felt a hatred for him. I told her so and told her I would go to any lengths to drive him away for good. By degrees she calmed me. She told me how Joe loved me and never complained of anything. I knew she meant that he didn't complain about me. She said he always did his duty with a strong hand, a quiet tongue, and a gentle heart.

"Surely it would be impossible to praise him too much. We must often speak of these things, for now I will be down here a great deal. I am not going to leave poor Joe alone."

Biddy said nothing.

"Biddy, don't you hear me?"

"Yes, Mr. Pip."

"Biddy, not to mention your calling me Mr. Pip, which seems foolish, have the goodness to tell me what you mean by not answering me."

"Are you quite sure then that you will come to see him often?" asked Biddy, looking at me under the stars with clear and honest eyes.

"Oh, dear," I said, as though she were to blame. "You're showing the bad side of your nature again. Don't say any more, if you please. I am shocked at you."

I treated her coldly during supper and when I went to my little room to sleep. I was restless all night, thinking what an injury and an injustice Biddy had done me.

Early in the morning I was up and looking through one of the windows of the forge, watching Joe already at work with a glow of health and strength on his face.

"Good-bye, dear Joe. No, don't wipe if off. Give me your blackened hand. I shall be down soon and often."

"Never too soon, sir," said Joe, "and never too often, Pip."

Biddy was waiting for me at the kitchen door with bread and milk ready. "Biddy," said I when I gave her my hand at parting, "I am not angry, but I am hurt."

"No, don't be hurt," she pleaded sadly. "Let only me be hurt if I have been unfair."

Once more the mists were rising as I walked away. If I could have seen myself clearly in the cold light of morning, I would have seen that Biddy was right and I would not come back to visit.

22   *A Secret Partnership*

Herbert and I went from bad to worse in the way of increasing our debts. He came of age eight months before me. Since he had no money to inherit, it was an event of small importance in Barnard's Inn. But we looked forward to my twenty-first birthday, feeling sure my guardian would then say something definite. I had been careful to let him know when my birthday would arrive. The day before it I had a note from Wemmick saying that Mr. Jaggers would be glad if I would call on him at five o'clock on the afternoon of the day. I was convinced that something important was going to happen to me and went there in a state of some excitement.

My guardian was standing before the fire when I entered. "Well, Pip," he said, "I must call you Mr. Pip today. Congratulations. Take a chair, Mr. Pip," said my guardian.

As I sat down I felt at a disadvantage and remembered for some reason the time long ago when I was set down on a tombstone by someone who stood over me.

"Now, my young friend," my guardian began, "I am going to have a word or two with you. What do you suppose you are spending for your living?"

I had investigated my money matters so often I knew I had to tell him I had no idea.

"I thought so," said Mr. Jaggers and blew his nose with

an air of satisfaction. "Now I have asked *you* a question, my friend," he went on. "Have you anything to ask of *me*? If so, ask."

"If I am free to ask questions now, sir," I said, "I would like to know if my benefactor is to be made known to me today."

"No. Ask another."

"Am I to find out soon?"

"Skip that for a moment," said Mr. Jaggers, "and ask another."

"Have I anything to receive, sir?"

"I thought we would come to that." He called Wemmick, who came in, handed him a piece of paper, and then disappeared. "Now, Pip," he said, "you have been drawing money here pretty freely. You are, of course, in debt. I don't ask what you owe, because you don't know. And if you did know, you wouldn't tell me. You'd say it was less. Oh, yes, you would. You think you wouldn't, but you would. Now take this piece of paper and tell me what it is."

"It is a bank note," said I, "for five hundred pounds."

"I'm sure you consider it a generous sum of money. It is your own, Pip, a present to you this day as a start of your expectations. You will get this generous sum every year, and you will have it until the person who gives it to you appears. As I have told you before, I am only the agent. I follow instructions and am paid for doing so. I think they are unwise, but I am not paid for giving my opinion about them."

I began to express my gratitude to my benefactor for the generosity with which I was treated. He stopped me. "I am not paid, Pip," said he coldly, "to carry your words to anyone."

After a pause I said, "There was a question just now, Mr. Jaggers, which you asked me to save for a moment. May I ask it now?"

"What is it?" said he.

"Is it likely," I said, "that my unknown friend will soon come to London or will ask me to come anywhere else?"

Mr. Jaggers stared at me with his dark, deep-set eyes. "Now, here," he said, "I must remind you of the evening when we first met in the village. What did I tell you then?"

"You told me that it might be years before that person appeared."

"Just so," said Mr. Jaggers. "That's my answer."

As we gazed at each other, my breath came faster in my strong desire to get something out of him. "Do you suppose it will still be years from now, Mr. Jaggers?" I asked.

He shook his head. "I'll be plain with you, my friend Pip," he said. "That's a question I must not be asked. Answering it might get me in trouble. When the person we are talking about appears, my part in this business will cease. It will not be necessary for me to know anything about it. And that's all I have to say."

I had an idea that Miss Havisham had not taken him into her confidence about her plan for Estella and me. He was either angry about this or he really did object to that scheme, and would have nothing to do with it. He was watching me carefully while I thought this out. "If that is all you have to say, sir," I remarked, "there can be nothing left for me to say."

He nodded in agreement and asked me where I was going to dine. I said at home with Herbert and asked him if he would be our guest. He said he would but insisted on walking home with me to see that I went to no special preparation for him. While he was getting ready to start, I went out to talk to Wemmick.

When I had been given the five hundred pounds, an idea had come into my head which had been there often before. It seemed to me that Wemmick would be a good person to consult about it. He was all ready to go home when I came out into his office. "Mr. Wemmick," said I, "I want to help out a friend and would like your opinion about it. This friend is trying to get on in business but has no money. I want to help him start."

"With money down?" said Wemmick.

"With some money down," I said, "and the rest to come out of my expectations."

"Mr. Pip," said Wemmick, "you might better throw your money into the Thames. Serve a friend with it, and you'll lose it. You'll probably lose the friend too."

"And that is your final opinion, Mr. Wemmick?"

"That is my opinion in this office."

I thought I saw a loophole. "But what would be your opinion in your castle?" I asked.

"Mr. Pip," he said, "the castle is one place and the office another. You can't ask about my castle ideas in this office."

"Very well," I said, much relieved, "then you can depend on my looking you up at home."

Mr. Jaggers was ready then, and we went to Barnard's Inn. I couldn't help wishing that he had something like the Aged to make him more human. He made the whole world seem suspicious, and with him I had an uncomfortable twenty-first birthday dinner. He was a thousand times better informed and cleverer than Wemmick. Yet I would a thousand times rather have had Wemmick to dinner. He made even the cheerful Herbert feel sad and guilty.

The next Sunday I made a trip out to the castle. The drawbridge was up, but when I rang, the Aged let me in. "My son, sir," said the old man, "rather expected you today and left word that he would be back soon from his afternoon's walk."

I nodded at the old gentleman, and we went in and sat down by the fire.

"You made my son's acquaintance at his office, I suppose?" he asked me. I nodded. "I have heard that my son is wonderful at his business of the law."

Curious to know what the old man thought of Mr. Jaggers, I roared at him but could not make him understand.

"I am hard of hearing, sir," he said.

I pretended to be surprised.

"Yes," he went on, "hard of hearing. But my son is a good lawyer, and little by little he has fixed up this beautiful property for me."

I was wondering what to say when I was startled by a sudden click in the wall on one side of the chimney. A little wooden flap fell out with the word "John" on it. The old man exclaimed, "My son's come home!" and we both went out to the drawbridge. The Aged was so delighted to work it that I did not even offer to help.

With Wemmick was a lady whom he presented to me as Miss Skiffins. She was two or three years younger than Wemmick, and she seemed a good sort with great respect for the Aged. I found out that she was a frequent visitor to the castle. When I complimented Wemmick on the clever way he had for letting the Aged know he was coming, he showed me how by pulling a wire on the outside of the chimney, a little door opened letting out one card that said "John" and another that said "Miss Skiffins."

I appreciated his cleverness. "Well, you know," he said, "it's pleasant and useful to the Aged. Of all the people who come to this gate only he and Miss Skiffins and I know how to pull the wires and let the names fall out."

"And Mr. Wemmick did it all with his own hands and his own head," said Miss Skiffins proudly.

While she was taking off her things, Wemmick invited me to take a walk with him around the property. I realized he did this to give me a chance to find out what his castle opinions were as to my scheme. So I started at once. I told him I was worried about Herbert Pocket. I told him how we had first met and fought and how poor his father was.

I told him how much Herbert had done for me and how little I had been able to do for him in return, in fact had probably harmed him with my expectations. I even hinted at the fact that Miss Havisham might have helped him instead of me if I had not come along just when I did. I told him Herbert was fair and generous and honest.

For all these reasons and because I loved him I wanted to use some of my fortune for him. I told Wemmick I wanted to use a hundred or so a year of my present income to buy Herbert some sort of partnership, though he must never in the world suspect I was doing it. I ended by laying my hand on Wemmick's shoulder and saying, "I can't help coming to you. I know I am being a bother. That is your fault for bringing me here."

"Well, you know, Pip," said Wemmick, "this is devilish good of you. I'll look him up and go to work for you."

"I thank you ten thousand times," I said.

"No, I thank you," he said. "After dealing with crooked people so much, it's good for me to know there is someone as generous as you."

Miss Skiffins was preparing tea and the Aged was making toast when we went in. We ate and drank as cozy as could possibly be. I felt as cut off from everything as though the moat were thirty feet wide and as many deep. Nothing could disturb the peace of the castle.

After Miss Skiffins had washed up the dishes, Wemmick invited the Aged to read the paper to us, explaining to me that this was the custom because it gave the old gentleman great satisfaction to read the news aloud. "Just nod at him every now and then when he looks up, and he'll be as happy as a king," he said.

So the Aged read on, and whenever he looked at us we all expressed the greatest interest and amazement and nodded until he went on reading again. Wemmick and Miss Skiffins sat side by side, and as I watched them from a dark

corner, I saw his arm gradually stealing around her waist and appearing at her other side. At that moment she unwound his arm and slowly put it down on the table in front of them. All of this she did with complete calm. By and by I noticed his arm beginning to disappear again and then appear on the other side of Miss Skiffins. She put it back again. This went on all through the Aged's reading. Finally he read himself to sleep. After Wemmick had fixed us something warm to drink—and I noticed that he and Miss Skiffins drank out of the same glass—I said good night and went home. Of course, I knew better than to offer to take Miss Skiffins home.

In less than a week I had a letter from Wemmick, saying that he had made some progress in the affair I had talked to him about and would be glad to have me come to see him. So I went out to Walworth several times and met him in London several times, though never at his office. The result was that we found a fine young man in the shipping business who wanted intelligent help and some capital and who would before long want a partner. I paid him half of my five hundred pounds and arranged to pay more out of my income and out of my property when it came to me.

The whole business was managed so cleverly that Herbert had no suspicion of my share in it. I shall never forget his beaming face when he came home one afternoon and told me that he had met a young businessman named Clarriker who had taken a great liking to him. He believed he had found an opening at last. Day by day his hopes grew stronger and his face brighter. I was even happier than he. At length all arrangements were made and he entered the business. At last my expectations had done some good to someone.

23 *A Cold Heart*

The lady with whom Estella was sent to live, Mrs. Brandley, was a widow with one daughter several years older than Estella. She had a position in society and visited and was visited by numbers of people. There was very little common interest between her and Estella, but they were useful to each other. In the early days before she withdrew from the world, Miss Havisham had been a friend of Mrs. Brandley.

In the house in Richmond I suffered every kind of torture that Estella could make me suffer. She knew me so well that she used me to tease other admirers. Because she had known me so long, she took me entirely for granted. When I was with her my love for her seemed as hopeless as if I were her secretary or a poor relation. It enraged her other lovers to hear her call me by my first name and to hear me call her by hers. It gave me no pleasure or security.

She had admirers without end, and my jealousy made others admire her even more. I saw her often at Richmond. I used to take her and the Brandleys out on the river in my boat. We went to plays, operas, concerts, and parties, through all of which I pursued her. They were all miseries to me. I never had one hour's happiness with her. Yet I never stopped hoping for the happiness of having her with me all my life.

All the time through this period of our lives, she acted as though we had been forced on each other. At other times she would seem to pity me. "Pip," she said to me one evening at Richmond, "will you never be warned against being attracted to me?"

I should have replied that love is blind. I felt always that I should not force my attentions on her because she had to obey Miss Havisham. I was sure that this put me at a disadvantage with her and perhaps turned her against me because she often had no choice about having me with her.

"At any rate," I said, "I couldn't be warned this time, for you wrote me to come."

"That's true," said Estella with the cold careless smile that always chilled me. "The time has come when Miss Havisham wishes to have me visit her for a day. You are to take me there and bring me back if you will. She doesn't want me to travel alone and dislikes having me bring my maid. You know she has a horror of seeing strange people. Can you take me?"

"Can I take you, Estella!"

"So you can. Come day after tomorrow please. You are to use my money to pay everything."

This was all the preparation I had for that visit or for others like it. Miss Havisham never wrote. I never saw her handwriting. We went down on the day appointed and found everything there unchanged. Miss Havisham was even fonder of Estella than she had been before. There was something dreadful in the way she looked at her and embraced her and admired her beauty and watched me admiring it. "How does she use you, Pip?" she asked me again eagerly. She was even more dreadful that night when we sat by the fire. Holding Estella's hand in hers, she asked her to tell again and again about the men who were in love with her. As she sat with her hand on her cane and her chin resting on it, her hurt and diseased mind made her seem like a very ghost.

I saw again plainly that Estella had been trained to get revenge on all men for Miss Havisham and that she was not to be given to me until she had done her worst. This seemed to me to be the reason she had been assigned to me from the start. Then she could attract and torment admirers who had no chance of winning her. And I, too, was to be held off to the last possible moment. It was natural that my guardian would not admit that he knew of such a scheme. The shadow of the dark and unhealthy house was on all of us.

It happened during this visit that Estella and Miss Havisham spoke harsh words to each other. It was the first time I had ever seen them quarrel. "What!" said Miss Havisham, glaring at the girl. "Are you tired of me?"

"Only a little tired of myself," replied Estella, moving over to the fireplace, where she stood looking down at the fire.

"Be truthful, you ungrateful girl!" cried Miss Havisham, striking the floor with her cane. "You are tired of me."

Estella looked at her calmly. Her beautiful face showed cruel indifference.

"You cold, cold-hearted girl!" exclaimed Miss Havisham.

"What?" said Estella coldly. "Are you blaming me for being cold? You? I am what you have made me. Take all the praise and all the blame. Take all my success and all my failure. They're yours."

"Look at her!" cried Miss Havisham bitterly. "Look at her so hard and thankless. She was brought up here. I gave her all the tenderness my bleeding heart could hold."

"I had nothing to say about it," said Estella. "I was scarcely old enough to walk or talk when I was brought here. But what do you want? You have been very good to me and I owe everything to you."

"Love," replied Miss Havisham.

"You have it."

"I have not."

"Adopted mother," said Estella, never raising her voice or showing either anger or tenderness, "I have said that I owe everything to you. All I possess is freely yours. All that you have given me you may take back again. Beyond that I have nothing. And if you ask me to give you what you never gave me, that is impossible."

"Did I never give her love!" cried Miss Havisham, turning wildly to me, "a love free from jealousy? Let her call me insane if she wishes."

"Why should I of all people call you insane?" answered Estella. "No one who lives knows your purposes as well as I do. I have sat beside you on that little stool learning your ideas and looking up into your face when it was strange and frightening to me."

"You have soon forgotten those times," moaned Miss Havisham.

"No, not forgotten," said Estella. "When have I forgotten what you taught me and failed to live by it? Who taught me to be hard? Be fair to me."

"But why are you so proud and so hard to me? Estella, don't be proud and hard to me."

Estella looked at her for a moment with a kind of calm wonder, not in the least disturbed. "I cannot think," she said, "why you should be so unreasonable when I come to you after a separation. I have never forgotten how badly you were treated. If I cannot return your love, it is because you yourself have taught me never to love anyone. You must accept me as I have been brought up to be."

I left the room then, and in sadness of heart went out to walk for an hour or so in the courtyard and around the ruined garden. When I at last got up courage to return, I found Estella sitting at Miss Havisham's knee taking some stitches in one of her old tattered pieces of clothing. Afterward Estella and I played cards as in the past, only we were skillful now and played French games as the evening passed.

My room was in the separate building across the courtyard. It was my first night at Miss Havisham's, and sleep refused to come. At last when the night had worn away to two o'clock, I got up and dressed and crossed the yard into the main house. I was no sooner in the hallway when I saw Miss Havisham walking along it and moaning as she went. She carried a candle in her hand and was an unearthly sight in its light. I saw her open the door of the room which held the bridal cake and walk in. Soon she came back to her own room and then went back and forth between the two, never stopping her low crying. I could not get out without her seeing me, and so until dawn came, I watched her walking and crying.

Before we left the next day there was no reference made to the disagreement between Estella and Miss Havisham. And in none of the four times I went back there was it repeated. There was no difference in Miss Havisham's manner to Estella except possibly a touch of fear.

It was not long after our first visit that I found out to my rage and horror that Bentley Drummle had been seeing Estella and that she allowed him to do so. A little while after that, he was with her often and he and I were always meeting each other when he called on her. He kept after her in a dull, persistent way, and Estella led him on. Sometimes she discouraged him and sometimes flattered him. Sometimes she acted as though she knew him well and sometimes scarcely remembered who he was.

The Spider, as Mr. Jaggers had called him, was used to lying in wait, however, and had the patience of his sort. Added to that, he had a stupid confidence in his money and his family importance. So he patiently watched Estella and outstayed many brighter men.

At a certain fancy ball in Richmond, Estella outshone all other beauties. Drummle was with her so much, and with her consent, that I decided to speak to her about him. I took the first opportunity, when she was waiting for Mrs. Brandley to take her home. I was with her, for I almost always accompanied them to and from such places.

"Are you tired, Estella?"

"I shouldn't be. I have my letter to Miss Havisham to write before I go to sleep."

"Telling her about tonight's conquest?" said I. "Surely a poor one, Estella."

"What do you mean? I didn't know there had been any."

"Estella," said I, "look at that fellow in the corner who is staring over here at us."

"Why should I look at him?" answered she with her eyes on me instead.

"That is the very question I want to ask. It makes me miserable that you should encourage a man so looked down on by everyone. You know he is generally hated."

"Well?" said she.

"You know he is stupid and bad tempered. You know he has nothing but money, don't you?"

"Well?" said she, opening her lovely eyes wider.

"Well, that is why I am so unhappy when you let him pay attention to you."

I wanted to think that she was leading him on to make me jealous. But I could believe nothing of the kind.

"Pip," said she, "don't be foolish about the way you feel. It's not worth discussing."

"Yes, it is," said I. "I cannot bear to have people say you are throwing yourself away on a stupid boor, the lowest of the crowd."

"I can bear it," said Estella.

"I have seen you give him looks and smiles this very night such as you never give me."

"Do you want me then," said Estella, turning to look at me seriously, "to deceive and trap you?"

"Do you deceive and trap him, Estella?"

"Yes, and many others—all of them but you. Here is Mrs. Brandley. I'll say no more."

24 *A Shocking Discovery*

I was twenty-three. I had not heard another word about my expectations. More than a year before we had left Barnard's Inn and now lived in the Temple* down by the river. I had left Mr. Pocket's, though I read regularly for many hours a day. I still had found nothing to do, possibly because my fortunes were on the whole so uncertain. Herbert's affairs were progressing favorably.

One night when he had gone on business to Marseilles, I was alone and lonely without him. It was miserable weather, stormy and wet, with wind so furious that high buildings in town had been damaged and trees in the country torn away. The papers carried accounts of shipwreck and death at sea. Herbert and I lived at the top of the last house in the row, and the wind rushing up from the river that night sounded like the roaring of cannon. Rain dashed against the windows as though I were in a lighthouse. Lamps in the halls and in the courtyard below had been blown out.

I read until eleven o'clock and then sat thinking about the storm outside. Suddenly I heard a step on the stairs. Remembering that the lights there were out, I picked up my reading lamp and went to the top of the stairs. "Is there someone down there?" I called out, looking down.

*The Temple: a district in London enclosed by a wall with gates—formerly the headquarters of an ancient society. Many of England's famous writers once lived there.

"Yes," said a voice from the darkness beneath. "I want someone on the top floor, Mr. Pip."

"That is my name. Is there something the matter?"

"Nothing the matter," replied the voice. And a man came up and appeared in the light of my lamp. In an instant I had seen a face that was strange, looking at me as if pleased. The man was comfortably but roughly dressed, like a traveler on the sea. He had long gray hair and seemed to be about sixty years old. He was muscular and strong and browned by the sun and wind. As he climbed the last stair, I saw with stupid amazement that he was holding out both hands to me. "What is your business?" I asked him.

"My business?" he repeated. "I will explain it, master, if you will let me come in."

I was a bit angry because he seemed to know me and expected me to know him too. Still, I asked him as politely as I could to explain himself. He looked around him in the strangest way, as if he had a right to admire the place. Then he pulled off his coat and hat, and I saw that he was quite bald on the top of his head.

Again he held out his hands to me. "What do you want?" said I, wondering if he was crazy.

"It is disappointing to a man," he said in a rough voice, "after having come so fur and waiting to come for so long. But you're not to blame for that. Give me half a minute please."

He sat down before the fire and put his hand to his head. I looked him over carefully and did not like what I saw. Again I did not know him.

"There's no one near, is there?" he said, looking over his shoulder.

"Why do you, a stranger, come into my rooms at this time of night asking questions?" I said.

"You're a good sport," he answered, shaking his head affectionately. "I am glad you've growed up to be like that."

Then I knew him! Even yet I remembered nothing definite about him, but still I knew him. If the wind and the rain could have swept us to the churchyard where we first stood face to face, I could not have known my convict more surely than I knew him now as he sat in the chair by my fire. He did not need to take a file from his pocket and show it to me or walk shivering across the room hugging himself with his arms. I knew him before he gave me any of those clues, though a minute before I had had no idea who he was.

He again held out both his hands, and not knowing what else to do I gave him mine. He raised them to his lips, kissed them, and still held them. "You acted nobly to me, my boy. And I have never forgot it."

"Wait a minute," I said. "If you are grateful to me for what I did when I was a little child, I hope you have reformed now. It wasn't necessary for you to come here to thank me. Still, there must be something good in the feeling that has brought you here. But surely you must understand—"

He looked at me so oddly that my words died away. "You was saying," he remarked, "that surely I must understand. What must I understand?"

"That I cannot be friends with you because of what happened in the past. I hope you have turned over a new leaf. I am glad that you feel grateful to me. But our ways are very different. You are wet, and you look tired. Will you drink something before you go?"

"I think I will drink afore I go."

I made him some hot rum and water, trying to keep my hand steady as I did so. The way he stared at me made that hard. When I finally handed him his glass, I saw with amazement that his eyes were filled with tears. I felt touched and sorry about the way I had treated him. "I hope," I said, "that you will not think I spoke harshly to you just now. I did not mean to do so and am sorry about it. I wish you well."

He stretched out his hand. I gave him mine, and then he drank and dried his eyes on his sleeve.

"How are you living?" I asked him.

"I've been a sheep farmer and a cattleman among other things away in Australia," he said, "many thousand miles of stormy water from here."

"I hope you have done well?"

"I've done wonderful well. No man who went there along with me as has done near as well as me. I'm famous for it."

"I am glad to hear it."

"I like to hear you say so, dear boy."

Without trying to understand what he meant, I asked, "Have you ever since seen a messenger you once sent me?"

"Never set eyes on him. I warn't likely to."

"He came faithfully and brought me the two one-pound notes. I was a poor boy then, as you know, and they were a little fortune to me. But I have done well since, and you must let me pay them back." I took out my purse.

He watched me as I spread out the notes and handed them to him. Still watching me, he folded them together, set fire to them at the lamp, and dropped the ashes into the tray. "May I be so bold," he said then with a smile that was like a frown, "as to ask how you have done well since you and me was out on them lone cold marshes?" He emptied his glass, got up, and stood by the fire, looking steadily at me. Only then I began to tremble. When I could force myself to speak, I told him that I had been chosen to inherit some property.

"Might a poor wretch ask what property?" said he.

I stammered, "I don't know."

"Could I make a guess, I wonder," said the convict, "at your income since you come of age? Is the first figure five?"

With my heart beating heavily, I stood up and looked wildly at him.

"About a guardian you had," he went on. "It must have been a lawyer. Would the first letter of his name be J?"

All the truth of my position came upon me. Its disappointments and dangers and disgraces rushed at me and made me struggle for breath.

"The man who employed that lawyer—me!—come over seas to Portsmouth and wanted to find you. However did I find out where you were? Why, I wrote to a person in London. What person?"

I could not have spoken one word to save my life. I stood still and looked wildly at him until the room swam before me. He caught me as I was about to faint, put me on the sofa, and bent on one knee in front of me. The face that I now well remembered and that I shivered at was very near to mine.

"Yes, Pip, dear boy, I've made a gentleman of you. It's me what had done it. I swore that time sure as ever I earned a guinea that guinea would go to you. I swore that if ever I got rich you should get rich. I lived rough so that you could live smooth. I worked hard so that you wouldn't have to work. Do I tell this so that you must feel you owe me something? Not a bit. I tell it for you to know that the hunted dog wot you kept alive got so far ahead that he could make someone into a gentleman. And Pip, you're him! You're that gentleman that I made."

If he had been some terrible beast I could not have hated and dreaded this man more.

"Look'ee here, Pip. I'm your second father. You're more to me than any son. I've saved money only for you to spend. When I was a shepherd in a lonely hut seeing no faces but those of sheep till I half forgot wot men's and women's faces were like, I see yourn. I drops my knife many a time when I was eating there and I says, 'Here's the boy again on them misty marshes a looking at me whiles I eat. Lord strike me dead,' said I, 'but wot if I gets liberty and money I'll make that boy a gentleman!' And I done it! Why, look at these lodgings, dear boy, fit for a lord!"

He laid his hand on my shoulder. I shuddered at the thought that it might be stained with blood.

"It warn't easy or safe for me, Pip, to leave them places where I lived. But my mind was made up to do it. At last I done it. Dear boy, I done it!"

I tried to get control of myself.

"Where will you put me to sleep, dear boy?" he asked presently. "To sleep long and sound. For I've been sea tossed and sea washed for months and months."

"My friend and companion," said I, rising from the sofa, "is away. You must have his room."

"He won't come back tomorrow, will he? Because look'ee here, dear boy, caution is necessary."

"What do you mean?"

"It's death for me if I am caught. I was sent away for life. It's death to come back. I would certainly be hanged if took."

This was the last straw. The miserable man, after loading me with his gold and silver chains for years, had risked his life to come to me. I held it in my keeping. If only I had loved him instead of shrinking from him it would have been easier. Then my heart would have led me to protect him.

I closed the shutters so that no light would show outside. Then I locked the doors. While I did so he stood eating and drinking, and I could see my convict at his meal on the marshes again. It almost seemed that he would stoop down to file at his leg.

I closed Herbert's door on the stairs and showed him where he would sleep. He asked for some "gentleman's linen" to wear in the morning and so went to bed.

I sat by the fire for an hour or more too stunned to think. Finally I began to understand how wrecked I was and how the ship in which I sailed had gone to pieces. Miss

Havisham's intentions toward me had all been a mere dream. Estella was not meant for me. I had been used as a convenience and as a torment for greedy relatives. I was only a model with no heart, for Estella to practice on. These were my first griefs. The deepest pain of all was the thought that I had deserted Joe for a convict, guilty of crimes I did not know about and apt to be taken from the rooms to be hanged.

I could not go back to Joe and Biddy now when I most needed their comfort and help. I was too ashamed of myself. Now I could never never undo what I had done.

With every gust of wind I imagined someone was coming. I remembered plainly that I had always thought of my convict as a dangerous man. The other convict had insisted that he had tried to murder him. I had seen him in the ditch fighting like a wild beast. I even began to feel afraid to be shut up here alone with him.

I took a candle and went in to look at him. His face was grim in his sleep. But he slept quietly though he had a pistol lying on the pillow. I locked him in before I returned to my chair. Gradually I slipped down and lay on the floor. When I awoke the clocks were striking five. The candles had burned out and the fire was dead. The wind and the rain were still raging in the blackness outside.

Part 3

Proving That What a Man Is, Not What He Has, Is All Important

25 *Plans Worked Out*

With morning I realized how impossible it would be for me to keep my dreadful visitor hidden in my rooms. I had no boy to wait on me now, but I was looked after by two women who were always around when they were not wanted and who were full of curiosity about everything. It seemed a good idea for me to tell them that my uncle had unexpectedly come from the country and was staying with me.

I went out to get the night watchman to bring in his lantern and help me light my lamp. In feeling my way down the dark stairs, I stumbled over a man crouching in the corner. He did not answer when I asked him what he was doing there. I found the watchman and urged him to come quickly, telling him on the way back about the man. We searched the staircase from the bottom to the top but did not find anyone there. Then it occurred to me that he might have slipped into my rooms. So, lighting my candle from the watchman's lantern, I looked everywhere, including the room where my guest lay sleeping. All was quiet.

It troubled me that there should have been a stranger lurking about on that night of all nights. I asked the watchman whether he had seen anyone around. "The night was

so bad, sir, I don't remember anyone since eleven o'clock when a stranger asked for you."

"My uncle," I said.

"And the person with him."

"Person with him!" I exclaimed.

"I judged the person to be with him," answered the watchman. "The person stopped when he stopped to ask me about you, and they both went in this direction."

The watchman had not noticed what sort of man it was. I got rid of him soon, not wanting to arouse his curiosity. I was very much troubled. It seemed to me that I was filled with doubt and fear about everything.

I lighted my fire and sat down before it, gradually falling into a light sleep from which I awoke every now and then. Finally, with the coming of daylight, I got up and tried to think. I was still too dazed to make any sort of plan. I looked out at the gray, wet morning. I moved from room to room, shivering and thinking how miserable I was.

Finally the women arrived and I told them about my uncle and ordered breakfast for both of us. Then I washed and dressed, and so, in a sort of dream, I sat down by the fire and waited for—*him*—to come to breakfast.

When the door opened and he came out, I thought he had even a worse look by daylight. "I do not even know," I said, speaking low as he took his seat at the table, "by what name to call you. I have given out that you are my uncle."

"That's it, dear boy, call me uncle. On shipboard I took the name Provis. I might as well keep it now unless you'd like another.

"What is your real name?" I asked him in a whisper.

"Magwitch," he answered in the same tone, "with the first name Abel."

"When you came in at the gate last night and asked the watchman the way here, was there anyone with you?"

"With me, dear boy? No."

"But there was someone there?"

"I didn't take particular notice, not knowing the ways of the place. But I think there was a person come in along with me."

"Are you known in London? Were you once known in London?"

"Not over and above, dear boy. I was in the country mostly."

"Were you—tried—in London?"

He nodded. "The last time. First knowed Mr. Jaggers that way. Jaggers was for me. And what I done is worked out and paid for."

He ate his breakfast then with loud noises, and all his actions were rude and greedy. He had lost some of his teeth and turned his food around in his mouth like a hungry old dog. If I had had any appetite to start with, he would have ruined it.

"I'm a heavy eater, dear boy," he said, when he had finished his meal. "I wouldn't have got into so much trouble if I could have gone without food. Likewise I must have my smoke." He took a black pipe from his pocket, filled it, and lighted it with a live coal from my fire. Then he went through his favorite action of holding out both his hands for mine. "And this," said he, as he patted my hands, "is the gentleman what I made. It does me good for to look at you, Pip. All I want is to sit round and look at you, dear boy."

I freed my hands as soon as I could. Now I found that I could begin to think about what had happened to me. I began to realize what I was chained to.

"I mustn't see my gentleman walking in the muddy streets," he went on. "My gentleman must have horses to ride and horses to drive and horses for his servants, too."

He took out a huge thick pocketbook bursting with papers and threw it on the table.

"There's something worth spending in that, dear boy.

It's all yours. There's more where that came from, too. I've come from the old country to see my gentleman spend his money like a gentleman. That'll be my pleasure."

"Stop!" said I, filled with fear and dislike. "I want to know what to do about you. I want to know how you are to be kept out of danger, how long you are going to stay, what plans you have. And I want to know how to prevent your being recognized and arrested."

"Well, dear boy, that danger ain't so great unless I am informed on. There's Jaggers and there's Wemmick, and there's you. Who else could report me to the police?"

"Is there no chance that someone will recognize you in the streets?"

"Well, there ain't much. Years have rolled away, and who's to gain by it? If the danger had been fifty times as great, Pip, I'd have come to see you just the same."

"How long will you stay?"

"How long?" he said, taking his pipe out of his mouth as he stared at me. "I'm not agoing back. I've come for good."

"Where are you to live? What is to be done with you? Where will you be safe?"

"Dear boy," he answered, "there's wigs and there's glasses and black clothes. Others has done it before and what others has done before others can do again. As to where and how to live, dear boy, give me your opinions."

"You talk calmly now," said I, "but you were very serious last night when you swore it was death."

"And so I swear it *is* Death," said he, "and Death by hanging in the street not far from here. And you should fully understand how serious it is. What of it, when what's done is done? To go back now 'ud be worse. As to what I dared now, I'm an old bird as has dared traps years and years. If Death is to come, let him come. I'll face him and I'll believe in him then."

It seemed to me that I should find him some quiet lodgings nearby. He could take them when Herbert came back in two or three days. I must tell Herbert all about him. It would be a relief to share my troubles. Mr. Provis, however, was not sure Herbert should be told. He wanted to see my friend first. "And even then," said he, pulling a greasy little black Bible out of his pocket, "we'll have him swear on this." I remembered how he had made me swear not to tell about him in the churchyard long ago.

As he was dressed in clothes like a sailor's, we considered next what he was to wear. I persuaded him that he should be made to look like a well-to-do farmer. About three o'clock in the afternoon I went out, leaving him in my rooms with instructions not to open the door for anything. First I found a room for my uncle, Mr. Provis, in a respectable lodging house the back of which faced the Temple and could almost be seen from my windows. Then I went from shop to shop buying things to change his appearance. This over with I went to Mr. Jaggers's office. He was at his desk, but got up when I entered, and stood by the fire. "Now, Pip," said he, "be careful. Don't tell me anything. I don't want to know anything. I am not curious."

Of course I saw that he knew the man had come.

"I merely want, Mr. Jaggers," I said, "to assure myself that what I have been told is true. I have been informed by a person named Abel Magwitch that he is the benefactor so long unknown to me."

"That is the man," said Mr. Jaggers—"in New South Wales."*

"I don't hold you responsible, sir, for my mistakes and wrong ideas. But I always supposed it was Miss Havisham."

"As you say, Pip," said Mr. Jaggers coldly, "I am not at all responsible for that."

---

* New South Wales: a province in Australia.

"And yet it looked so like it, sir," I pleaded sadly.

"Not a particle of evidence, Pip," said Mr. Jaggers. "Take nothing on looks. Take everything on evidence."

"I have no more to say," I said with a sigh.

"And Magwitch—in New South Wales—having at last made himself known to you, you will understand, Pip, how carefully I have always stuck to facts. I wrote Magwitch when I first heard from him that I would tell you only facts. I also wrote him a warning. He hinted once at an idea he had of seeing you in England some day. I warned him against it. I told him that he could probably not get a pardon; that he was to stay away from here his whole life; that if he came back he would be in danger of death. No doubt he took my warning."

"No doubt," said I.

"Wemmick tells me," said Mr. Jaggers, staring hard at me, "that he has received a letter mailed in Portsmouth from a man from New South Wales named Provis. This letter asked for your address to give to Magwitch. Wemmick sent it. Probably it is, through Provis that you have learned about Magwitch—in New South Wales."

"The information came through Provis," I said.

"Good day, Pip," said Mr. Jaggers. "Glad to have seen you. In writing Magwitch—in New South Wales—or in communication with him through Provis, say that I will send you a complete statement of your long account together with the cash balance. Good day, Pip."

I left the office realizing that for his own safety Mr. Jaggers would never admit to me or himself that Provis was really Magwitch and that he was not in New South Wales but right here in London. Wemmick was out. He could have done nothing for me anyway. I went back home, where I found the terrible Provis smoking his pipe and drinking rum in safety. Next day the clothes I had ordered arrived and he put them on. It seemed to me that they did not make him look any different. To me he was still my convict escaping on the marshes. It even seemed to me that he dragged one of his legs as though there was still a chain on it. His long life alone had given him a fierce manner that no clothes could tame. In all his ways of sitting and standing and eating and drinking he seemed to me still a prisoner and a criminal.

He continued to be a dreadful mystery to me. When he fell asleep of an evening, I would sit and look at him, wondering what he had done and accusing him in my mind of all the crimes in the world. Often I had an urge to run away from him. I loathed him so much more every day that I think I really would have left him in spite of all he had done for me if Herbert had not been coming back. One night I actually did get out of bed and start to dress in my old clothes, intending to leave him there with everything I owned and enlist for India as a private soldier.

A ghost could not have been more terrible to me in those lonely rooms in the long evenings and long nights, with the wind and the rain always rushing by. A ghost could not have been arrested or hanged because of me as he could be. He amused himself by playing with a ragged pack of cards and keeping score by sticking his penknife into the table. He asked me to read to him. "Foreign language, dear boy!" Though he could not understand a word, his pride in my ability was endless. The more he admired me and the fonder he was of me, the more I shrank away from him.

All of this went on about five days. It seemed to me like a year. Expecting Herbert all the time, I dared not go out except when I took Provis for an airing after dark. At last one evening when dinner was over and I had fallen asleep quite worn out, I was awakened by welcome footsteps on the stairs. Provis, who had been asleep too, started up, and in an instant I saw his knife shining in his hand.

"Quiet! It's Herbert!" I said. And Herbert came bursting in happily. "Handel, my dear fellow, how are you? I feel as though I'd been gone for a month. Why, you've grown thin and pale. Handel, my friend—I beg your pardon."

He was stopped by seeing Provis. My convict, staring at him steadily, was putting away his knife and feeling in his pocket for something else.

"Herbert, my dear friend," I said, while he stood staring and wondering, "something very strange has happened. This is a visitor of mine."

"It's all right, dear boy," said Provis, coming forward with his little black Bible. "Take it in your right hand," he said to Herbert. "Lord strike you dead on the spot if you ever squeal on me in any way. Kiss it."

"Do as he wishes," I said to Herbert. So Herbert, looking at me in friendly uneasiness and surprise, did so. Provis immediately shook hands with him and said, "Now you're on your oath, you know. And believe me on my oath as Pip'll make a gentleman of you, too."

26 *The Convict's Story*

Herbert felt as amazed and as disturbed as I did about the arrival of Provis. We could hardly wait until we were alone to talk things over. My convict seemed jealous of Herbert and did not leave for his lodgings until midnight. When he had gone, I felt the first relief I had had since his arrival. How wonderful it was to have a friend to help me solve my problems!

"What," said I to Herbert, "is to be done?"

"My poor Handel," he answered, holding his head, "I am too stunned to think."

"So was I when the blow first fell. Still, something must be done. He wants to spend more money on me—to buy horses and carriages and all sorts of expensive things. He must be stopped somehow. Yet the dreadful truth is that he loves me dearly."

"Poor Handel," Herbert said.

"Even if I never took another penny from him," I went on, "think what I owe him already. I am heavily in debt— with no expectations now. I have been trained to do no work. I'm not fit for anything."

"You would be useful to us at Clarriker's, I'm sure. I'm working up to a partnership, you know."

Poor fellow! He had no idea my money was doing it for him.

"On the other hand," Herbert went on, "you can't desert this man now. He is ignorant and fierce. For years he has thought of nothing but coming back to see you. He has risked his life to come. If you turned your back on him now and made him think that all his work for you was in vain, he would have nothing left to live for. He would certainly give himself up to the police, and it would be all your fault."

I had had some such idea right from the start and was horrified by it now. Even if I didn't desert him and he was arrested anyway, I would still be the cause of his destruction. What could we do?

"I think the first and main thing to be done," said Herbert, "is to get him out of England. You will have to go with him. Only that will persuade him to leave. Maybe we could use that other convict as an excuse to get him away—or something else in his life."

"I know nothing of his life," I told Herbert. "It has almost driven me crazy to sit here with him at night so closely connected with him in a way, and yet knowing nothing about him except that he was the terrible man who for two days in my childhood frightened me to death."

"Handel," said Herbert, "are you sure you must break with him?"

"Herbert, you can ask me that?"

"But you care enough about him to save his life because he has risked it for you. Then you must get him out of England, before you give him any idea you want to part with him. We'll work it all out together, dear old boy."

We shook hands on it and I told Herbert the only way we could find out about Provis's past was to ask him.

"Then let's ask him at breakfast tomorrow morning," said Herbert.

That decided, we went to bed. I had wild dreams and awoke unrested and filled with the fear which never left me that Provis would be found and arrested.

At breakfast he was full of plans for us. He urged me to begin looking for a fashionable place where we could live and he could stay with me. When he had finished eating, I said to him, "After you were gone last night, I told my friend about the fight you had with another man on the marshes so long ago. You remember?"

"Remember!" he said. "I think so!"

"We want to know something about that man and about you. Isn't this a good time for you to tell us about yourself?"

"Well," he said after some thought, "you're under oath, you know, both of you. And what I did is worked out and paid for now."

So he sat down and told us his story.

"Dear boy and Pip's comrade, I'm not going to tell you my life like a story in a book. In jail and out of jail, in jail and out of jail. That's my life up to the time when Pip was my friend. I've been done everything to—except hanged. I've been whipped and worried and drove. No idea where I was born. First thing I can remember I was stealing turnips for a living. Someone had run away from me and left me alone and cold.

"I don't know how I know my name is Abel Magwitch. Everyone who looked at me when I was small drove me away or put me in jail. So when I was still a poor ragged little creature, they said I was hard. 'This is a terrible hard one,' they says to prison visitors, picking me out. 'He just lives in jails, this boy.'

"So, tramping, begging, stealing, working sometimes when I could, I grew to be a man. A deserting soldier learned me to read. And a traveling circus man learned me to write. At the races over twenty years ago, I met a man whose skull I'd crack with this poker if I had him here. His right name was Compeyson, and he had been to good schools and had learning. He was a smooth talker and he knew how to get along with nice people. He was good-looking, too. One night the landlord of an inn I used to go to led me up to him when he was sitting at a table with some other people. 'I think this is a man might suit you,' he told Compeyson. Compeyson looks me over and I look him over. He has a watch and chain and a ring and a fine suit of clothes. 'You look as though you're out of luck,' " he says to me.

" 'I've never been in it much,' I say. (I'd just come out of jail.)

" 'Maybe yours is going to change,' says Compeyson. 'What can you do?'

" 'Eat and drink,' I says, 'if you'll find the materials.'

"Compeyson laughed, and the next night took me on to be his man and partner. His business was stealing, forging checks, passing stolen bank notes, and such like. He figured out all the tricks and then let other men do the work for him. He had no more heart than an iron file, and he had the head of the Devil.

"There was another in with Compeyson called Arthur. He was dying of some slow disease and was nothing but a shadow. Him and Compeyson had been in some bad deal with a rich lady some time ago, and they'd made a pot of money by it. Compeyson had gambled most of his away. So Arthur was dying poor and out of his head half of the time. Compeyson's wife—whom he kicked mostly—was having pity on him when she could, and Compeyson was having pity on nothing and nobody.

"I might a took a warning by Arthur, but I didn't. So I went to work for Compeyson and become just a tool for him. Arthur lived in the top of Compeyson's house. The second or third time I ever see him he come tearing into Compeyson's parlor late at night and he says to Compeyson's wife, 'Sally, she really is upstairs with me now and I can't get rid of her. She's all in white and she's awful mad and she has a shroud hanging over her arm and she says she'll put it on me at five in the morning.

" 'I don't know how she got there,' says Arthur, shivering with fear, 'but she's standing at the foot of my bed. And over where her heart's broke—you broke it—there's drops of blood.'

"Compeyson spoke brave, but he was always a coward. 'Go along with this crazy sick man,' he says to his wife, 'and Magwitch, lend her a hand, will you?' But he never went near Arthur himself.

"Compeyson's wife, being used to him, give him some liquor to quiet him down, and by and by he rested until nearly five o'clock. Then he starts up screaming, 'Here she is! Here she is! She's coming up to the bed with the shroud. Don't let her touch me with it! Don't let her lift me up to put it over my shoulders! She's lifting me up! Keep me down!' Then he lifted himself up straight and was dead.

"Compeyson thought it was good riddance for us. He didn't care. Him and me was soon busy. And that man made me his slave. I was always in debt to him, always under his thumb, always in danger. He was younger than me but smart and educated. My missus as I had the hard time with—Stop, though. I ain't brought *her* in—"

He looked up in a confused way before he went on with his story. "There ain't no need to tell about everything," he said then. "The time I had with Compeyson was the hardest ever in my life. I was arrested twice or three times in the four or five years it lasted, but evidence was lacking. At last me and Compeyson was both in jail on a charge of passing stolen money and other things, too. Compeyson says to me, 'We'll have separate defenses and we won't work together on them.' I was so miserable poor I sold all the clothes I had except what hung on my back afore I could get Jaggers.

"When we was brought to trial I noticed what a gentleman Compeyson looked with his curly hair and his black clothes and his white handkerchief, and what a common sort of wretch I looked. And all the evidence was heavy on me and light on him. It seemed as though I was always the one that did all the bad deeds, and he got all the profits.

"And Compeyson's lawyer made it seem that I had been the leader in crime and the worst of the two of us. Compeyson had been to school along of people who were important. And he had belonged to clubs and societies and such like. And it was me that had been tried afore and put in all sorts of jails. And Compeyson could make fancy speeches—with verses in them, too. All I could say was, 'Gentleman, this man at my side is all bad.' And when the verdict come it was recommended that Compeyson be shown mercy because he had a good character and got in bad company. And it was me that never got a word but Guilty. Then I says to Compeyson, 'Once out of this court I'll smash that face of yourn.' And Compeyson asks the judge to be protected and gets two guards. When we're sentenced he gets seven years and me fourteen. The judge is sorry for him, but thinks I'm an old offender who will probably come to worse."

My convict had become so excited he had to wipe the sweat off his face and neck and arms before he could go on.

"I had told Compeyson I'd smash his face in, and I swore to the Lord I'd do so. We were in the same prison ship, but I couldn't get at him for a long time, though I tried. At last I caught him and got one good one at him when I was grabbed. They put me in the black hole of the ship, but I escaped and got to shore. I was hiding among the graves there wishing I was in one of them when I first see my boy."

He gave me a look of affection which I hated, though I felt great pity for him.

"But I had been told Compeyson was out on them marshes. I think he escaped to get away from me, not knowing I was ashore too. I hunted him down. I smashed his

face. 'And now,' says I, 'the worst thing I can do to you, caring nothing about myself, is to drag you back.' And I'd have swum out, towing him by the hair if it had come to that.

"Of course he got the best of it up to the very end—his character was so good. They said he'd escaped to get away from being murdered by me. I was put in chains, brought to trial again, and sent away for life. I didn't stop for life, dear boy and Pip's comrade, being here now."

He slowly took out his pipe, filled it, and began to smoke.

"Is he dead?" I asked after a silence. "Compeyson?"

"He hopes I am, if he's alive, you may be sure," he said with a fierce look. "I never heard no more of him."

Herbert had written something which he passed to me. I read, "Young Havisham's name was Arthur. Compeyson is the man who pretended to be Miss Havisham's lover."

I nodded to Herbert. Neither of us said anything and both looked at my convict as he sat smoking by the fire.

27 *Farewell to Dreams*

Two worries were always strongly present in my mind. The first was that Compeyson was still alive and would in some way discover that Provis had returned to England. I could not doubt that if this should happen, Compeyson would not hesitate to turn my convict over to the police. It would be an easy and a safe way to get rid of the man he feared so terribly. The second was the wide distance now between Estella and me. What a contrast presented by her in her pride and beauty and the man I sheltered! Never would I breathe a word to her about Provis. Still, I felt that I ought to see both her and Miss Havisham before I left England.

The day after Provis had told us his story I went out to Richmond. Estella had gone to the country, I was told by her maid, and might come back to Richmond again for only a short while. This was the first time she had ever gone to Miss Havisham's without me. That night I consulted Herbert after I had taken Provis home, and we decided that I should follow Estella for a visit. Meanwhile Herbert and I would consider what excuse we could give Provis for getting him out of the country. He was anxious for us to start living on a grander scale. It occurred to both of us that we could take him abroad by water with the excuse that we could buy things there for our new life. Leaving him in charge of

Herbert and with the mean excuse that I was going to see Joe, I left for Miss Havisham's.

I started out early on a miserable rainy morning. When the coach drew up to the Blue Boar, whom should I see coming out of the inn, toothpick in hand, but Bentley Drummle. We both pretended not to see each other. It was poison to me to see him in the town, for I knew very well why he had come. We both went into the coffee room, where he had just finished his breakfast and where I ordered mine. Finally he spoke to me. "Are you pretending not to know me?" he said.

"Oh, it's you, is it?" said I.

"You have just arrived?" he asked.

"Yes," said I. "Have you been here long?"

Then we both looked down at our feet and said nothing for a while.

"I've been here long enough to be tired of it," said Drummle at last.

"Are you staying long?"

"Can't say," answered Drummle. "Are you?"

"Can't say," said I.

"There are marshes around here," he said. "I'm going out for a ride to explore them. They tell me there are out-of-the-way villages among them with little inns—and blacksmith shops. Waiter! Is my horse ready?"

"Look here, sir, the lady won't ride today. The weather's bad."

"And I won't be having dinner here because I'm dining at the lady's."

Then Drummle glanced at me with a look of triumph on his fat face that cut me to the heart. Finally I said, "Mr. Drummle, I didn't ask for this conversation. I don't think it's a very agreeable one. Let me suggest that we have nothing to do with each other hereafter."

"That suits me fine," said Drummle. "But don't lose

your temper. Haven't you lost enough without that?"

"What do you mean, sir?"

"Waiter!" said Drummle by way of answering me. "You quite understand that the young lady is not riding today and that I am dining at the young lady's?"

"Quite so, sir."

Boiling with rage as I was, I felt that we could not go on talking without bringing in Estella's name, which I could not bear to have him mention. I was glad that three farmers came in to eat just then so that we no longer had the place to ourselves. Drummle went out, and through the window I saw him mounting his horse in his usual brutal way and calling for a light for his cigar. A man appeared from somewhere to give it to him. Though I could not see his face, his slouching shoulders and ragged hair reminded me of Orlick.

In too bad a mood to care much whether it was he or not, I went out to the never-forgotten old house that it would have been so much the better for me never to have entered, never to have seen.

In the room where the dressing table stood I found Miss Havisham and Estella. Estella was knitting and Miss Havisham was looking on. When they saw me I felt that they both noticed a change in my appearance.

"And what wind blows *you* here, Pip?" asked Miss Havisham. She seemed rather embarrassed.

"Miss Havisham," I said, "I went to Richmond yesterday to speak to Estella. Finding that some wind had blown her here, I followed. What I had to say to her I will say before you in a few minutes. It will not surprise or displease you. I am as unhappy as you can ever have meant me to be."

Miss Havisham stared steadily at me. Estella did not look up.

"I have found out who my benefactor is. It is not a

happy discovery. It will never make me better off in reputation or in fortune or in anything. There are reasons why
I can say no more than that. I must keep another person's
secret."

While I considered how to go on, Miss Havisham repeated, "The secret is someone else's."

"When you first had me brought here, Miss Havisham,
from the little village I wish I had never left, I suppose I
really did come here as any boy might have, as a kind of
servant."

"Yes, Pip," said Miss Havisham, "you did."

"And Mr. Jaggers—"

"Mr. Jaggers," said Miss Havisham in a firm tone, "had
nothing to do with it and knew nothing about it. It was just
a coincidence that he was the lawyer of your benefactor
too."

I could tell from the look on her face that she was telling
the truth.

"But when I made the mistake of thinking my benefactor was you, you led me on."

"Yes," she said, "I let you go on."

"Was that kind?"

"Who am I," cried Miss Havisham, with such sudden
rage that Estella looked at her with surprise, "who am I, for
heaven's sake, that I should be kind?"

It was weak of me to have complained to her and I told
her so. "I was paid generously for coming here, and I have
asked these questions only for my own information. Now I
have another purpose in what I will say, an unselfish one.
In letting me think as I did, Miss Havisham, you were
punishing your self-seeking relatives?"

"I was. They even wanted to believe I was helping you.
Why should I have told them the truth? You made your
own mistakes. I never made them."

Waiting until she was quiet again, I went on, "Ever

since I went to London, I have been constantly with one family of your people. They believed, just as I did, that you were my benefactor. But you deeply wrong Mr. Pocket and Herbert if you don't believe they are generous and honest and incapable of anything mean."

"They are your friends," she said.

"They made themselves my friends even when they thought you were giving me what might have been theirs. Sarah Pocket and Georgiana and Camilla were not my friends, I think."

I could see I had made some impression on her. "What do you want for them?" she asked.

"Miss Havisham," I said, "if you could spare the money to do something for my friend Herbert—something he must not know about—I could show you how."

"Why is he not to know?" she asked.

"Because I started to help him, without his knowing it, more than two years ago. I don't want him to know now. Why I can't go on, I cannot explain. It is part of someone else's secret."

She sat gazing at the fire while Estella knitted on. Then she turned her attention to me again. "What else?" she asked.

"Estella," I said, turning to her now with my voice trembling, "you know I love you. You know I have loved you long and dearly."

She raised her eyes to my face and looked at me without showing any feeling.

"I would have said this sooner if it hadn't been for my long mistake. That led me to hope Miss Havisham meant us for each other. When I thought you had no choice about your future, I kept still. But I must say it now."

Estella shook her head.

"I know," I said, "that I have no hope that you will ever be mine, Estella. I don't even know what may become of me very soon, how poor I may be, or where I may go. Still, I love you. I have loved you ever since I first saw you in this house."

Looking at me perfectly unmoved, she shook her head again.

" It would have been cruel of Miss Havisham to torture me all these years with a vain hope if she had realized the importance of what she was doing. But I think she didn't. I think that in her own suffering she forgot mine, Estella."

I saw Miss Havisham put her hand to her heart and hold it there as she sat looking by turns at Estella and me.

"It seems," said Estella calmly, "that there are ideas and feelings I don't understand. When you say you love me, I understand the words, but nothing more. I have no feelings in my heart. I have tried to warn you of this, but you thought I didn't mean it. Now do you think so?"

"I hoped you could not mean it. You, so young and beautiful. It is against nature."

"It is my nature," she answered. "It is the way I have been trained. I would not even bother to explain this to anyone else. It is all I can do for you."

"Is it not true," said I, "that Bentley Drummle is in town and pursuing you? That you encourage him and that he is riding with you today?"

She seemed a little surprised that I should know it, but said, "Quite true."

"You cannot love him, Estella."

"What have I told you?" she answered in anger. "Do you still think that I do not mean what I say?"

"You would never marry him, Estella?"

She looked toward Miss Havisham and thought a minute. Then she said, "Why not tell the truth? I am going to be married to him."

I dropped my face in my hands but was able to control myself better than I would have expected. When I raised my face again, I saw such a terrible look on Miss Havisham's face that it impressed me even in my own grief.

"Estella, dearest Estella, do not let Miss Havisham lead you into this fatal step. Push me aside—you have already done so—but give yourself to a worthy person. Miss Havisham gives you to Drummle only to injure the many far better men who really love you. There must be one among them who loves you as dearly as I do. Take him, and I can bear it better for your sake."

My seriousness surprised her and would have aroused her sympathy if she could have understood me. "I am going to be married to him," she said in a gentler voice. "Preparations are being made, and I shall be married soon. Why do you blame my mother by adoption? It is my own idea."

"Your own idea to throw yourself away on a brute?"

"To whom should I give myself?" she answered with a smile. "To a man who would realize at once that I have nothing to give him? I'll do well enough, and so will my husband. Don't blame Miss Havisham for what I am doing. She wanted me to wait and not marry yet. But I am tired of the life I am living and want to change. Say no more. We will never understand each other."

"Such a mean, stupid brute," I urged in despair.

"Don't be afraid of my being a blessing to him," said Estella. "Come. Here is my hand. Shall we part on this, you romantic boy—or man?"

"O Estella!" I said, while my tears fell on her hand. "Even if I stayed in England and could hold up my head, how could I see you Drummle's wife?"

"Nonsense," she answered. "You will forget this in no time. You will get me out of your thoughts in a week."

"Out of my thoughts! You are part of my existence, part of myself. You have been with me every moment since I came here, the rough, common boy whose heart you wounded even then. Your presence and your influence have been with me everywhere and always will be. To the last hour of my life you will be a part of me. God bless you. God forgive you!"

I held her hand to my lips, and so I left her. But afterward I remembered that while Estella looked at me only with unbelieving surprise, Miss Havisham, her hand still covering her heart, stared at me with pity and remorse.

So much had happened that when I came out the light of day seemed darker than when I went in. By and by I started to walk all the way to London. I could not bear to sit in a coach and talk to people. I could not go back to the inn and see Drummle there. I could do nothing half so good for myself as tire myself out.

It was past midnight when I crossed London Bridge. I was not expected until tomorrow, but I had my keys and could get in without disturbing Herbert. The night watchman looked at me closely as I entered the gate. Then he handed me a note, saying, "The messenger that brought it said would you be so good as to read it by my lantern."

Much surprised, I took the note. On the outside were the words, "Please read this here." I opened it and read in Wemmick's handwriting, "Don't go home."

28   *Safe Lodgings*

Turning from the Temple gate as soon as I had read the warning, I made my way to Fleet Street and there took a coach to an inn I knew of. Here I got a bed for the night. And what a long, anxious night it was! From all corners of the room the words, "Don't go home," seemed to echo back to me. For hours I lay awake. Why I was not to go home and what had happened at home and whether Provis was safe at home were questions occupying my mind so busily that there was room for few other thoughts. Even when I thought of Estella and how we had parted that day forever, the caution, "Don't go home," was always in my mind. When I finally dozed, worn out in mind and body, the words were still so close to the surface in my mind that I roused up and felt as though I were losing my mind.

I had left directions to be called at seven. It was plain that I must see Wemmick before seeing anyone else. It was plain, too, that I must see him at his castle, not at the office. It was a relief to get out of the room where I had spent such a miserable night. I needed no second knocking on the door to get me up. The towers of the castle came into my view at eight o'clock. The little servant happening to arrive at the same time, we crossed the drawbridge together and entered the house. Wemmick was making tea for himself and the Aged. Through an open door I could see the old man in bed.

"Hello, Mr. Pip," said Wemmick, "you did come home then."

"Yes," I answered, "but I didn't *go* home."

"That's all right," said he. "I left a note for you at each of the Temple gates on a chance. Which gate did you come to?"

I told him.

"I'll go around to the others some time during the day and destroy the notes," said Wemmick. "It's a good rule never to leave written evidence if you can help it. You never know what use it may be put to. Now, would you mind toasting the sausages for the Aged?"

When I said I would do so, he sent the maid out to do something else, and so we were alone.

"Now, Mr. Pip," said Wemmick, "you and I understand each other. This is a confidential matter, as some of our others have been. This is away from my office."

I agreed. I was so nervous that I had already set fire to the Aged's sausages and had to blow it out.

"I accidentally heard yesterday morning," said Wemmick, "being in a certain place where I once took you—I won't mention names—"

"I understand you," I said.

"I heard there by chance yesterday morning," Wemmick went on, "that a certain person from a different part of the world, where people are sometimes sent whether they want to go or not, had made a great stir in those parts by disappearing and being no more heard of. As a result of his leaving, guesses as to where he went were being raised. I also heard that you had been watched at your rooms and might be watched again."

"By whom?" I said.

"I wouldn't go into that," said Wemmick. "It wasn't told to me. I just heard it."

He took the sausage from me, laid out the Aged's breakfast neatly on a little tray, and took it in to him.

"This watching of me at my rooms," I went on when he had returned, "is definitely connected with the person you have referred to, isn't it?"

Wemmick looked very serious. "I couldn't be sure it was, right at the start," he said. "But it either is or it will be or it's in great danger of being."

I saw that he did not feel, because of his position at his office, as though he could tell me as much as he knew. I realized how much he was doing already and did not press him. I told him, however, that I would like to ask him a question and he could feel free to answer it or not, as he thought best. "You have heard of a man of bad character whose real name is Compeyson?" I asked.

He nodded.

"Is he living?"

He nodded again.

"Is he in London?"

He gave me one last nod and went on with his breakfast. "Now," he said, "questioning being over, I come to what I did after what I heard. I went to your home to look for you, and not finding you there, I went to Mr. Herbert at Clarriker's. Without mentioning any names or going into any details, I gave him to understand that it would be better while you were away to keep any third person he might know out of sight."

"Herbert was greatly puzzled as to what to do?"

"He was, especially when I said it would not be safe to take the other person too far away at present. Mr. Pip, there's no place like a big city to hide in. Don't come out too soon. Lie close. Wait until things slacken before you come out of hiding, even to go away to foreign parts."

I thanked him for his advice and asked him what Herbert had done.

"Mr. Herbert, after being completely upset for half an hour, thought of a plan. He mentioned to me a secret that he is courting a young lady who has a bedridden Pa. That Pa, having worked on a ship all his life, now lies in bed in a bay window where he can see the ships sail up and down the river. You know the young lady most likely?"

"Not personally," said I.

The truth was that she had objected to me. She thought I was an expensive companion who was doing Herbert no good. Consequently, she had not been anxious to meet me, and Herbert had thought it better that I wait a while before making her acquaintance. When I had begun to pay secretly for Herbert's career, I felt better about everything, and Clara felt better about me because Herbert had begun to do so well. We had for a long time been sending messages to each other through Herbert, though I had never seen her. I didn't tell Wemmick about all this, however.

"The house with the bay window," said Wemmick, "is kept by a very respectable widow who has a furnished upper floor to let. Mr. Herbert asked me what I would think of it as a temporary home for the person we're talking about. For three reasons I thought well of it. First, it's off the beaten track. Second, without going there yourself, you could always get reports from Herbert. And, after a while when it seems wise, you could always ship the person right from there on board a passenger ship."

Much comforted by these thoughts, I thanked Wemmick again and again, and asked him to go on.

"Well, sir, Mr. Herbert went into the affair with a will. By nine o'clock he had housed the person quite successfully. At your lodgings it was understood that he had been called to Dover. In fact, he was even taken a piece down the Dover road. Now, another great advantage to you of all this is that it was done without you while you were miles away and busy otherwise. This takes away suspicion from you and confuses things. For the same reason, I suggested that you stay away from home last night. It brings in more confusion, and you want confusion."

Wemmick, having finished his breakfast here, looked at his watch and began to get his coat on. "And now, Mr. Pip," said he, "I have probably done the most I can do. But if I can ever do more, I shall be glad to do it. Here's the address. There can be no harm in your going there tonight to see how things are before you go home. But after you have gone home, don't go back there. You are very welcome, I am sure, Mr. Pip. And let me impress one important point on you. Use this evening to get hold of his money. You don't know what may happen to him. Don't let anything happen to his property."

I was sure I couldn't explain to Wemmick how I felt about that, so I didn't try.

"I must be off now," said he. "If you have nothing important to do until dark, I would advise your staying here. You look very much worried. It will do you good to have a perfectly quiet day with the Aged. Good-bye, Aged Parent," he shouted cheerfully.

"All right, John. All right, my boy," piped the old man from his room.

I soon fell asleep before Wemmick's fire, and the Aged and I enjoyed one another's company by falling asleep before it more or less all day. When it was quite dark, I left him preparing the fire for toast. I gathered from the number of tea cups and from his glance at the two little doors in the wall that Miss Skiffins was expected.

29 *Followed*

It was eight o'clock before I got down to the river front. The place I was looking for was far from easy to find. It was called Mill Pond Bank, Chink's Basin, and when I had at last discovered it, it turned out to be an open kind of place, where the wind from the river had room to turn itself around. There were even two or three trees still growing there. I selected from the few queer houses on Mill Pond Bank one with a wooden front and three stories of bay windows with the name Mrs. Whimple on the door. My knock was answered by an elderly woman of a pleasant appearance. She was followed at once by Herbert, who led me into the parlor and shut the door. It was strange to see his familiar face quite at home in that very unfamiliar room and section.

"All is well, Handel," said Herbert, "and he is quite satisfied, though eager to see you. My dear girl is with her father. When she comes down, I'll introduce you to her, and then we'll go upstairs. That's her father."

I had noticed an alarming growling overhead and had probably looked surprised.

"I am afraid he's a bad old rascal," said Herbert, smiling, "but I have never seen him. Don't you smell rum? He is always at it. You can imagine how good it must be for his gout. He insists on keeping all the provisions in his room and weighing them out just as he used to do when he was on shipboard. A man with gout in his right hand must find it hard to cut cheeses."

220

We heard another furious roar upstairs.

"To have Provis for a lodger is quite a godsend to Mrs. Whimple," said Herbert, "for of course people in general won't stand that noise. Mrs. Whimple is the best of housewives. I really don't know what my Clara would do without her. For Clara has no mother of her own, Handel, and no relations in the world but old Gruffandgrim. That's my name for her father," he explained when I looked startled. "His real name is Mr. Barley."

Just then a very pretty slim, dark-eyed girl of twenty or so came in. Herbert, blushing, presented her to me as Clara. She was a most charming girl—like a fairy whom old Barley had captured and made to wait on him.

"Look here," said Herbert, showing me the basket that Clara had carried in. "Here's poor Clara's supper served out by her father every night."

Clara seemed resigned to her father's methods. She was so natural and attractive as she stood with Herbert's arm around her that I would not have had anything happen to their engagement for all the money in the world. I was looking at her with pleasure and admiration when there was a growl and a roar and a dreadful bumping noise from upstairs. "Papa wants me, darling," said Clara to Herbert and ran away.

"What a terrible old shark he is," said Herbert. "What do you suppose he wants now?"

"I don't know," said I. "Something to drink?"

"That's probably it," said Herbert. "He keeps his grog already mixed in a little tub on the table."

When Clara had come back, Herbert took me upstairs to see my convict. In his two rooms at the top of the house, which were fresh and airy, I found him comfortably settled. He did not seem to be afraid, and for some reason was much gentler than he had been before. I decided to say nothing to him about Compeyson, for I was afraid his hate for the man would send him out to find him and thus destroy himself. I asked him first of all whether he trusted Wemmick's judgment and sources of information.

"Ay, ay, dear boy," he said with a grave nod. "Jaggers knows."

"I have talked with Wemmick," said I, "and have come to tell you what warning and advice he gave me." So I told him how Wemmick had heard in Newgate Prison that he was suspected of being in England and my rooms were being watched; and what Wemmick said about getting him abroad after he had stayed in hiding for some time. I told him Wemmick thought I should stay away from him until he left to go abroad.

He was reasonable throughout. He had taken a chance on coming back, he said, and had always realized it. He would do nothing rash now and had no fears of his safety with such good help.

Herbert now came forward with an idea. "We are both good with boats, Handel," he said, "and could take Provis down the river ourselves when the right time comes. Then we would not need to hire boatmen, who might be suspicious. You could start at once to keep a boat at the Temple stairs and go out rowing regularly. Then no attention would ever be given you later."

We all liked this scheme and agreed that Provis would always pretend not to notice us if we rowed past his home, but should pull down the shade in his east window whenever he saw us as a signal that things were all right with him.

When everything was arranged I rose to go, telling Herbert that he and I had better not go together. "I don't like to leave you here," I said to Provis, "though I'm sure that you're safer here than you would be near me. Good-bye."

"Dear boy," he answered, clasping my hands, "I don't

know when we may meet again, and I don't like good-bye. Say good night."

We left him standing on the landing outside his door and holding a lamp to light us on our way. Looking back at him, I thought of the first night of his return when our positions were reversed. I little thought then that my heart could ever be as heavy and anxious at parting from him as it was now. On the way down Herbert told me that Provis was known in his new lodgings as Mr. Campbell, a good friend of Herbert's for whom he was responsible.

When I had said good night to the pretty girl and the motherly woman with whom she lived, I felt that Chink's Basin, filled with youth and hope and love, was quite a different place from what I had expected. And then I thought of Estella and our parting and went home very sad.

Next day I got a boat and started going out for practice, sometimes alone, sometimes with Herbert. Nobody paid any attention to me after I had been out a few times. Whenever we passed Mill Pond Bank, we saw the shade toward the east pulled down. Herbert went down there at least three times a week, bringing me back news that was never alarming. Still, I knew there was cause for alarm, and I could not get over the feeling of being watched. I was always full of fear for the rash man in hiding. Herbert found it pleasant to stand at one of our windows and think of the river as flowing toward Clara. But I thought with dread that it was flowing toward Magwitch and that any black mark on its surface might be his pursuers going swiftly, silently, surely to take him.

Some weeks passed in this way without bringing any change. We waited for Wemmick and he made no sign. If I had never known him as a friend and away from his office, I might have doubted him.

My worldly affairs began to look very gloomy, and I was pressed for money by more than one tradesman to whom I was in debt. I began to know what it was like to need ready cash and to get some by selling some of my jewels. I was quite determined not to take more money from my benefactor in the present uncertain state of affairs. I had sent him by Herbert his unopened pocketbook, and I felt a kind of satisfaction over not having spent any of his money since he had come home.

As time went on I had a sad feeling that Estella was married. Afraid of finding it out for sure, I would not read the newspapers, and I begged Herbert never to speak to me of her. It was an unhappy life I lived with one fear stronger than all others in my mind. Still, no new cause for alarm arose. I waited in a state of constant restlessness and suspense. I rowed my boat and waited, waited, waited, as I best could.

Sometimes when the tide wasn't right for me to get home easily, I would leave my boat a bit down the river to be brought up to the Temple stairs later. I liked doing this because it made people around the water front more used to seeing me and my boat. As a result of this, I had two meetings which I shall tell of now.

One afternoon late in February I came ashore at dusk after rowing down the river to Greenwich and back. It had been a fine bright day, but had become foggy as the sun dropped, and I had to feel my way among the boats pretty carefully. Both going and coming I had seen the signal in his window. All well. As it was a raw evening and I was cold, I thought I would have dinner at once. The theater where we had seen Mr. Wopsle play was in that neighborhood, and rather than sit alone at home, I decided to stop in and see a play after I had had my dinner.

Mr. Wopsle was still there, playing all sorts of small parts. That evening he appeared first as an important government official and next as a magician. There was nothing remarkable about either the play or Mr. Wopsle's part in it.

What was strange was that at his second appearance he, having nothing much to do or say on stage, devoted his time to staring in my direction as if he were lost in amazement.

I could not make him out and sat thinking of his strange actions until the play was over. When I came out of the theater, I found him waiting for me at the door. "How do you do," said I, shaking hands as we went down the street together. "I saw that you saw me."

"Saw you, Mr. Pip," he answered. "Yes, of course I saw you. But who else was there?"

"Who else?"

"It is the strangest thing," said Mr. Wopsle, "and yet I could swear to him. Whether I would have noticed him if you hadn't been there, I can't be sure. Yet I think I would."

I looked around me as I had grown used to doing these days, for his words gave me a chill.

"Oh, he can't be in sight," said Mr. Wopsle. "He went out before I left the stage. I saw him go. I had an idea he must be with you, Mr. Pip, till I saw that you were quite unaware of him, sitting behind you like a ghost."

I said nothing, being suspicious of this poor actor as I was of everyone. Perhaps he had been set by someone to make me mention Provis, though I knew it could not have been Provis sitting near me.

"You'll hardly believe what I am going to tell you, Mr. Pip. It's so strange I would hardly believe it myself if you told me."

"Indeed?" said I.

"Mr. Pip, you remember in old times a certain Christmas Day, when you were still a child and some soldiers came to Gargery to get a pair of handcuffs made?"

"I remember it very well."

"You remember there was a chase after two convicts, and we joined in and Gargery carried you on his back?"

"I remember it very well."

"You remember we came up with the two in a ditch and one of them had been beaten and knocked in the face by the other?"

"I see it all before me."

"And the soldiers lighted torches and put the two in the center and we went on with them over the black marshes with the torchlight shining on their faces?"

"Yes," said I, "I remember all that."

"Then, Mr. Pip, one of those two prisoners sat behind you tonight. I saw him over your shoulder."

"Steady!" I thought. Then I asked him, "Which of the two do you suppose you saw?"

"The one who had been beaten," he answered promptly, "and I'll swear I saw him."

"This is very curious," said I, trying to act as though it was nothing at all to me. "Very curious indeed." I can't describe the terror I felt at Compeyson's being behind me "like a ghost." For if he had ever been out of my thoughts since the hiding had begun, it was at this moment when he was closest to me. I could not doubt that he was there because I was there.

I questioned Mr. Wopsle as to when the man had come in. He could not tell me, for at first he had not identified him at all, though he had thought of him as having some vague connection with me and the old village times. He had been prosperously dressed in black. There were no scars on his face.

After I had treated Mr. Wopsle to some refreshments, we parted. It was between twelve and one when I reached home. No one was near me.

Herbert and I had a very serious council. There was nothing to be done but to let Wemmick know what had happened. I wrote to him at once and went out and posted the letter. No one was near, but from that time on we were more cautious than ever, if that was possible.

30 *Powerful Hands*

The second of the two meetings I have referred to occurred about a week after the first. One afternoon as I was strolling along the street, a large hand was laid upon my shoulder. It was Mr. Jaggers's hand, and he passed it through my arm.

"As we are going in the same direction, Pip, we may walk together. Where are you bound for?"

"I don't know. I haven't made up my mind."

"If you are going to dine," said Mr. Jaggers, "come and dine with me."

I was going to excuse myself when he added, "Wemmick's coming." So I changed my excuse into an acceptance. We went first to the office, where I waited while he got ready to leave. As I stood by the fire, its rising and falling flames made the two casts on the shelf look as though they were playing a gruesome game of bo-peep with me.

We all three went to Mr. Jaggers's home together in a coach. As soon as we got there, dinner was served. Though I realized that Wemmick was now away from his castle, I tried to catch his eye once in a while in a friendly fashion. But it was not to be done. He was as cold and distant to me as if there were twin Wemmicks and this was the wrong one.

"Did you send that note of Miss Havisham's to Mr. Pip?"

Mr. Jaggers asked soon after we began dinner.

"No, sir," replied Wemmick, "it was going by mail when you brought Mr. Pip in. Here it is."

"It's a note of two lines, Pip," said Mr. Jaggers, handing it to me, "sent to us because Miss Havisham was not sure of your address. She wants to see you on a little matter of business you mentioned to her. When can you go?"

"If Mr. Pip intends going at once," said Wemmick to Mr. Jaggers, "he needn't write an answer."

Taking this as a hint that it was best not to delay, I said I would go tomorrow.

"So, Pip," said Mr. Jaggers then, "our friend the Spider had played his cards and won the prize."

It was as much as I could do to agree.

"Hah! He's a promising fellow—in his way—but he may not have it all his own way. The stronger one of them will win in the end. But we have to find out first which one is stronger. If he should beat her—"

"Surely," I interrupted, with a burning face and heart, "you do not seriously think he is bad enough for that, Mr. Jaggers?"

"I didn't say so, Pip. I am just considering the affair. A fellow like our Spider either beats or cowers—either gets the strength on his side or gives in to the stronger one. So here's to Mrs. Bentley Drummle. May the question be settled to the lady's satisfaction. Now Molly, Molly, Molly, how slow you are today."

She was at his elbow putting a dish on the table when he spoke to her. As she stepped back, nervously making some excuse, a certain movement of her hands attracted my attention.

"What's the matter?" said Mr. Jaggers.

"Nothing, only the subject we were speaking about is rather painful to me," I said.

The action of her fingers was like the action of knitting!

She stood looking at her master, not understanding whether she was free to go or not. Her look was very attentive. Surely I had seen exactly such eyes and hands on a memorable occasion very lately!

He told her to go, and she glided out of the room. But I could see her as plainly as if she were still there. I looked at her hands, her eyes, her flowing hair. I compared them with twenty years of a brutal husband and a stormy life. I looked again at the hands and eyes of the housekeeper and looking, remembered the feeling I had when I last walked with Estella in Miss Havisham's ruined garden. I remembered how the same feeling had come back when I saw her face and when I had ridden with her in a carriage through a sudden glare of light in a dark street. The only clue I needed had been supplied to me when, thinking of Estella, I had looked at this woman with her knitting fingers and her attentive eyes. Then I felt absolutely certain that this woman was Estella's mother.

Mr. Jaggers had seen me with Estella. He probably knew about the feeling I had for her. He nodded when I said the subject was painful for me, clapped me on my back, and went on with his dinner.

Only twice more did the housekeeper appear. Then her stay in the room was short, and Mr. Jaggers was sharp with her. But her eyes were Estella's eyes. If she had appeared a hundred times, I could not have been more sure that my idea was the truth.

It was a dull evening, for Wemmick had little or nothing to say, waiting only to answer questions put to him by his chief. He seemed to me the wrong twin all the time, with only a faint resemblance to Wemmick of the castle.

We left together early. We had not gone a dozen yards before I found that I was walking arm in arm with the right twin and the wrong one had quickly evaporated into the evening air.

"Well!" said Wemmick, "that's over. He's a wonderful man, but I'm always on edge when I dine with him, and I dine more pleasantly at ease."

I felt that this was a good statement of the case and told him so.

"Wouldn't say it to anybody but yourself," he answered. "I know that what is said between you and me goes no further."

I asked him if he had ever seen Miss Havisham's adopted daughter, Mrs. Bentley Drummle. He said no.

"Wemmick," said I, "do you remember telling me before I first went to Mr. Jaggers's house to notice his housekeeper?"

"Did I?" he replied. "I dare say I did."

"A wild beast tamed, you called her. How did Mr. Jaggers tame her, Wemmick?"

"That's his secret. She's been with him many a long year."

"I wish you would tell me her story. I feel a particular interest in it. You know that what is said between you and me goes no further."

"Well," replied Wemmick, "I don't know her story; that is, I don't know all of it. But I'll tell you what I do know. Twenty years or so ago she was tried for murder at the Old Bailey and was acquitted. She was a very handsome young woman and I believe had some gypsy blood in her. Anyhow, you can imagine it must have been hot blood."

"But she was acquitted?"

"Mr. Jaggers was for her," continued Wemmick with a meaning look. "He worked her case in a quite surprising way. It was a desperate cause and it came to him at the start of his career. Everyone admired the way he conducted it. In fact, it may almost be said to have made him.

"The murdered person was a woman a good ten years older, very much larger, and very much stronger. It was a case of jealousy. They had both been tramps, and this woman who is now Mr. Jaggers's housekeeper had been married very young to a man who was also a tramp. She was a jealous woman to the point of fury.

"The murdered woman—closer to the man's age than his wife—was found dead in a barn. There had been a violent struggle, perhaps a fight. She was bruised and scratched and torn and had been held by the throat at last and choked. There was no suspicion directed against anyone but this woman. Jaggers rested his case on the idea that it wasn't likely anyone as small as she could have committed the crime. You may be sure he never called attention to the strength of her hands then, though he sometimes does now.

"Well, sir!" Wemmick went on, "it happened, don't you see, that this woman was so cleverly dressed from the time of her arrest that she looked much smaller than she really was. In particular, her sleeves were so made that her arms had a very frail look. She had only a bruise or two on her—nothing for a tramp—but the backs of her hands were torn. The question was, was it with fingernails?

"Now, Mr. Jaggers showed that she had struggled through a lot of briers which were not so high as her face but which she couldn't have gone through and kept off her hands. Bits of the briers were found in her skin, some of them with little spots of blood and shreds of her dress on them. These were used as evidence in court. Jaggers made another good point. As proof of her jealousy it was testified that she was suspected at the time of the murder of frantically destroying her three-year-old child by this man to get revenge on him. But Mr. Jaggers reminded the court that she was not being tried for the murder of her child. He proved, too, that her scratches were caused by briers. He was altogether too much for the jury, and they gave in."

"Has she been in his service ever since?"

"Yes. But not only that. She went to his service as soon as she was freed, tamed as she is now. She has been taught one thing and another in the way of her duties, but she was tamed from the start."

"Do you remember the sex of the child?"

"Said to have been a girl."

"You have nothing more to say to me tonight?"

"Nothing. I got your letter and destroyed it."

We said good night and I went home with something new to think about but no relief from the old thoughts.

31 *The Fire*

The next day I went down by coach to Miss Havisham's. I got off while we were still out in the country and walked the rest of the distance. I wanted to get into the town quietly by back roads and to leave in the same way. It was late in the afternoon as I walked slowly along hearing in the distance the cathedral chimes. They seemed to be telling me that everything was changed and that Estella had gone away forever.

An elderly servant opened the gate for me. A lighted candle stood in the dark passage inside as of old. I took it and went upstairs alone. Miss Havisham was not in her own room but in the large one across the hall. I saw her sitting by the fire, lost in thought. There was an air of utter loneliness about her. I pitied her in spite of the deep injury she had done me. As I stood looking at her, I thought that I too had become a part of the wrecked fortunes of the house.

"It is I, Pip," I said when she looked up at me. "Mr. Jaggers gave me your note yesterday, and I came at once."

"Thank you," she said, and I brought a chair and sat down beside her. She looked at me almost as if she was afraid of me. "I want," she said, "to go on with a subject you mentioned to me when you were here before. I want to show you that there is still something human in my heart.

234

You said, speaking for your friend Herbert, that you could tell me how to do something useful and good—something you would like done. What is it?"

I began to tell her about the secret partnership I had bought for Herbert, but she did not seem to listen, and I stopped. After many minutes of silence she said, "Do you grow silent because you hate me too much to bear to speak to me?"

"No, no," I answered. "How can you think so, Miss Havisham? I stopped because I thought you were not following what I said."

"Perhaps I was not," she answered, putting her hand to her head. "Begin again. Tell me."

She rested her hand on her stick and looked at the fire, seeming to make a strong effort to pay attention. I went on with my explanation and told her how I had hoped to complete the business with my own money but could not do so. The cause of that, I reminded her, was someone else's secret, not mine.

"So!" she said, "and how much money is needed to complete the purchase?"

I was rather afraid of stating it, for it sounded like a large sum. "Nine hundred pounds."

"If I gave you the money for this purpose, would you keep my secret as you have kept your own?"

"Quite as faithfully."

"And your mind will be more at rest?"

"Much more at rest."

"Are you very unhappy now?"

She asked this question in a tone of sympathy unusual with her. I could not answer at once, for my voice failed me. She put her arm on the head of her cane and laid her head on it.

"I am far from happy, Miss Havisham. But I have other causes of grief than any you know of. They are the secrets

I have mentioned."

"It is noble of you to tell me you have other causes for unhappiness. Is it true?"

"Only too true."

"Can I only help you, Pip, by helping your friend? Is there nothing I can do for you yourself?"

"Nothing. Thank you for the question, but there is nothing."

She presently rose from her seat and took from her pocket a notebook yellow with age and bound in tarnished gold, and wrote in it with a gold pencil that hung around her neck. "You are still on friendly terms with Mr. Jaggers?" she asked.

"Quite. I dined with him yesterday."

"This is an order to him to pay you the money for your friend." She read me what she had written, and it was direct and clear. She handed me the notebook with her trembling hand, and taking the pencil from around her neck, gave me that too. "My name is on the first leaf," she said. "If you can ever write under it, 'I forgive,' even though it is long after my broken heart is dust, please do."

"Oh, Miss Havisham," I said, "I can do it now. There have been bad mistakes. My life has been a blind and thankless one. But I need forgiveness far too much myself to be bitter against you."

To my amazement, even to my horror, she dropped on her knees at my feet. To see her with her white hair and her worn face kneeling there gave me a terrible shock. I begged her to rise, and got my arms around her to help her up. But she only pressed my hand and wept. I had never seen her shed tears before, and in the hope that they might bring her relief, I bent over her without speaking.

"Oh!" she cried in despair. "What have I done? What have I done?"

"If you mean what have you done to me, it's very little,

Miss Havisham. I would have loved her under any circumstances. Is she married?" It was a needless question, for a new sadness in the sad old house had told me so.

"Yes," she answered, crying out again, "What have I done?"

I did not know how to answer her or to comfort her. I knew she had done a terrible thing in taking a young child and poisoning its mind with her own wild hatred and wounded pride. I knew that in living as she did she had kept away from herself all the natural and normal influences of life. I knew that her mind had finally grown diseased as all minds must that think and brood on themselves only and forget their God. I could not look at her now without pity. She had punished herself too completely by the life she had let her sorrow make for her.

"Until you spoke to Estella the other day, until I saw in your face the same kind of love that I once felt for someone, I didn't realize what I had done."

"Miss Havisham," I said, "your conscience need not trouble you about me. But Estella is a different case. If you can ever undo what you have done to her in training her as you have, it will be a hundred times better than grieving over the past."

"Yes, yes, I know it. Pip, my dear, believe this. When she came to me, I meant only to save her from misery like my own. But as she grew more and more beautiful, I gradually did worse. With my praises and my jewels and my teachings, I stole her heart away and put ice in its place."

"It would have been better to let her have a normal heart that could be bruised and broken."

"If you knew all my story," she pleaded, "you would have some pity on me and a better understanding of me."

"Miss Havisham," I said, as tactfully as I could, "I do know your story and have known it ever since I left here. It has filled me with great pity. Does our long acquaintance give me an excuse to ask about Estella as she was when she first came here? Whose child was she?"

She shook her head.

"You don't know? But Mr. Jaggers brought her here. Will you tell me how that came about?"

She answered carefully in a low whisper. "I had been shut up in these rooms a long time. I told him then that I wanted a little girl to bring up and love and save from my fate. I had first seen him when I withdrew from the world. Then I had read about him in the paper and had sent for him to manage my affairs. He told me he would look around for an orphan child. One night he brought her here asleep, and I called her Estella. She was two or three years old then. She knows nothing but that she was left an orphan and I adopted her."

In my own mind I was sure that Mr. Jaggers' housekeeper was her mother. But what could I gain by asking more questions or staying longer? I had gotten what I wanted for Herbert. Miss Havisham had told me all she knew of Estella. I had forgiven her. So we parted.

It was almost dark when I went downstairs and out into the air. I wanted to walk around the place a little before leaving. I had a feeling that I would never be there again. I went to the ruined garden and walked to the corner where Herbert and I had had our fight and around the paths where Estella and I had gone. It was so cold there, so lonely, so dreary! Finally I came out through the gate where I had wept because Estella had scorned me.

Before I left forever, I wanted to be sure that Miss Havisham was all right. Going upstairs again, I looked into the room where I had left her and saw her sitting close to the fire with her back toward me. In a moment as I turned to go quietly away, I saw a great flaming light spring up. In the same moment she ran toward me shrieking with a whirl of fire blazing all around her.

I had a heavy overcoat on and another thick one over my arm. I threw her down and wrapped her up in them. Then I dragged the cloth from the table for the same purpose, and with it all the rotten things that had been on it so long. We were on the floor struggling like enemies. The closer I covered her the more wildly she shrieked and tried to free herself. I moved only by instinct, not from either thought or plan.

Then I looked around and saw the disturbed spiders and beetles running over the floor, and the servants rushing in. I still held her with all my strength like a prisoner. I doubt if I even knew who she was or why we had struggled until I saw the burnt shreds of what had been her clothing falling in a black shower around us.

She was unconscious, and I was afraid to have her moved or touched. I held her until the doctor came and was astonished then to see that both my hands were burned. I had not even felt them. She was laid on the huge table to have her injuries dressed. She was badly but not dangerously burned. The shock to her nerves was much more serious. When I saw her again an hour later, she lay where I had seen her strike her stick and had heard her say she would die someday. She still had some of her horrible bridal look, for they had covered her to the throat with white cotton wool, and she lay with a white sheet over her.

Estella, I learned from the servants, was in Paris. The doctor promised that he would write her, and I took it on myself to inform Herbert's father of the accident.

One time that evening she came to and spoke of what had happened. Toward midnight she wandered in her mind, moaning constantly, "What have I done!" and then, "When she first came, I meant to save her from misery like mine." And then, "Take the pencil and write under my name, 'I forgive her.' " All of this she repeated again and again.

I could be of no more help there. And I had, nearer home, reasons for anxiety and fear that were constantly on my mind. So I decided during the night that I would return by the early morning coach. About six in the morning I leaned over and touched her lips with mine, just as she was saying, again and again, "Take the pencil and write under my name, 'I forgive her.' "

32 *Hidden Truths*

My hands had been dressed two or three times in the night and again in the morning. My left arm, which I had to carry in a sling, was badly burned to the elbow and somewhat so as high as the shoulder. It was very painful, but I could move my fingers. My hair had been singed but not my head or face.

Herbert spent the day taking care of me. He was a kind and patient nurse. At first I suffered more in mind than in body. I kept seeing the glare of the flames and smelling the smoke. If I dozed for a minute, I was awakened by Miss Havisham's cries. Herbert, seeing this, tried his best to keep my thoughts occupied. Neither of us spoke of the boat I might soon have to row, but we both thought of it. I agreed—without words—to cure my burns in the shortest possible time.

Toward night we began to talk of affairs down the river. "I sat with Provis last night a good two hours, Handel," said Herbert. "Clara had to spend the evening with Gruffandgrim. He kept pounding on the floor whenever she was out of sight, I doubt that he will live very long, though. What with rum and fits of temper, I should most certainly say that his days are nearly over."

"And then you will be married, Herbert?"

"How can I take care of the dear child otherwise? But

241

I was speaking of Provis. Do you know, Handel, he improves? He told me a great deal more about his life last night. You remember his breaking off here about some woman he had had great trouble with?"

His words gave me a start.

"I had forgotten that, Herbert, but I remember, now you speak of it."

"Well! He told me about it, and a dark, wild story it is. Shall I tell you? Or would it worry you now?"

"Tell me by all means. Every word."

"It seems that the woman was young and jealous and spiteful, Handel, to the last degree—murder!"

"How did she murder? Whom did she murder?"

"Well, perhaps that's too terrible a name for it," said Herbert, "but she was tried for it. Mr. Jaggers defended her. It was another and a stronger woman that was the victim, and there had been a struggle in a barn. Who began it and how unfair it might have been, nobody knows. How it ended

is certainly not doubtful, for the victim was found choked to death."

"Was the woman found guilty?"

"No, she was acquitted. This young woman and Provis had a little child of whom he was quite fond. On the evening of the murder Provis's wife came to him for a moment and swore that she would kill that child (who was with her then) and that he would never see it again. Then she disappeared. What is wrong, Handel? You seem to be breathing too fast."

"Perhaps I am, Herbert. Did the woman keep her threat?"

"There comes the worst part of Provis's life. She did."

"That is, he says she did."

"Why, of course," answered Herbert in surprise. "He says it all. I have no further information. Provis doesn't say whether he treated the child's mother badly or well. But she had lived with him four or five years, and he pitied her and was forgiving toward her. So, fearing he would have to testify in court about the child and thus be the cause of his wife's death, he hid himself and kept from the trial. After she was freed, she disappeared. Thus he lost both the child and the child's mother."

"I want to ask—"

"Just a little more. That evil man Compeyson, worst villain of all villains, knew that Provis had been in hiding and knew why. Afterward, he used the knowledge as a way to keep his victim poorer and work him harder."

"I particularly want to know, Herbert, when all of this happened."

"Let me remember what he said—I think it was twenty years ago. Almost directly after that he joined Compeyson. How old were you when you came upon him in the church-yard?" he asked.

"I think almost seven."

"It had happened three or four years before that. He said you reminded him of his little lost girl, who would have been about your age."

"Herbert," I said, "look at me."

"I am looking, my dear boy."

"Touch me. You are not afraid that I have a fever or that the accident last night has affected my mind?"

"No dear, boy," said Herbert, after looking me over. "You are rather excited, but you are yourself."

"I know I am. And the man we have in hiding down the river is Estella's father!"

I don't know exactly why I was so anxious to prove Estella's parentage. When I heard Herbert's story, I could scarcely be kept from going to Mr. Jaggers that very night. Only the knowledge that I would probably make my injuries worse by neglecting them kept me home. But early next morning I was on my way to the office. Wemmick and Mr. Jaggers were together going over the office accounts when I arrived. I had to give them the story of the whole accident, of course. I had sent only a brief notice of it to Mr. Jaggers before. When it was over, I produced Miss Havisham's order for the nine hundred pounds for Herbert. Mr. Jaggers handed it to Mr. Wemmick to write the check. Then he said to me, "I am sorry, Pip, that we can do nothing for *you*."

"Miss Havisham was good enough to ask me," I replied, "whether she could do something for me, and I said no."

"I should not have told her no if I had been you," said Mr. Jaggers. "But every man ought to know his own business best."

As I thought the time had now come for saying what I had planned, I turned to Mr. Jaggers. "I did ask something of Miss Havisham, sir," I said. "I asked her to give me some information about her adopted daughter, and she gave me all she had."

"Did she?" said Mr. Jaggers. "I don't think I would have done so if I had been Miss Havisham. But she ought to know her own business best."

"I know more about Miss Havisham's child than she does herself, sir. I know her mother."

"Mother?" repeated Mr. Jaggers, looking inquiringly at me.

"I have seen her mother within the past three days. You, sir, have seen her still more recently."

"Yes?" said Mr. Jaggers.

"Perhaps I know more of Estella's history than even you do," said I. "I know her father, too."

A certain way that Mr. Jaggers acted convinced me that he did not know who her father was. I had suspected this from Provis's account to Herbert that he had kept out of his wife's affairs and had not been Mr. Jaggers's client until several years later. Then he would have had no reason for admitting the relationship.

"So you know the young lady's father, Pip?" said Mr. Jaggers.

"Yes," I replied, "and his name is Provis—from New South Wales."

Even Mr. Jaggers started when I said those words. He covered his surprise at once, but I had noted it. I dared not look at Wemmick to see how he had taken the news.

"And on what evidence, Pip," said Mr. Jaggers cooly, "does Provis make this claim?"

"He has never made it," said I. "He has no idea or belief that his daughter is still alive."

My reply, I could see, was completely unexpected. Mr. Jaggers folded his arms and looked at me with stern attention as I told him what I knew and how I knew it. To keep from him what Wemmick had told me, I let him think that Miss Havisham was my only source of information.

"Hah!" said Mr. Jaggers at last when I had finished. "Let us go on with our business now, Wemmick."

But I didn't intend to be put off in this way, and I appealed to Mr. Jaggers to be more friendly and honest with me. I reminded him of what a blow it had been to me to learn where my money had come from. I told him I had been frank with him and expected him to act in the same way toward me. I told him I wanted information from him about Estella because, even though I had lost her, she was still dearer to me than anything in the world. As he still kept silent, I turned to Wemmick and said, "Wemmick, I know you have a kind heart. I have seen your pleasant home and your old father and your cheerful, playful way of life. Say a word for me to Mr. Jaggers."

I have never seen two men look more oddly at each other than Mr. Jaggers and Wemmick did. At first I thought Wemmick might lose his position at once. Then I saw something like a smile on Mr. Jaggers's face. "What's all this?" he said to Wemmick. "You with an old father and with cheerful, pleasant ways!"

"Well," said Wemmick, "since it don't interfere with business, let it be so. I shouldn't wonder if you are planning a pleasant home of your own one of these days when you are tired of all this work."

Mr. Jaggers nodded and actually sighed. "Pip," he said, "I'll give you an idea of what might have happened. Remember, I admit nothing."

I said I understood.

"Let's say," said Mr. Jaggers, "that the woman had her child hidden, but had to tell her lawyer so. At the same time he was looking for a child to take to an old but rich lady for adoption."

"I follow you, sir."

"The lawyer had lived in the midst of evil, and he had often seen children with that sort of background brought into court and imprisoned and whipped and neglected and sometimes even hanged when they grew up. In his daily business nearly all the children he saw came to no good end."

"I follow you, sir."

"Here was one pretty little child who could be saved. The father thought she was dead and dared not make a fuss about it. The lawyer had the woman in his power. He told her that if she would give up the child he would do all in his power to free her from the charge of murder. And whether she was saved or not, the child would still be in good hands."

"I understand you perfectly."

"The woman's mind, Pip, had been unsettled by her feelings and by her fear of death. When she was set free she came to the lawyer to be protected. He took her in and kept her from going back to her old wild ways because she was in his power. Then the child grew up and was married for money. The father and mother, though living only a short distance apart, are completely unknown to each other. The secret is still a secret and would always have been one if you hadn't found out about it.

"Now, for whose sake would you tell the secret? It would not help the father to learn about the mother. The mother is safest right where she is. If the daughter found out about her parents, she would be completely disgraced after an escape of twenty years. What then could you gain by letting anyone know the secret?"

I looked at Wemmick, whose face was very serious. He touched his lips to advise me to keep silent. I did the same to indicate I would do so. Mr. Jaggers did the same. "Now, Wemmick," he said then, "where were we when Mr. Pip came in?" This ended our interview.

Watching them for a little while, at their work, I saw them look at each other oddly now and then. I suppose it was because they had shown their human and unprofessional side for the first time since they had been working together, and it embarrassed them.

33 *The Mysterious Note*

With my check in my pocket I went to Clarriker's and finished paying for Herbert's partnership. It was the only good thing I had done since I first learned of my great expectations. Clarriker told me that his company was doing so well he would soon be opening a branch office in the East. Herbert, as his partner, would take charge of it. So, even if my own future had been secure, I would still have been separated from my friend. I felt as though I had lost my last anchor and was drifting with the winds and waves. My reward was Herbert's joy over his own plans and his happiness.

It was now March. My left arm had taken so long to heal that I was still unable to get a coat on. I could use my right arm, though it was badly scarred. On a Monday morning when Herbert and I were at breakfast, I received the following letter from Wemmick:

"Burn this as soon as you read it. Early in the week or possibly Wednesday, you might do what you know of if you feel like it. Now burn."

Herbert and I considered what to do. We could no longer disregard my being disabled. "I have thought it over again and again," said Herbert, "and I think we could take Startop with us. He's an honorable fellow and fond of us and a good

248

boatman. We could tell him very little, only that it is most important for us to get Provis away."

I had thought of him more than once.

"Where will you go?" asked Herbert.

It did not seem important where we headed for, as long as it was out of England, and I said so. Foreign steamers left London at about the turn of high water. We could go down the river on the falling tide and wait in some quiet spot until a steamer came along. Then we could pull off to it and get on board.

We went at once to find out what steamers would be leaving. There was one bound for Hamburg which suited our purpose best, though we found out about others too. Then I went to get passports and Herbert found Startop, who agreed to help us. The plan was that he and Herbert would row. I would steer, and Provis would be our passenger. We made final plans for Provis to be ready on Wednesday and to come down to the water to get in our boat as soon as he saw us approach.

When I got home, I found a letter in our mailbox addressed to me—a very dirty letter, though not badly written. It had been delivered by hand and said, "If you are not afraid, come to the old marshes tonight or tomorrow night at nine. Come to the little house by the floodgates near the limekiln.* If you want information about your uncle Provis, you'd better come right away and tell no one. You must come alone. Bring this with you."

I had had enough on my mind without this strange letter. I could not tell what to do now. The worst of it was that I must decide quickly or I would miss the afternoon coach which would get me down there in time for that evening. The next night would be too close to the time set for our flight. And perhaps the information offered would

*Limekiln: an open-air pit in which lime is made from limestone rocks.

have something to do with the flight itself. I decided to go—chiefly because of the reference to my uncle Provis. Following the instructions of the letter to keep it a secret, I wrote a note to Herbert. I told him that I had decided to run down to see how Miss Havisham was, since I was going away for such a long time. I had just time to get my coat, lock up, and reach the coach as it was pulling out.

Then for the first time since the letter came, I had a chance to think. The morning had been a very upsetting one, for Wemmick's message, no matter how long we had awaited it, had been a surprise at last. Now I could not be sure I should have come, and wondered whether I would not leave the coach and go back. I did not trust unsigned letters. Still, the reference to Provis was important. If harm should come to him through my not going, how could I ever forgive myself?

I found a small and rather unknown inn when I reached the town, and while my dinner was being prepared, went to inquire about Miss Havisham. She was still very ill, though somewhat better. Upon my return, the landlord cut my meat for me, since I was not able to do it myself. Meanwhile, not recognizing me, of course, he entertained me by telling me my own story. According to him, Pumblechook had made my fortune for me and now I would have nothing to do with him. That is what the old humbug had been telling everyone since I had left for London. His lies would have had no importance for me if they had not shown me how good Joe was by comparison. Joe never complained to anyone about the way I had treated him. Neither did sweet Biddy. And they both had so much cause to complain! I felt humble and ashamed as I sat by the fire an hour or two before it was time for me to go to the marshes. I had looked in my pocket for the letter some time before that. I couldn't find it and was worried for fear that I had dropped it in the coach.

It was a dark night, though the full moon rose as I

walked along. There was a cold wind, and the marshes were very gloomy. I hesitated, half persuaded to go back. But I had no excuse for returning. So, having come there with no desire to do so, I went on in the same way. The lime-kilns were nowhere near my old home or the sea wall where I used to sit with Joe, but in the opposite direction. As I walked, my back was turned to the convict ships and the lights on them. I seemed to have the whole world around me to myself. It was a half hour before I reached the kiln. The lime was burning with a stifling smell, but the fires had been built up and left, and no workmen were around. I saw a light in the old house I was heading for. I knocked at the door. While I waited for someone to come, I noticed that the gates were deserted and broken, and the house about to tumble down. There was no answer, and I knocked again. Then I tried the latch.

The door opened, and inside I saw a lighted candle on a table, a bench, a ladder that led to a loft, and a chair. "Is there anyone here?" I called, but no one answered. Then I looked at my watch, and finding that it was past nine, called again, "Is anyone there?" There being no answer, I went to the door and looked out; seeing nothing, I turned back into the house. I knew someone must have been there lately, or the candle would not be burning. I picked it up to judge from the wick how long it had been lighted when suddenly it was put out violently and I was caught in a noose which had been thrown over my head from behind. "Now," said someone with a curse, "I've got you!"

"What is it?" I cried, struggling. "Who is it? Help! Help!"

My arms were pulled close to my sides and the pressure on my bad arm caused me terrible pain. A man's strong hand was put over my mouth to quiet my cries. His hot breath was close to me, and I struggled in vain. "Now," said the voice, "call out again and I'll make short work of you."

Faint and sick with the pain in my arm and dazed with

the shock of what had happened to me, I realized the threat might be carried out and kept still to ease my arm a little. The pain of it was torture. Finally the man let me alone and began to strike a light. I waited breathlessly to see who he was. Then a beam flashed up and showed me—Orlick! Seeing him, I knew that I was in a dangerous position indeed. After he had lighted the candle, he sat down by the table with his hands folded and looked at me. I could see that I was fastened to a ladder standing against the wall.

"Now," said he when we had looked at each other for some time, "I've got you."

"Let me go," said I. "Why did you get me here?"

"Ah," he answered, "I'll let you go to the moon. All in good time. I've got you here because I mean to get rid of you all by myself. One keeps a secret better than two. Ah, you enemy! You enemy!"

His enjoyment of my position had a viciousness in it that made me tremble. He picked up a gun from the corner by his side. "Do you recognize this?" he said, making as if he would aim at me. "Speak, wolf!"

"Yes," I answered.

"You lost me my place at Miss Havisham's, didn't you?"

"What else could I do?"

"That would be enough without anything else. How dared you come between me and a young woman I liked? You always give Old Orlick a bad name to her."

"You gave it to yourself. I couldn't have harmed you if you'd been all right."

"You're a liar. You told her you'd take any pains and spend any money to drive me out of the country." These were the words I had said to Biddy in our last interview. "Now I'll tell you something. It would be worth all your money to get me out of the country tonight." He snarled like a tiger.

"What are you going to do to me?"

"I'm going to have your life." He stared at me and drew his hand across his mouth as though it watered for me. "You was always in Old Orlick's way since you was a child. You goes out of his way tonight. You're dead."

I felt that I had come to the edge of the grave. I looked wildly around for a way to escape, but there was none.

"More than that," he said, "I won't have a rag or a bone of you left on earth. I'll put your body in the kiln."

I thought of what that would mean. Estella's father would think I had deserted him and would be taken and die accusing me. Even Herbert would doubt me. Joe and Biddy would never realize how sorry I had been about them. No one would know the agony I had passed through.

"Now, wolf," said he, "afore I kill you like any other beast, I'll take a good look at you. Oh, you enemy!"

I would not have cried out again even if it might have done some good. I would die rather than give him that satisfaction. If I could have killed him, even if it had cost me my life, I would have done it.

He had been drinking. His eyes were bloodshot. "Wolf," said he, "it was you as did for your evil-tempered sister."

"It was you, villain!" said I.

"It was your doing," said he. "I come upon her from behind as I come on you tonight. I give it to her. I left her for dead, and if there had been a lime kiln near her like the one near you, she wouldn't have come alive again. But it was you did it. You was favored and Old Orlick was bullied and beat. You done it. Now you pays for it."

He drank again and became fiercer. There was not much left in the bottle. I realized that he was working himself up to make an end of me as soon as the bottle was empty. I knew that every drop it held was a drop of my life. And I knew that when he had made an end of me, he would go slouching off to town as he had done in my sister's case.

When he had drunk the second time, he picked up the candle so as to throw its light on me and stood looking at me. "Wolf," he said, "I'll tell you something more. It was Old Orlick that you fell over on your stairs in London that night. And why was Old Orlick there? I'll tell you something more. You and Biddy have pretty well driven me out of this country as far as making an easy living goes. I've took up with new companions and a new master. Some of 'em writes my letters when I wants them wrote. I've had it in mind to kill you ever since you was down to your sister's burying. So I've followed you around. And when I looks for you I finds your uncle Provis."

I could see all my plans over with as my life ran out.

"You with a uncle!" Orlick went on. "Why, I knowed you at Gargery's when you was a child, and you hadn't no uncle then. But when Old Orlick heard that your uncle Provis wore the leg chains what Old Orlick had picked up and hit your sister with—"

He waved the candle so close to me he almost burned my face.

"Ah!" he cried, laughing at me. "Old Orlick knowed you was burnt. He knowed you was running away with your uncle Provis. And I'll tell you something more, wolf. There's someone who's smarter than your uncle Provis. There's someone won't have Magwitch—yes, I know his real name—in the same land with him. Someone who'll see to it he doesn't leave England alive. Beware of Compeyson, Magwitch, and the gallows!"

I had no hope left. He took the cork out of his bottle and threw it away. He swallowed his last few drops of liquor slowly. Then violently and swearing horribly he threw the bottle from him and stooped. I saw in his hand a hammer with a heavy handle.

Then at last I shouted with all my might and struggled with all my might. At the same instant I heard shouts and saw people rushing in at the door. Orlick jumped over the table and flew out into the night.

Sometime later I found that I was lying on the floor with my head on someone's knee. Opening my eyes, I looked in the face of Trabb's boy. "I think he's all right," he said, "but ain't he just pale though!" Then I saw I was leaning against—Herbert!

"Herbert! Great heavens!" I said, "and our old friend Startop." Then I had a terrible fear. "Has the time gone by?" I asked. "What night is tonight?"

"It is still Monday night," said Herbert. "And you have all tomorrow—Tuesday—to rest in, Handel. How badly are you hurt? Can you stand?"

"Yes, yes," I said. "I have no hurt but my arm."

They did what they could for it. It was badly swollen, and I could scarcely bear to have it touched. They made fresh bandages of their handkerchiefs and put it back in the sling. In a little while we were on our way back to town, Trabb's boy leading the way with a lantern.

On the way Herbert told me how he had come to my rescue. In my hurry I had dropped the letter open in our rooms. He had become uneasy when he read it and had decided to follow me at once with Startop. In the town they had come upon Trabb's boy, who agreed to guide them out to the marshes. They had circled around the old house by the floodgates, and upon hearing me cry out had rushed in to save me.

Because of what we had to do with Provis so soon, we gave up all idea of trying to catch Orlick and set out at once for London. It was daylight when we reached the Temple. I went to bed and lay there all day. I was terrified for fear I would become ill and unable to carry out my plans for the next day.

We did not get in touch with Provis in any way all that day. Yet every footstep and every sound frightened me into thinking he had been taken. As the day came to an end and darkness arrived with no bad news, I began to worry about my arm, which pained fiercely. They kept me very quiet all day, took constant care of my arm, and gave me cooling drinks. Whenever I dozed I wakened with the fear that Wednesday had passed.

Wednesday morning was dawning when I looked out of the window and watched the sun rise over the river and the bridges and the rooftops. As I saw sparkles of light on the water, I felt strong and well again. Herbert and Startop were still asleep. I could not dress without help, but I made up the fire and got the coffee ready. In good time they too got up strong and well and we looked out at the tide that was still flowing towards us. "When it turns at nine o'clock," said Herbert cheerfully, "look out for us and stand ready, you over there at Mill Pond Bank!"

34   *A Try for Freedom*

It was one of those March days when the sun shines hot and the wind blows cold. I took with me a bag filled only with a few necessities, as I did not know where I might go and when I might return. I was interested only in Provis's safety. For a passing moment before I left I stopped at the door to look back and wonder whether I would ever see my rooms again.

The boat was ready for us, and we went on board. It was then about high tide. Our plan was to row down the river until dark, by which time we would be below Gravesend, between Kent and Essex. Here the river is broad and empty and there are few inhabitants along its banks. We could find a lonely inn and spend the night there. A steamer bound for Hamburg and one for Rotterdam would leave London about nine o'clock on Thursday morning. We would try to stop the first one. If we failed we would have the second one to try for.

I was relieved to be following out my plan at last. The crisp air and the sunlight filled me with new hope. It grieved me, though, to be of so little use in the boat. My two friends, however, were the best oarsmen possible. They started out with a steady stroke that was to last all day.

In those times there were very few steamboats on the Thames. Early as it was that morning there were many

258

boats being rowed. We did not attract any attention. We soon passed London Bridge and were in the midst of shipping. We saw Scottish steamers loading and unloading and looking immensely high out of the water. We saw tomorrow's steamers for Rotterdam and for Hamburg and took particular note of them. My heart beat fast as we approached Mill Pond Bank.

"Is he there?" said Herbert.

"Not yet."

"Right. He was not to come down till he saw us. Can you see his signal?"

"I think I do—now I see it. Pull in, Herbert."

In a minute he was on board and we were off again. He wore a boatman's coat and had a black canvas bag. He looked as much like a river pilot as my heart could wish.

"Dear boy!" he said, putting his arm on my shoulder as he took his seat. "Faithful dear boy. Well done. Thank ye, thank ye!"

Finally we were out in the open river with the confusion of shipping behind us. I had seen no signs of our being suspected. We had not been followed by any boat. Provis, perhaps because of the miserable life he had led, was the least anxious of any of us. He was not indifferent to danger—he told me he hoped to live to see me one of the finest gentlemen in a foreign country—but he did not believe in worrying about it until it had actually arrived.

"If you knowed, dear boy," he said to me, "what it means to sit by my dear boy and have my smoke after being indoors day after day, you'd envy me."

"I think I know what it means to be free," I answered.

"Ay," he said, shaking his head seriously, "you've never been under lock and key as I've been so much."

I wondered then why he had risked his freedom just to come to me. Perhaps he had had so little freedom without danger that taking chances was part of his very life. Soon he said, "You see, dear boy, when I was t'other side of the world, I was always thinking of this side. It was very dull there, even if I was growing rich. Magwitch could come and go and nobody cared. It ain't like that here."

"If all goes well," I said, "you will be perfectly free and safe again within a few hours."

"Well," he said, drawing a long breath, "I hope so."

"And think so?"

He smiled at me in the gentle way he had these days and dipped his hand in the water. "Ay, I 'spose I think so, dear boy. We're slipping so soft and pleasant through the water. But I was thinking just now—we can't see to the bottom of the next few hours any more than we can to the bottom of this river. And we can't stop those hours any more than I can hold this water in my hand."

"From your face I would think you're a little sad," I said.

"Not a bit of it, dear boy. It comes of us flowing so quiet, like Sunday. Maybe I'm growing a trifle old besides."

He put his pipe back in his mouth and sat as calm and contented as if we were already out of England. The air felt cold on the river, but the sunlight was cheering. The tide was still with us when we were off Gravesend. As Provis was wrapped in his coat, I purposely passed close to the floating custom house and out in the middle of the stream alongside two emigrant ships and under the bows of a large transport loaded with soldiers. But when the tide turned, we kept near the shore, as much out of the strength of the current as possible.

Our oarsmen were still not tired, for they had let the tide carry the boat along every now and then. They took a quarter of an hour's rest on the shore, however, while we ate the food we had brought with us. The country was like my own marshlands, flat and dull, with the river twisting and turning in the distance.

We pushed off again and went as far as we could. It was much harder work now against the tide, but Herbert and Startop rowed and rowed until the sun went down. As darkness was near and the moon did not rise early, we decided we had better look for the first lonely tavern we could find. I watched for one while my friends went on rowing four or five more dull miles. It was very cold now. At this gloomy time we all got the idea that we were being followed. Whenever the tide slapped against the shore, one or the other of us would be sure to look in that direction. We were nervous and suspicious whenever we passed any little creeks along the river bank. Sometimes one of us would say in a low voice, "What was that noise?" or, "Is that a boat in the distance?" Aterward we would all fall silent and I would be impatient of the sound made by the oars.

At last we saw a light and a roof and soon afterward ran up beside a little landing. I stepped ashore and found that the light was in the window of an inn. It was dirty enough and probably often visited by smugglers. But there was a good fire, eggs and bacon to eat, and two double bedrooms we could have. Only the landlord, his wife, and a dirty helper were there. We all came ashore, pulling the boat up for the night. We ate a good meal by the fire and then went upstairs. Herbert and Startop were to have one bedroom, Provis and I the other.

While we were at dinner, the helper, who was sitting in the corner, asked me if we had seen a four-oared galley* with two passengers in it going up the river. When I said no, he decided it must have gone down the river then, though it had headed upstream when it left the inn. One man in it had stopped for beer. The helper thought it was probably from the floating customhouse, though the landlord did not agree. The helper was sure a boat would not

*Galley: a small, open boat used by government officials.

go up and down the river unless the men in it were looking for someone.

This conversation made us all very uneasy. There was a dismal wind blowing around the house and I had a feeling that we were caged and threatened. A boat waiting around in such an unusual way as to attract notice from those on shore seemed suspicious. When I had persuaded Provis to go to bed, I went outside with my two companions and we talked things over. Whether to stay at the house until nearly time for the steamer, about one in the afternoon, or to start out early in the morning was the question. On the whole, we thought it better to stay where we were until an hour or so before the steamer would come by and then get out in her path and drift with the tide. Having settled this, we went in and to bed.

I lay down with most of my clothes on and slept well a few hours. When I awoke, the wind had risen and was making the sign on the inn rattle and creak. I got up and looked out of the window. In the dim light of the cloudy moon I saw two men looking into our boat. They went by under the window, looking at nothing else. Then they walked away from the river across the marshes. My first idea was to wake up my friends. Then I remembered how tired they were and did not do so. Feeling very cold, I lay down to think the matter over and fell asleep again.

We were up early. As we all walked back and forth together after breakfast, I told what I had seen during the night. Again Provis was the least anxious of any of us. It was very likely that the men belonged to the customhouse, he said quietly, and had no thought of us. I tried to persuade myself that this was so—as it easily might be. However, I suggested that he and I walk down the river to a point we could see in the distance, and have the boat pick us up there. Since everyone thought this was a good idea, we left after breakfast without saying anything at the tavern.

He smoked his pipe as we went along and sometimes stopped to pat me on the shoulder. It seemed as though I, not he, were in danger, and he was encouraging me. We talked very little. As we neared the spot for which we were heading, I begged him to stay out of sight while I went to look around. There was no galley off the point nor anywhere near it. Then our boat came along and we got on board and rowed out into the track of the steamer. By that time it was ten minutes of one and we began to look for her smoke. It was half past one before we saw it and behind it the smoke of another steamer. As they were coming on at full speed, we got the bags ready and then said good-bye to Herbert and Startop (neither Herbert's nor my eyes were dry), when I saw a four-oared galley shoot out from the riverbank a little way ahead of us and row out into the same track.

We could now see the steamer rounding a bend and coming straight toward us. I called Herbert and Startop to keep out in the river so she would see us waiting for her and advised Provis to sit very still, wrapped in his coat. He answered cheerily, "Trust me, dear boy," and sat like a statue. Meanwhile, the galley, skillfully handled, had let us come up to her and was now beside us. Leaving just room enough for the movement of the oars, she stayed beside us, drifting when we drifted and pulling when we pulled. Of the two passengers, the one who was steering looked at us attentively. The other, wrapped up much as Provis was, whispered some instruction to the man steering. Not a word was spoken in either boat.

"The Hamburg steamer is coming first," Startop told me in a low voice. She was nearing us then. The sound of her paddle wheels grew louder and louder. I felt as if her shadow was on us when the galley hailed us. I answered.

"You have a returned convict there," said the man who was steering. "That's the man wrapped up in the coat. His name is Abel Magwitch, known as Provis. I arrest that man and call on him to give himself up and you to assist!"

At the same moment he ran his boat into us. Our boat was being held fast before we knew what he was doing. There was at the same time great confusion aboard the steamer among the passengers, who were watching all this. The paddle wheels had stopped, but the ship was coming directly to us. In the same moment, the man steering the galley seized Provis's shoulder and both boats swung around with the force of the tide. Still in the same moment Provis leaned forward and pulled the coat from the other passenger. I recognized at once the face of the other convict of long ago, who I now knew was Compeyson. Now it had a

look of terror on it that I shall never forget. There was a loud cry on board the steamer and a loud splash in the water. I felt our boat sink from under me.

An instant later I was taken on board the galley. Herbert and Startop were already there, but the two convicts were gone. Everyone was silently and eagerly watching a struggle that was going on in the water. Presently a dark object was seen heading toward us on the tide. It was Magwitch, swimming but not swimming freely. He was taken on board and at once chained by the wrists and the ankles. Nothing stirred in the water. The second steamer now came up at full speed. She was hailed and stopped. There was still no sign of life from the water, and I felt sure that Magwitch's enemy was gone at last. Finally the steamers went on their way, and we pulled in to the shore by the inn we had just left. Here I was able to take care of Magwitch—Provis no longer—who had some very bad injury on his chest and a deep cut in his head.

He told me he thought he had been struck on the head by the keel of the steamer when he came up out of the water. The injury to his chest, which made breathing very painful, he thought he had received against the side of the galley. He told me that he and Compeyson had gone down fiercely locked in each other's arms. There had been a struggle underwater, he had freed himself, and swam away. I believed what he told me.

When I asked permission to buy dry clothes for my convict at the inn, the police officer consented gladly. But he took charge of everything the prisoner had on him. So the pocketbook which I once had had was now in his possession. I was also given permission to accompany Magwitch to London.

The people at the inn were told to watch for the body of the drowned man. We stayed there until the tide turned, and then Magwitch was taken down to the galley and put on board. Herbert and Startop were to get to London by land as soon as they could. We had a sad parting, and when I sat down at Magwitch's side, I felt that there was my place as long as he lived. For now all my disgust for him had melted away. In the hunted, wounded, chained creature who held my hand, I saw only a man who had meant to be my benefactor. I saw a man who had felt affectionate and graceful and generous toward me for years. I saw a much better man than I had been to Joe.

His breathing became more difficult and painful as night came on. Often he groaned. I tried to hold him in a comfortable position on my good arm. I hated to realize that I could not be really sorry he was badly hurt. It would be much better for him to die. I was sure there were still people living who would be willing to identify him. I could not hope that he would be treated gently. He had shown up in the worst possible light at his first trial. He had broken out of prison and been taken again. He had been sent to Australia and told to stay out of England for the rest of his life but had come back. He had been the cause of the death of the man who had had him arrested.

As we went back toward the setting sun we had left behind us yesterday, I told him how sorry I was to think he had come home because of me. "Dear boy," he said, "I'm quite content to take my chance. I've seen my boy, and he can be a gentleman without me."

No, that would not be possible. Even if I had wanted to go on living like a gentleman, I could not. I understood Wemmick's hint now. If he were convicted, all he owned would be claimed by the government.

"Lookee here, dear boy," he said, "it's best as a gentleman should not be seen with me now. Only come to see me as if you come by chance with Wemmick. Sit where I can see you when I am brought into court for the last time. I don't ask no more."

"I will never move from your side," said I, "when I am permitted to be near you. Please God, I will be as true to you as you have been to me."

I felt his hand tremble in mine and he turned his face away. I heard what sounded like a sob. I was glad he had said what he did. It gave me an idea that I might never have thought of until too late. He need never know that I would not get his money after he was gone.

35 *A Pleasant Interval*

He was taken to the police court the next day. As it was necessary to send for an old officer of the prison ship from which he had once escaped to identify him, he was not brought to trial immediately. His case was set for a month after the arrival of the witness. I had gone to Mr. Jaggers's home as soon as I reached London to get him to help me. He told me, however, that the case would be over in five minutes when the witness was there, and no power on earth could prevent its going against us.

I told Mr. Jaggers I did not want Magwitch to know that I would not get his money. He was very angry with me for letting it slip through my fingers. He said we might later try to get some of it, though my claim on it was very slight. I was not related to my convict. He had never put in writing his desire for me to have his wealth. I decided and ever after stuck to my resolution not to attempt the hopeless and heartbreaking task of trying to get it.

Compeyson's body was found many miles from the scene of his death and so horribly disfigured that he could be identified only by some notes in a case in his pocket. These contained a list of Magwitch's possessions in New South Wales, and we concluded he had hoped to get a reward from turning his victim over to the police. Magwitch, poor fellow, never found out that I would never be rich.

At this dark time of my life, Herbert came home one evening and told me that he would have to leave for Cairo very soon to open the branch office there. "I am afraid I must go, Handel, when you most need me," he said.

"Herbert, I shall always need you, because I shall always love you. I shall not be lonely, though. You know I am always with him every minute that I am permitted to be. I would be with him all day long if I could. And when I come away, my thoughts are with him."

We were both horrified by what had happened to my convict and hated to talk about it.

"My dear fellow," said Herbert, "before we part, let us talk about you. Have you thought of your future?"

"No, I have been afraid to think of any future."

"But yours *must* be considered, Handel. In this office of ours we want to have a—"

I saw he did not want to mention a position so small, so I said, "A clerk."

"A clerk. And it is entirely likely that he may some day become a partner. In short, my dear boy, will you come with me? Clara and I have talked about it again and again. The dear little thing begged me this evening to say that if you will live with us when we are married, she will do her best to make you happy. We would get along so well, Handel."

I thanked them both heartily but said I could not yet decide. My mind was too filled with my troubles for me to think clearly. "But if you think, Herbert," I said, "that you can leave the matter open for a little while—"

"For any while," said Herbert. "Six months, a year!"

"Not so long as that," said I. "Two or three months at most."

Herbert was delighted when we shook hands on this arrangement and said he now had courage to tell me that he would probably have to leave at the end of the week.

"And Clara?" said I.

"She still must stick to her father, but he can't live much longer. Then I shall come back for her and we will be married."

On Saturday of that same week I said good-bye to Herbert as I put him on a coach which would start him on his trip east. On my way home I met Wemmick, who had just come from my room. I had not seen him alone since Provis and I had tried to get out of the country. Now he told me how sorry he was that we had failed—and how especially sorry he was that I had lost all that money.

"What I think of, Wemmick, is the poor owner of the money."

"Yes, to be sure," said Wemmick. "Of course there can be no objection to your being sorry for him. I'd give a five-pound note myself to get him out of it. But what I look at is this. The late Compeyson knew so much about him and was so determined to have him caught I don't think he could have been saved. But the property *could* have been saved."

I invited Wemmick to come to my rooms for a while and have a drink with me. He did so but seemed very fidgety. Finally he said, for no apparent reason, "What do you think of my taking a holiday on Monday, Mr. Pip?"

"Why, I suppose you haven't done such a thing in a year."

"Twelve years," said Wemmick. "Yes, I am going to take a holiday. More than that; I'm going to take a walk. More than that; I'm going to ask you to take a walk with me."

I was going to say I wasn't much in the mood for it just at that time when he said, "I know you are out of sorts, Mr. Pip. But if you could oblige me, I'd take it kindly. It ain't a long walk, and it's an early one, say from eight to twelve. Couldn't you stretch a point and manage it?"

He had done so much for me at various times this

seemed like a little thing to do for him. I said I would manage it, and he was so pleased that I was pleased, too.

On Monday morning at eight I rang the bell at the castle gate and was received by Wemmick, who seemed to be rather dressed up. The Aged was nowhere around. We started off on our walk, and soon Wemmick said suddenly, "Hello! Here's a church!"

There was nothing very surprising in that. But I *was* surprised when he said as though he had just had a brilliant idea, "Let's go in!"

We went in and looked all around. In the meantime Wemmick had pulled something out of his pocket. "Hello!" he said. "Here's a couple of pairs of gloves. Let's put 'em on."

As the gloves were white kid ones, and as Wemmick was beginning to smile, I had my strong suspicions. Then I saw the Aged enter at the side door with a lady.

"Hello!" said Wemmick. "Here's Miss Skiffins! Let's have a wedding."

That lady was now putting on a pair of white kid gloves too, and so was the Aged—but he had so much trouble with his that Wemmick had to help the old gentleman pull them on while I held him around the waist to keep him steady. Then the clergyman appeared, and we lined up before the altar. Carrying out his game that none of this had been planned beforehand, I heard Wemmick say to himself as he took something out of his pocket, "Hello! Here's a ring!"

I acted as best man. The Aged was supposed to give the lady away. He was so absentminded, however, that the minister asked twice, "Who giveth this woman to be married to this man?" And Wemmick had to interrupt the ceremony to say, "Now, Aged Parent, you know, who giveth?" To which the Aged replied before saying that *he* gave, "All right, John, my boy, all right." Then the wedding proceeded.

Afterward we all had breakfast at a pleasant little inn

a mile or so away. We had an excellent breakfast. I drank to the new couple, to the Aged, to the castle. I kissed the bride when I left and made myself as agreeable as I could.

Wemmick came to the door with me, and I again shook hands and wished him joy. "Thankee!" said Wemmick, and then in a low voice, "All of this is a castle affair, you understand."

"I understand. Not to be mentioned at the office."

Wemmick nodded. "After what you let out to Jaggers the other day, he might better not know about this. He might think my brain was softening or something like that."

36 *The Death Sentence*

Provis lay in prison very ill during the whole time between his arrest and his trial. He had broken two ribs. They
had wounded one of his lungs, and he breathed with great
pain and difficulty, which increased daily. He could not
speak above a whisper because of his injury and so talked
very little. But he was always ready to listen to me. It became
the first duty of my life to say to him and to read to him
what I knew he ought to hear.

After the first day or so he moved into the infirmary.
This gave me chances to be with him that I would not have
had otherwise. Although I saw him every day, it was for
only a short time. And each day he changed for the worse,
becoming slowly weaker and weaker.

He acted like a man who was tired out, and who had
stopped struggling against his fate. Sometimes he gave me
the impression, in a whispered word or two, that he wondered whether he would have been a better man in different
circumstances. But he never excused himself for what had
happened in his past.

Now and then when I was there, the people who took
care of him would refer to his bad reputation. Then he would
smile and give me a trustful look as if he were sure that I

had seen some good in him even when I was a child. He was humble and gentle, and I never knew him to complain.

Mr. Jaggers asked to have his trial postponed. Since the court knew that this request was made because he would not live much longer, it was refused. The law required that he be brought to trial before he died. When he was finally brought into court, he was seated in a chair. No objection was made to my standing close to him and holding the hand that he stretched out to me. The trial was very short and very clear. Whatever could be said for him was said—that he had become a hard worker in Australia and had lived there lawfully and honorably. But nothing could deny the fact that he had gone against the law by coming home. The judge and jury could do nothing else but find him guilty.

I shall never forget the last day of the trial when sentence was passed on him and on thirty-two other prisoners—men and women—with him. I even remember the drops of April rain on the windows, which glittered in the rays of the April sun. I stood just outside the railing holding his hand in mine. There had been sobbing and weeping among the prisoners and shrieks from the women. But all was still now. A great gallery full of people looked on, as though they were at the theater.

Then the judge addressed them, singling out for special attention my convict. He had been, said the judge, a breaker of the law since he was a child. He had been imprisoned and punished again and again and had at last been exiled for a period of years. With great boldness and violence he had escaped and been sentenced again to exile* forever. Then for a time, far away from England, he had lived a peaceable and honest life. But in a fatal moment he had

*Exile: forced removal from one's country.

decided to come back again to the country from which he had been sent away. For a time he had succeeded in escaping justice. Then he had been seized as he was about to run away and had caused the death of the man who had reported him to the police. The punishment for his return to England being death, he must prepare himself to die.

The sun was striking through the great windows of the courtroom as he rose. "My Lord," he said, "I have already received my sentence of death from God, but I bow to yours." Then he sat down again, and for a minute there was a

silence, until the judge went on to pronounce sentences of death on all the others, and they filed out of the room. He went last of all because of having to be helped from his chair and to go very slowly. He held my hand to the last.

I hoped and prayed that he would die before his sentence would be carried out. In dread of his living on, I began that night to write a petition to the Home Secretary telling how he came home for my sake. I wrote as earnestly and as sadly as I could. When I had sent that in, I wrote other petitions to important men, even to the King himself. For several days and nights I took no rest except when I fell asleep in my chair. In restlessness and pain of mind I roamed the streets in the evenings, wandering by the offices and houses to which I had sent my letters. I felt more hopeful when I was near them.

The daily visits I could make him were shorter now, as he was kept more strictly. Nobody was hard with him or with me, however. The officer in charge always told me that he was worse, and other sick prisoners in the room with him gave me the same report.

As the days went on, I noticed more and more that he would lie calmly looking at the ceiling with no light in his face until I spoke to him. Sometimes he was unable to speak. Then he would press my hand as an answer, and I would understand his meaning very well. On the tenth day I saw a much greater change in him. He eyes lighted up when I came in. "Dear boy," he said as I sat down by his bed, "I thought you was late. But I knowed you couldn't be."

"It is just the time I always come," I said. "I waited for it at the gate. I never want to lose a minute of my time with you."

"Thankee, dear boy, God bless you. You've never deserted me, dear boy."

I pressed his hand in silence, for I could not forget that I had once meant to desert him.

"And what's best of all," he said, "you've been more comfortable because of me."

He lay on his back, breathing with great difficulty. No matter how much he loved me, the light left his face every now and then, and a cloud came over it.

"Are you in much pain today?"

"I don't complain."

"You never do complain."

He had spoken his last word. He smiled, and I understood his touch to mean that he wanted me to lift my hand and lay it on his breast. I put it there, and he smiled again and put both his hands on it.

The time I was allowed to be with him ran out as we stayed this way. But, looking around, I found the governor of the prison standing near me. He whispered, "You needn't go yet." I thanked him and asked, "May I speak to him if he can hear me?"

The governor and the police officer left me alone with him. The light came back to his face and he looked at me lovingly.

"Dear Magwitch," I said, "I must tell you now at last. You understand what I say?"

He pressed my hand gently.

"You had a child once, whom you loved and lost."

He pressed my hand more strongly.

"She lived and found important friends. She is living now. She is a lady and very beautiful. And I love her!"

With a last faint effort and with my help, he raised my hand to his lips. Then he gently let it sink on his own breast again with his own hands lying on it. The calm look came back to his face, and his head dropped quietly on his breast.

Remembering the passages from the Bible we had read together, I thought of the two men who went into the Temple to pray. I knew there were no better words I could say beside his bed than, "Lord, be merciful to him a sinner!"

37 Return of a Faithful Friend

Now that I was entirely alone, I gave notice that I would leave my rooms in the Temple as soon as I could do so legally. Meanwhile, as I was in debt and had scarcely any money, I decided I would try to sublet the apartment. I would have worried more about the state of my affairs if I had not realized I was growing very ill. I had put sickness off for a long time. I knew it was surely coming on me now.

For a day or two I lay on the sofa or on the floor —anywhere I happened to sink down—with a heavy head and aching limbs, with no purpose and no strength. Then there came one long night of misery, and in the morning I could not even sit up in bed and think. Dimly confused by fever, I saw that two men were looking at me. "What do you want?" I asked. "I don't know you."

"Well, sir," said one of them, bending down and touching me, "you're arrested for a debt of a hundred and twenty pounds. It's a jeweler's bill, I think."

I made an attempt to get up and dress myself. When I next noticed them, they were still standing by the bed looking at me. I still lay there.

"You see the state I am in," I said. "I would come with you if I could, but it is quite impossible. If you take me from here, I think I shall die on the way."

Perhaps they argued with me or tried to make me believe I was not so bad off. I don't remember. I only know they did not move me. I can recall little about that time except that I had a fever and suffered greatly. I was often out of my head and struggled with people who were with me, sometimes believing they were murderers, sometimes realizing they had come to do me good. All these people sooner or later looked like Joe to me.

After I had passed the worst stage of my illness, I began to notice that it was always Joe who came to me. I opened my eyes in the night, and in the big chair by my bed was Joe. I opened my eyes in the day, and sitting by the open window smoking his pipe was Joe. I asked for a cooling drink, and the dear hand that gave it to me was Joe's. I sank back on my pillow, and the face that looked at me so hopefully and tenderly was Joe's.

At last one day I got up courage and said, "Is it Joe?"

And the dear old home voice answered, "Which it air, old chap."

"Oh Joe, you break my heart. Look angry at me, Joe. Tell me how ungrateful I am. Don't be so good to me."

For Joe had laid his head down on the pillow beside me and put his arm around my neck in his joy that I knew him at last.

"Dear old Pip, old chap," said Joe, "you and me was ever friends. And when you're well enough to go out for a ride—what fun!"

After which Joe went over to the window and stood with his back toward me wiping his eyes. I was too weak to go over to him. I lay there whispering, "O God bless him. God bless this gentle good man!"

Joe's eyes were red when he next sat down beside me. I was holding his hand, and we both felt happy.

"How long have I been sick, Joe?"

"It's the end of May, Pip. Tomorrow is the first of June."

"And have you been here all the time, dear Joe?"

"Pretty near, old chap. For as I says to Biddy when the news of your being ill was brought by letter, you might be among strangers and might like a visit from an old friend like me. And Biddy's words were, 'Go to him without a minute's loss of time.' "

There Joe stopped and told me I was not to be talked to very much. I was to take food often whether I wanted it or not, and I was to follow his orders. So I lay quiet while he wrote a note to Biddy with my love in it.

Evidently Biddy had taught Joe to write. As I lay in bed watching him, it made me, in my weak state, cry with pleasure to see the pride with which he went about his letter. He sat down at my desk, chose a pen as if he were picking out a tool, and tucked up his sleeves as if he were going to work with a crowbar or a sledgehammer. He held on to the table with his left elbow, and when he finally began, made every stroke as slowly as if it were six feet long. When he had signed his name, he got up, and standing over the table, looked at his work from every angle with the greatest satisfaction.

I waited until the next day to ask him about Miss Havisham. He shook his head when I wanted to know if she had recovered. "Is she dead, Joe?"

"After you was took ill," said Joe, "she lingered about a week more."

"Dear Joe, have you heard what became of her property?" I asked.

"Well, old chap," said Joe, "it do appear that she settled the most of it on Miss Estella. But she had wrote out a little note in her own hand a day or so before the accident leaving a cool four thousand to Mr. Matthew Pocket. And why do you suppose, Pip, she left that to him? Because of Pip's account of Matthew!"

This gave me great joy. It made perfect the only good thing I had ever done. I asked Joe what she had left to her other relatives.

"Miss Sarah, she have twenty-five pounds a year to buy

pills. Mrs. Camels (I knew he meant Camilla) have five pound to buy candles to put her in good spirits when she can't sleep at night."

This sounded quite suitable. "And now," continued Joe, "Old Orlick's been a bustin' into a house—Pumblechook's. He took the cash box and drank his wine and ate his food and stuffed his mouth full of plants to prevent his crying out. But Pumblechook knowed Orlick and Orlick's in the county jail."

We finally caught up on all the news. I gained strength slowly but surely. Joe stayed with me, and I imagined I was little Pip again. For Joe was so gentle with me that I was like a child in his hands. He would sit and talk with me with his simple, protecting ways of the past so that I would half believe that all my life since our days together in the old kitchen were a bad dream.

When the day finally came that I could go out for a ride, Joe carried me down and put me in the carriage, as if I were still the small helpless creature to whom he had given generously all his love. Joe got in beside me and we drove together into the country. It was Sunday, and when I heard the church bells and looked at the spring loveliness around me, I felt that I should be thankful to be alive. I laid my head, in my weakness, on Joe's shoulder as I had laid it long ago when he had taken me out somewhere and I was tired. As we rode together, we talked as we used to talk lying on the grass at the old sea wall. There was no change in Joe. He was just as faithful, just as perfect.

When we got back again and he lifted me out and carried me upstairs, I thought of that important Christmas Day when he had carried me over the marshes. We had not yet talked about my change of fortune, and I did not know how much of my experiences he had heard about.

"Have you heard, Joe," I asked him one evening sometime later, "who my benefactor was?"

"I heerd," replied Joe, "as it was not Miss Havisham, old chap, but it were a person what sent the person what give you the bank notes at the Jolly Bargemen."

"So it was."

"Astonishing!" said Joe in the calmest way.

"Did you hear that he was dead, Joe?"

"I think as I *did* hear something or another like that."

"If you would like to hear about it, Joe—"

"Lookee here, old chap," he said, bending over me, "ever the best of friends, ain't us, Pip?"

I was ashamed to answer him.

"Very good," said Joe, as if I *had* answered. "Then why go into subjects unnecessary between friends? Suppose you did keep little matters to yourself when you were a child? You probably kept them because you were afraid of your poor sister and knowed as how I couldn't always stand between you and her. Biddy spent a deal of time with me before I left helping me to view it in this light. Now you must not be overdoing but must have your supper and be put to bed."

The tact with which Joe closed the subject and the kindness of Biddy in talking to him about me as she had done made a great impression on me. I still wondered whether Joe knew how poor I was. Something else about him worried me. As I became stronger and better, he grew less at ease with me. When I was weak and dependent on him, the dear fellow had called me by the old names, "old Pip, old chap," that now were music to my ears. I too had fallen into the old ways, only thankful that he would let me do so. I had to face the fact now that he was afraid I would again turn my back on him when I was well.

The third or fourth time we went out walking I happened to say to him, "See, Joe! I am strong now. I can walk by myself."

"Which do not overdo it, Pip," said Joe. "But I shall be

glad to see you well, sir."

The last word hurt me. I pretended I was weaker than I was and asked Joe for his arm. He gave it to me thoughtfully. I was thoughtful too. How could I stop this growing change in Joe? I was ashamed to have him know about my poverty. He would want to help me out of his savings, and that I could not let him do. I finally decided that, the next day being Sunday, I would wait until Monday and then tell him everything and tell him, too, about a plan I had for my future.

We had a quiet day riding in the country and walking in the fields. "I feel thankful that I have been ill, Joe," I said. "It has been a time to remember for me."

"Likewise for myself, sir," Joe answered.

"We have had a time together, Joe, that I can never forget. In the past I know I did forget our days together. These I shall never forget."

"Pip," said Joe, looking troubled, "there has been fun. And, dear sir, what has been between us, has been."

At night when I had gone to bed, Joe came into my room as always to ask me if I still felt well.

"Yes, dear Joe, quite."

"And you are always getting stronger, dear chap?"

"Yes, dear Joe, steadily."

He patted my shoulder with his big good hand and said in a husky voice, "Good night."

When I got up in the morning rested and strong, I was full of my plan to tell him everything without delay. I went to his room, but he was not there. On the breakfast table there was a short note from him.

Not wanting to be in the way I have left for you are well again dear Pip and will do better without

Joe

P.S. Ever the best of friends.

Enclosed in the letter was a receipt for all the debts which had caused me to be arrested. Up to that moment I had supposed that the people to whom I owed money were waiting until I had recovered. I never dreamed that Joe had paid the bills.

What could I do now but follow him back to the forge and there tell him everything and ask for his forgiveness?

Another idea had been growing stronger in my mind with each day. I would go to Biddy and tell her I was coming back with all my pride gone. I would tell her I had lost all I once hoped for, and I would remind her of the times when I had told her all that was in my heart. I would say to her, "Biddy, you once liked me very well, and I was more at peace with you than I have ever been with anyone else. If you can like me only half as well, if you can take me back like a forgiven child, I can be a little worthier of you now. And, Biddy, you can decide whether I shall work at the forge with Joe or at something else, or whether we shall go away together to a distant place where I have a position waiting for me. Dear Biddy, if you can tell me you will go through the world with me, you will make it a better world for me, and I will try to make it a better world for you." Such was my purpose. In three days I went down to the old place to carry it out.

38 *The Parting*

The news of my loss of fortune had traveled ahead of me. Even the Blue Boar had heard of it and greeted me without enthusiasm. It was evening when I arrived, much tired out by the trip which had once seemed so short to me. I was told that my usual bedroom was taken, probably by someone who had expectations. I'm sure my sleep was just as sound in the little back room I was given.

Early in the morning I walked to Miss Havisham's house. There were bills of sale posted all around and notice of a public auction of furniture. The house itself was to be sold for old building materials and pulled down. I stepped through the open gate for a minute and looked around uncomfortably, feeling like a stranger who had no business there.

When I got back to my breakfast in the coffee room, Mr. Pumblechook was waiting for me. "Young man," he said, "I am sorry to see you brought so low. But what else could be expected!"

I was too broken down by sickness to refuse to shake hands with him. He stood over me as I ate my meal, staring like a fish and breathing noisily as he always did. "He's little more than skin and bone," he remarked about me. "And yet when he went away from here—I may say with my blessing—he was as plump as a peach."

I remembered the way he had tried to win my favor when I had first learned of my good luck. There was a remarkable difference in his treatment of me now. "And are you going to Joseph?" he asked me.

"In heaven's name," I said, getting angry in spite of myself, "what does it matter to you where I'm going?"

This gave Pumblechook the chance he was waiting for. "Yes, young man," he said, "I will leave you alone. This is him," he said to the waiter at the door, "as I have rode in my carriage. This is him as I have seen brought up by his sister, my niece. Young man, you go to Joseph and tell him you have just seen your greatest benefactor and the founder of your fortunes. Tell him you've never even shown him common gratitude."

I was surprised that he would have the face to talk to me like this.

"Tell Joseph," he went on, "that your greatest benefactor doesn't repent of what he did for you. It was right and kind to do it, and he would do the thing all over again if he had a chance."

"It's too bad," I said scornfully, "that I haven't the least idea what on earth you have ever done for me."

But Pumblechook shook hands with the landlord and the waiter and walked out. I followed soon after and passed his little shop, where he was talking to a group of men, no doubt about my ingratitude, for they scowled at me as I walked by.

It was pleasant to turn toward Biddy and Joe. Their patience with me shone even brighter because of the old fraud who had just forced his attentions on me. I started for the forge with a feeling of great relief. The June weather was beautiful. The sky was blue, the larks flying high over the green corn, and the country more peaceful and beautiful than I had ever seen it. I thought as I walked along of the pleasant life I would lead there and the change for the better that would come over my character when I had Biddy at my side to guide me with her faith and her simple wisdom.

I had never seen the schoolhouse where Biddy taught, but I walked past it now and was disappointed to find that it was closed that day. No children were around and Biddy's house was closed. I hoped to see her busily at work.

But the forge was a very short distance off, and I went toward it under the spring green of the trees, listening for the clink of Joe's hammer. Long after I should have heard it and imagined that I did hear it, all was still. No sound of it traveled on the midsummer wind.

Almost fearing, without knowing why, to come in view of the forge, I saw it at last and saw that it was closed. There was no gleam of fire, no shower of sparks. All was shut and still.

But the house was not deserted, and the best parlor seemed to be in use. White curtains were fluttering, and the window was open and gay with flowers. I went softly toward it, meaning to peep in, when Joe and Biddy stood before me, arm in arm. At first Biddy gave a cry as if she thought it was my ghost, but in another moment she was in my arms. I wept to see her because she looked so fresh and pleasant. She wept because I looked so worn and white.

"But, dear Biddy, how nice you look."

"Yes, dear Pip."

"And, Joe, how nice you look."

"Yes, dear old Pip, old chap."

I looked from one to the other of them and then—

"It's my wedding day," cried Biddy in a burst of happiness, "and I am married to Joe!"

They took me into the kitchen and I laid my head down on the old table and cried a little while they stood over me. "He wasn't strong enough, my dear, to be surprised," said Joe. And Biddy said, "I ought to have thought of it, dear Joe, but I was too happy." They were both so glad and so delighted that I should have come by accident to make their day complete!

My first thought was one of great thankfulness that I had never breathed to Joe a word of my hope of marrying Biddy. How often while he was with me I had thought of telling him. How surely he would have known it if he had stayed with me another hour!

"Dear Biddy," I said, "you have the best husband in the whole world. And, dear Joe, you have the best wife in the whole world. She will make you as happy as you deserve to be, you dear, wonderful Joe!"

Joe looked at me with tears in his eyes.

"And Joe and Biddy both, let me thank you for all you have done for me that I have not repaid. I am going away in an hour or so—going abroad, where I have a position awaiting me. There I shall never rest until I have earned the money with which you kept me out of prison and have sent it to you. If I paid it a thousand times over, I could not make up to you what you have done for me."

They were both touched by my words and begged me to say no more.

"But I must say more. Dear Joe, I hope you will have children to love. I hope some little fellow, who will remind you of another little boy gone forever, will sit by the fireplace on a winter night. Don't tell him I was ungrateful and unjust. Only tell him that I honored you both because you were so good and true. Tell him I am sure he will grow up to be a much better man than I was."

"I am not going to tell him anything of that sort, Pip," said Joe, "and Biddy ain't either."

"And now tell me both of you that you forgive me. Let me hear you say the words so that I can carry the sound of them with me. Then I'll be able to believe that you can trust me and think better of me in the time to come."

"Dear old Pip, old chap," said Joe, "God knows as I

forgive you if I have anything to forgive."

"Amen! And God knows I do too," echoed Biddy.

"Now let me go up to my little old room and rest there a few minutes by myself. Then when I have eaten with you, go with me to the signpost, dear Joe and Biddy, before we say good-bye."

I sold all I had and paid my creditors as much as I could. Within a month I left England and went out to join Herbert. Within two months I was a clerk for Clarriker and Company. Within four months I was in complete charge of the branch office. For Clara's father died and Herbert went to England to be married.

Many a year went by before I became a member of the firm. I lived happily with Herbert and his wife, paid my debts, and wrote constantly to Biddy and Joe. It was not until I was a partner that Clarriker told Herbert what I had done for him years ago. Herbert was both amazed and touched, and we became even better friends thereafter. We never made a fortune with our business, but we had a good name and did very well. Much of our prosperity we owed to Herbert's hard work and ambition. I often wondered how I could ever have doubted his ability—probably because I then had no ability of my own.

39 *After Eleven Years*

For eleven years I had not seen Joe or Biddy, though they had been often in my thoughts. One evening in December, an hour or two after dark, I opened the old kitchen door and looked in so quietly that no one heard me. There, smoking his pipe by the fire, as strong and well as ever though a little gray, sat Joe. And there sitting on my own little stool, looking at the fire was—I again!

"We giv' him the name of Pip for your sake, dear old chap," said Joe, delighted when I sat down by the child's side. "We hoped he might grow a little bit like you, and we think he does."

I thought so too. The next morning I took him for a walk, and we talked at length, understanding each other perfectly. We went down to the churchyard. I set him on a tombstone, and he showed me the stone sacred to the memory of Philip Pirrip and Georgiana his wife.

"Biddy," said I when I talked with her later, as her little girl laying sleeping on her lap, "you must lend Pip to me one of these days."

"No, no," said Biddy gently, "you must marry."

"So Herbert and Clara say, but I don't think I shall, Biddy. I've settled down in their home. I am already quite an old bachelor."

Biddy kissed her little child and then put her good strong hand in mine. "Dear Pip," she said, "are you sure you don't grieve for her?"

"Oh, no, I think not, Biddy."

"Tell me as an old friend. Have you entirely forgotten her?"

"I have forgotten nothing that was ever important in my life. But that poor dream, as I once used to call it, has gone forever."

Still, I knew even when I spoke, that I planned that evening to visit the place where the old house had once been for her sake. For Estella's sake.

I had heard that she had led a most unhappy life. She had separated from her husband, who had treated her cruelly. I had heard of the death of her husband. He had been killed by a horse which he had ill treated. This had happened two years before. For all I knew, she had married again.

After dinner that night I started out for the old place. I walked so slowly on the way, looking at familiar spots and remembering old times, that it was almost dark when I arrived. There was no house now, no brewery, no building whatever left but the wall of the old garden. The cleared space was enclosed with a rough fence. Looking over it, I saw that some of the old ivy was still growing among the ruins. I opened the gate in the fence and went in.

Stars were shining through a light, silvery mist. The moon was coming and the evening was not dark. I could see where every part of the old house had been. As I stood there looking at the ruins, I saw someone standing in the midst of them alone. Whoever it was had been moving toward me, but now stood still. As I drew nearer I saw that it was a woman. Suddenly I heard my name and cried out, "Estella!"

"I am greatly changed," she said. "I am surprised that you know me."

The freshness of her beauty was indeed gone, but dignity and great charm remained. In her once proud eyes there was a sad soft light. And her once cold hand touched mine with warm friendliness. We sat down on a bench and I said, "After so many years it is strange that we should meet again, Estella, where we met for the first time. Do you come here often?"

"I have never been here since."

"I haven't either."

The moon began to rise, and for some reason I thought of the last calm look on the face of my dear convict. I thought of his pressure on my hand when I spoke the last words he had heard on earth.

Estella broke the silence. "I have often hoped and intended to come back," she said, "but have been kept away by many things. Poor old place!"

The first rays of the moon shone on the silvery mist and on the tears that fell from her eyes. Now knowing that I saw them, she said quietly, "Were you wondering as you came along why the place had been left like this?"

"Yes, Estella."

"The land belongs to me. It is the only thing I have not given up. Everything has gone from me little by little, but I have kept this."

"Will something be built here?"

"At last there will be. I came here to say good-bye to it. And you," she said, "still live away from England?"

"I still do."

"And you are doing well, I'm sure?"

"I work hard. Yes, I am doing well."

"I have often thought of you," said Estella.

"Have you?"

"Very often lately. For a long time I wouldn't let myself realize what I had thrown away when I turned my back on you. Since the death of my husband, I have let myself think of you again."

"You have always kept your place in my heart," I answered.

"I never thought," said Estella, "that I would be saying good-bye to you, too, when I say good-bye to this place. I am glad it has happened so."

"Are you glad to part with me again, Estella? To me, parting is a painful thing. The thought of our last parting has always been sad."

"But you said to me, 'God bless you; God forgive you.' If you could say that to me then, you will surely say it to me now. Now suffering has been my teacher. It has taught me to understand how much you used to love me. I have been through terrible experiences—but I am a better woman for them. Be as gentle and as good to me as you were in the past and tell me we are friends."

"We are friends," said I, rising and bending over her.

"And will continue friends, though we are not together?" said Estella.

I took her hand in mine, and we went out of that ruined place. As the morning mists had risen long ago when I first left the forge, so the evening mists were rising now. In the peaceful light of the moon I felt sure that I would never part from her again.

REVIEWING YOUR READING

Part 1

CHAPTER 1

Finding the Main Idea
1. The purpose of this chapter is to
   a. tell that Pip is an orphan **b.** introduce Pip and the stranger
   c. tell Pip's real name   **d.** show where Pip lives

Remembering Detail
2. Pip promised to bring the food and file to
   a. the edge of the river   **b.** the churchyard   **c.** an oak tree
   d. the sea wall
3. Pip's uncle was a
   a. blacksmith   **b.** cook   **c.** farmer   **d.** convict

Drawing Conclusions
4. The stranger wanted the file in order to
   a. repair a wagon   **b.** cut the chain from his leg   **c.** help a
   friend escape from prison   **d.** break into Pip's house

Understanding the Tone
5. Which of the following best describes Pip's attitude toward the
   stranger?
   a. respect   **b.** hate   **c.** envy   **d.** fear

Logic and Deeper Meaning
6. When the stranger refers to himself as "a person such as me,"
   he means
   a. an escaped convict   **b.** an unhappy person   **c.** a hungry
   man   **d.** a thief

THINKING IT OVER
1. The stranger tells Pip about a horrible young man who is hiding? Do you think he exists? Explain.
2. Does the stranger himself actually threaten to harm Pip? What does this say about him?

CHAPTER 2

Finding the Main Idea

1. In this chapter, the author mostly tells about
   a. how Pip kept his promise to the stranger   **b.** the young man with the stranger   **c.** how Joe protected Pip from Mrs. Joe   **d.** how the stranger thanked Pip for the food and the file

Remembering Detail

2. What was Tickler?
   a. a mean dog   **b.** a stick   **c.** a whip   **d.** a pet cat
3. The ''medicine'' Mrs. Joe gave Pip and Joe was
   a. cod-liver oil   **b.** herb tea   **c.** tar water   **d.** cold tea
4. When Pip took brandy from a jug in the pantry, he
   a. replaced it with water   **b.** replaced it with beer   **c.** replaced it with some brown liquid   **d.** hid the jug behind the flour

Drawing Conclusions

5. You can tell from the story that Mrs. Joe
   a. is difficult to get along with   **b.** has many friends
   c. is strict but kindhearted   **d.** adores children
6. You can tell from the story that Joe
   a. did not like Pip   **b.** usually paid no attention to Pip
   c. got along well with Pip   **d.** tolerated Pip

Understanding the Tone

7. In this chapter, Pip feels all of the following *except*
   a. guilty   **b.** relaxed   **c.** afraid   **d.** sympathetic

Logic and Deeper Meaning

8. When Pip told the stranger he had seen another man who had ''the same reason for wanting to borrow a file,'' he meant
   a. an escaped convict   **b.** a murderer   **c.** a thief
   d. a hungry man

THINKING IT OVER

1. Compare Mrs. Joe and Joe. How does each one treat Pip?
2. Thinking about things early in the morning, Pip says, ''I had seen the mist on the outside of my little window as though a goblin had been crying there all night and using the window for a handkerchief.'' What picture does the misty window make for him? What mood does this picture create? Look for more references to mist as you read on in the book.

CHAPTER 3

Finding the Main Idea

1. In this chapter, the author is mostly interested in telling about
   a. how Pip's family celebrated Christmas   **b.** the guests at dinner   **c.** the events that occurred that Christmas day
   d. how Uncle Pumblechook got a surprise drink

Remembering Detail

2. The brandy had been mixed with
   a. water   **b.** tar water   **c.** gin   **d.** sugar
3. When Pip ran from the dinner table,
   a. Mrs. Joe ran after him   **b.** Joe went to find him   **c.** he ran into soldiers at the door   **d.** he ran into Mrs. Joe

Drawing Conclusions

4. Pip did not enjoy Christmas dinner because
   a. he had stolen some brandy and the pork pie
   b. Joe ignored him   **c.** the stranger had promised to appear
   d. everyone asked him questions

Understanding the Tone

5. You can tell from this chapter that Mrs. Joe felt Pip was
   a. a nuisance   **b.** smart   **c.** helpful   **d.** a thief

Logic and Deeper Meaning

6. When Pip says, "Whenever Mrs. Joe had gone into the pantry, fear and remorse had gripped me," he means that he felt afraid and
   a. guilty   **b.** angry   **c.** upset   **d.** unhappy

THINKING IT OVER

What does the Christmas dinner tell you about the characters of the adults present: Mrs. Joe, Mr. Pumblechook, Mrs. Hubble, and Joe? Explain.

CHAPTER 4

Remembering Detail

1. The soldiers who came to the door were looking for
   a. a criminal   **b.** Pip   **c.** the blacksmith
   d. something to eat

2. The soldiers wanted Joe to
   a. repair one of their guns   **b.** shoe the soldiers' horses
   c. fix the lock on a pair of handcuffs   **d.** be a lookout for
   possible criminals

Drawing Conclusions

3. Pip was upset when he heard what the soldiers planned because
   a. he felt sorry for his "friend" in the marshes   **b.** he knew
   his stealing would be discovered   **c.** Joe was in trouble
   d. the best dinner of the year had been interrupted
4. The two convicts
   a. were friends   **b.** wanted Pip to help them   **c.** were
   enemies   **d.** recognized Pip

Understanding the Tone

5. While the soldiers were in the house, everyone was
   a. relaxed   **b.** afraid   **c.** anxious   **d.** excited

Logic and Deeper Meaning

6. You can tell that Pip's convict wanted revenge on the other
   convict more than he wanted
   a. his own freedom   **b.** food   **c.** a gun   **d.** money

THINKING IT OVER

Why did Pip's convict tell the soldiers that he had stolen food from
the blacksmith? Explain your answer.

CHAPTER 5

Remembering Detail

1. It was planned that when Pip got older, he would
   a. leave home   **b.** become a soldier   **c.** be apprenticed to Joe
   d. go to school
2. Biddy helped Pip by
   a. giving him small jobs to do   **b.** teaching him to read and
   write   **c.** giving him money   **d.** making excuses for him at
   school

Drawing Conclusions

3. Mrs. Joe didn't want her husband to learn to read and write
   because
   a. she didn't know how to read and write, either   **b.** it would
   take too much time   **c.** he would make fun of her   **d.** it
   would make him too important

Logic and Deeper Meaning
4. Riding in Uncle Pumblechook's carriage, Pip had tears in his eyes for all the following reasons *except:*
   a. he was excited about being away from home   **b.** he was sad to be leaving Joe   **c.** soapsuds were burning his eyes
   d. he was happy about being with Uncle Pumblechook

THINKING IT OVER
In Pip's village, most children did not go to school. Do you think the attitude there toward education has changed from what it was, almost 130 years ago? Explain.

CHAPTER 6

Finding the Main Idea
1. This chapter is mostly about how Pip
   a. becomes angry at Estella   **b.** feels ashamed of being poor
   c. learns who Miss Havisham is   **d.** meets Estella

Remembering Detail
2. The girl who answered Miss Havisham's bell was
   a. shy   **b.** proud and self-assured   **c.** friendly and nice
   d. laughing and joking
3. Miss Havisham's bridal gown was
   a. yellow with age   **b.** covered with beads and lace   **c.** in perfect condition   **d.** draped over a chair

Drawing Conclusions
4. You can tell that Miss Havisham's heart had been broken
   a. by Uncle Pumblechook   **b.** recently   **c.** by Estella's uncle
   d. on her wedding day

Understanding the Tone
5. Estella made Pip feel
   a. happy   **b.** ashamed and angry   **c.** fortunate   **d.** sad

Logic and Deeper Meaning
6. When the author says that Estella laughed at Pip "scornfully," he means that she
   a. thought very little of him   **b.** thought he was funny
   c. liked him a lot   **d.** was relaxed with him around

THINKING IT OVER

1. Why does Pip make up stories about Miss Havisham? What would you have done?
2. After one visit to Miss Havisham's, Pip has changed. Describe the change.

CHAPTER 7

Finding the Main Idea

1. This chapter tells mostly about
   a. how Pip is reminded of the convict   **b.** Pip's relationship with Joe   **c.** Mrs. Joe's good mood   **d.** how the convict remained safe

Remembering Detail

2. The clue that the strange man at the Three Jolly Bargemen knew Pip's convict was
   a. a wink   **b.** his half-shut eye   **c.** the way he tilted his hat
   d. the file

Drawing Conclusions

3. The stranger did not tell anyone about the two one-pound notes because
   a. he thought they would be a nice surprise   **b.** they were counterfeit   **c.** he might be accused of stealing them
   d. he did not want Joe and Mr. Wopsle to be suspicious of who he was

Logic and Deeper Meaning

4. Pip's convict had sent the stranger to
   a. harm Pip   **b.** pay Pip back for helping him   **c.** meet Joe
   d. give Pip another job to do

THINKING IT OVER

Pip said that it gave him nightmares to think about the money in the teapot. Why?

CHAPTER 8

Remembering Detail

1. All the time pieces in Miss Havisham's house
   a. were slow   **b.** had stopped at the same time   **c.** were fast
   d. were set every night

2. Miss Havisham's relatives came
   a. on her birthday   **b.** on Estella's birthday   **c.** twice a year
   d. once a month

Drawing Conclusions

3. You can tell that Pip and the man on the stairs
   a. would always be enemies   **b.** had been friends   **c.** would
   meet again   **d.** had met before

Understanding the Tone

4. When Pip was at Miss Havisham's house, he felt
   a. relaxed   **b.** happy   **c.** uncomfortable   **d.** afraid

Logic and Deeper Meaning

5. Miss Havisham does not allow her birthday to be mentioned
   because
   a. she does not like being old   **b.** it was on her birthday that
   her heart was broken   **c.** she dislikes celebrations   **d.** she is
   embarrassed by gifts

THINKING IT OVER

Miss Havisham's relatives visit her for their own selfish reasons.
What do you think the author's attitude toward these people is? Explain. Why doesn't her cousin Matthew Pocket visit her?

CHAPTER 9

Remembering Detail

1. The premium Miss Havisham gave Joe for Pip was
   a. several chickens   **b.** five pounds   **c.** twenty-five guineas
2. Pip didn't tell anyone about Miss Havisham and Estella except
   a. Mr. Pumblechook   **b.** Joe and Mrs. Joe   **c.** Joe
   d. Biddy

Drawing Conclusions

3. When Miss Havisham told Pip it was time to be indentured to
   Joe, Pip's sister was disappointed because
   a. she thought Pip would be a terrible blacksmith   **b.** she was
   hoping Miss Havisham would make them rich   **c.** Pip liked going
   to Miss Havisham's   **d.** Joe didn't need an apprentice

Understanding the Tone

4. You can tell from the story that around Miss Havisham, Joe is
   a. uncomfortable   **b.** relaxed   **c.** excited   **d.** worried

Logic and Deeper Meaning

5. When Miss Havisham tells Estella to "Break their hearts and have no mercy," she is referring to

a. blacksmiths **(b.)** boys and men **c.** poor boys **d.** ignorant people

THINKING IT OVER

Why does Mr. Pumblechook think he deserves credit for any good fortune that comes to Pip? Do you agree with him? Explain.

CHAPTER 10

Remembering Detail

1. On his visit to Miss Havisham's, Pip discovered that
   a. Miss Havisham had changed **b.** Miss Havisham wouldn't see him **c.** Estella had gone away to school **d.** Estella still disliked him

2. Mrs. Joe was hit with
   a. a hammer from the forge **b.** a sharp instrument
   c. a strong man's fist **d.** something blunt and heavy

3. After her accident, Mrs. Joe
   a. had a worse temper **b.** was patient and sweet
   c. recognized no one **d.** was unpredictable

4. After the attack, Mrs. Joe was cared for by
   a. Joe's aunt **b.** Pip **c.** Biddy **d.** Mr. Wopsle's great aunt

Drawing Conclusions

5. Pip's real reason for going again to Miss Havisham's was to
   a. thank her for the gift she had given him **b.** see if she was well **c.** see Estella again **d.** ask for more money

6. Orlick didn't like Pip because
   a. he was afraid Pip might take his job someday **b.** Pip told Joe when Orlick wasn't working **c.** Pip made fun of him
   d. Pip had refused to teach him to read

7. Orlick's quarrel with Mrs. Joe was not held against him because
   a. it happened after she was hit **b.** they had laughed about it later **c.** she quarreled often with everyone **d.** he had apologized afterward

Understanding the Tone

8. You can tell that Joe is
    a. a gentleman, afraid to fight **b.** a gentle but very strong man **c.** a demanding master **d.** a man with a quick temper

THINKING IT OVER

Pip thought that Orlick might be guilty of attacking his sister. What evidence did he have? What motive would Orlick have had?

CHAPTER 11

Remembering Detail

1. Pip confided in Biddy that he
    a. always disliked his sister **b.** had given aid to the convict **c.** wanted to be a gentleman **d.** wanted to marry her
2. Every year on his birthday, Pip
    a. went back to the spot where he met the convict **b.** put his small earnings into a bank account **c.** wrote to Estella **d.** visited Miss Havisham
3. Biddy promised Pip that she
    a. would always be around if he needed her **b.** wouldn't tell anyone about his hopes **c.** would never marry Orlick **d.** would always care for Mrs. Joe

Drawing Conclusions

4. Pip was upset that
    a. Biddy understood him **b.** Biddy thought he was silly **c.** he cared more for Estella than for Biddy **d.** he had confided in Biddy

Understanding the Tone

5. Biddy feels that Pip should
    a. be content with his position in life **b.** get as far ahead as possible **c.** be more ambitious **d.** not learn any more

Logic and Deeper Meaning

6. The ship's sinking on the river represents
    a. an improved lifestyle **b.** a stormy life **c.** calmness **d.** freedom

THINKING IT OVER

How does the meaning of "gentleman" today differ from the meaning Pip gave it?

CHAPTER 12

Remembering Detail

1. The gentleman who came into the Three Jolly Bargemen looking for Pip was
   a. someone he didn't recognize   **b.** the man Pip had met on the stairs at Miss Havisham's   **c.** Mrs. Wopsle's brother
   d. Miss Havisham's relative, Raymond

2. Mr. Jaggers asked Joe's permission to
   a. hire Pip at a high salary   **b.** make Pip a lawyer   **c.** take Pip away and make him a gentleman   **d.** send Pip on a vacation

3. The name of the person who was providing the offer to Pip was
   a. not revealed   **b.** Mr. Jaggers himself   **c.** Miss Havisham
   d. Estella

Drawing Conclusions

4. Joe invited the stranger into the best parlor because
   a. the stranger was a gentleman   **b.** the stranger insisted on it
   c. Joe thought the stranger was going to give him money
   d. Mrs. Joe was in the kitchen

Understanding the Tone

5. When Joe heard about Pip's good fortune, he was *not*
   a. happy for Pip   **b.** angry that Pip was leaving   **c.** amazed at the money Pip received   **d.** sad to be separated from his friend

6. On the night he learned of his good fortune, Pip felt
   a. happier than ever   **b.** lonelier than ever   **c.** proud of himself   **d.** satisfied

Logic and Deeper Meaning

7. An agent is
   a. someone who acts for someone else   **b.** a spy   **c.** a salesperson   **d.** a hired hand

8. A benefactor is
   a. a kind person   **b.** a wealthy person **c.** someone who provides a gift, often of money   **d.** someone who knows you

THINKING IT OVER

1. Pip has to agree to several conditions before he can receive his new fortune. What do you think of these conditions? Would you have accepted them? Explain.
2. If you were given a lot of money, how would you react? Do you think it would change your character? Explain.

CHAPTER 13

Remembering Detail

1. When Joe put Pip's indentures in the fire, it meant that
   a. Pip had become a master blacksmith   **b.** Joe was happy Pip was leaving   **c.** Pip was completely free   **d.** Joe was angry

Drawing Conclusions

2. You can tell that Pip thought his benefactor was
   a. an unknown relative   **b.** Miss Havisham   **c.** Matthew Pocket   **d.** Mr. Jaggers
3. Mr. Trabb treated Pip well because
   a. Pip had a lot of money to spend   **b.** he had always liked Pip   **c.** Pip had always been a good customer   **d.** he and Joe were good friends
4. Pip thought of Miss Havisham as his "fairy godmother" because
   a. she had always been so nice to him   **b.** he thought she was his benefactor   **c.** she always wore a wedding dress   **d.** they had been good friends

Understanding the Tone

5. In his new clothes, Pip felt
   a. ridiculous   **b.** at ease   **c.** handsome   **d.** uncomfortable

THINKING IT OVER

Do you think it was wrong of Pip to treat Joe the way he did? Explain.

Part 2

CHAPTER 14

Remembering Detail

1. When Pip arrived at Mr. Jaggers's office, Jaggers was
   a. waiting for him **b.** having dinner out **c.** in court
   d. talking with a client

2. Mr. Wemmick was
   a. Mr. Jaggers's office clerk **b.** being defended by Mr. Jaggers **c.** a friend of Mr. Jaggers **d.** Mr. Jaggers's business partner

3. Pip had met Mr. Pocket, Junior, before
   a. in the church graveyard **b.** at the Three Jolly Bargemen
   c. out on the marshes **d.** at Miss Havisham's house

Drawing Conclusions

4. You can tell that Mr. Jaggers thinks Pip would
   a. spend too much money **b.** be careful with his money
   c. be a success **d.** end up in jail

Understanding the Tone

5. During his first few hours in London, Pip felt
   a. excited **b.** depressed **c.** happy **d.** relaxed

Logic and Deeper Meaning

6. A clerk is
   a. a priest or minister **b.** a policeman **c.** someone who manages a household **d.** someone who does office work

THINKING IT OVER

What does Jaggers's office and his method of dealing with people who come to see him tell you about him?

CHAPTER 15

Remembering Detail

1. Herbert's father was
   a. Miss Havisham's brother-in-law **b.** Mr. Jaggers's cousin
   c. Miss Havisham's cousin **d.** Miss Havisham's friend

2. Herbert decided to call Pip

a. Philip **b.** Handel **c.** Sir **d.** The Harmonious Blacksmith

3. Herbert was studying to be
a. an accountant **b.** a lawyer **c.** a shipbuilder **d.** an importer of sugar and tobacco

Drawing Conclusions

4. Miss Havisham's half brother plotted against her because
a. their father was stricter with him than with her **b.** she had always disliked him **c.** he didn't like the man she was going to marry **d.** he thought she had influenced their father against him

Logic and Deeper Meaning

5. Miss Havisham was raising Estella to get revenge on men because
a. her father treated her badly **b.** her mother taught her to hate men **c.** her half brother and her intended husband betrayed her **d.** she had always disliked men

THINKING IT OVER

Pip asked Herbert to teach him correct table manners. Why? Do you think the same table manners would be correct today? Explain.

CHAPTER 16

Remembering Detail

1. Which of the following did Pip find odd about the Pockets?
a. The Pockets' servants lived better than their masters.
b. Mrs. Pocket was disorganized. **c.** Mr. Pocket had several pupils. **d.** The Pockets were friendly.
2. Mr. Wemmick advised Pip to take a careful look at
a. Herbert's arm **b.** Mr. Jaggers's handwriting **c.** his collection of statues **d.** Mr. Jaggers's housekeeper
3. Matthew Pocket was well educated and
a. nasty **b.** proud **c.** poor **d.** useless

Drawing Conclusions

4. You can tell that Mr. Wemmick's attitude toward his boss was
a. indifference **b.** respect **c.** fear **d.** hatred

Logic and Deeper Meaning

5. When Wemmick refers to one of Jaggers's ex-clients as a "rogue," he means that the man is a

a. Greek scholar **b.** tricky businessman **c.** dishonest, mischievous person **d.** French soldier

THINKING IT OVER

Describe the education that Pip was to be given. How is this different from the way someone would be educated today?

CHAPTER 17

Remembering Detail

1. Mr. Wemmick lived in a

a. tiny "castle" **b.** huge apartment **c.** small townhouse **d.** one-room apartment

2. The Aged was

a. Mr. Wemmick's mother **b.** Wemmick's name for Miss Havisham **c.** an old woman who cooked for Wemmick **d.** Mr. Wemmick's father

3. Jaggers referred to Bentley Drummle as

a. the spider **b.** the worm **c.** Sir Drummle **d.** Mr. B.

4. Mrs. Jaggers's housekeeper, Molly,

a. walked with a limp **b.** was tall and clumsy **c.** had fiery eyes **d.** had exceptionally strong wrists

Drawing Conclusions

5. No thief would dare rob Mr. Jaggers because

a. his skill as a criminal lawyer was so great **b.** he owned a vicious watchdog **c.** he had the house guarded **d.** he had important friends

Understanding the Tone

6. At Mr. Jaggers's dinner party, everyone felt

a. somber **b.** lively **c.** tense **d.** depressed

THINKING IT OVER

Compare Mr. Wemmick's personality at the office with his personality at home. Which one appeals to you more? Explain.

CHAPTER 18

Remembering Detail

1. Whom was Pip ashamed to have Joe meet?
a. all his friends **b.** Bentley Drummle **c.** Herbert **d.** Mr. Wemmick

Drawing Conclusions

2. Pip was glad that Herbert called him Handel when he said good-bye because
a. Pip did not sound like the name of a gentleman **b.** Handel was the name he had given to the driver **c.** he didn't want to be recognized on the coach **d.** he was afraid the convicts might ask about him in his village

3. Joe came to see Pip in order to
a. show him that he had advanced in learning **b.** see if they could still be friends **c.** tell him Estella wanted to see him at Miss Havisham's **d.** tell him news of home

Logic and Deeper Meaning

4. Pip decided to stay at the Blue Boar because
a. there was no room for him at Joe's **b.** Joe would not want him to stay at his place **c.** Biddy didn't want to see him
d. he knew he would be uncomfortable around Joe

THINKING IT OVER

Pip has changed since he came to London. Do you like the "old" Pip or the "new" Pip better? Explain your answer.

CHAPTER 19

Remembering Detail

1. Pip thought it was Miss Havisham's plan to
a. ask Pip to take her shopping **b.** set Pip up in business
c. give Pip and Herbert money **d.** bring Pip and Estella together

2. Pip knew that Estella would
a. not make him happy **b.** nevery marry him **c.** make him very happy **d.** never leave him

3. Estella told Pip that she
   a. had never loved anybody   **b.** loved him   **c.** wished she loved him   **d.** loved another man
4. Miss Havisham wanted Pip to
   a. leave Estella alone   **b.** ask Estella to marry him   **c.** visit Estella once a year   **d.** love Estella

Drawing Conclusions

5. Pip decided not to visit Joe because
   a. Joe had not invited him   **b.** it was too far to go   **c.** Estella would have disapproved   **d.** Miss Havisham told him not to

Understanding the Tone

6. When he thought about his love for Estella, Pip felt
   a. miserable   **b.** confident   **c.** content   **d.** angry

Logic and Deeper Meaning

7. Pip asked Jaggers what Estella's last name was because
   a. he wanted to send her letters   **b.** he wanted to confirm what Estella had told him   **c.** Miss Havisham had told him to ask   **d.** Estella reminded him of someone he had seen

THINKING IT OVER

In what ways has Estella changed in the years she and Pip have been separated? How is she still the same? Why does Pip feel both happy and sad about seeing her?

CHAPTER 20

Remembering Detail

1. Mr. Jaggers would defend only those prisoners
   a. whom he believed to be innocent   **b.** who paid him well   **c.** whom he liked   **d.** who were intelligent
2. Estella came to London on her way to
   a. Richmond   **b.** France   **c.** Hammersmith   **d.** Miss Havisham's

Drawing Conclusions

3. At this point in the story, Pip is
   a. about 25   **b.** almost 21   **c.** just 18   **d.** just 21
4. Estella and Pip felt that Jaggers
   a. knew very little except about criminal law   **b.** was very direct   **c.** talked too much   **d.** knew secrets about them

Understanding the Tone

5. Toward Pip, Estella felt

    a. indifferent   **b.** loving   **c.** friendly   **d.** mean

THINKING IT OVER

Pip is always miserable when he is with Estella. Why does he continue to see her? Do you agree with him? Explain.

CHAPTER 21

Remembering Detail

1. Biddy told Pip she would like to

    a. get a job as a teacher   **b.** marry him   **c.** go away to London   **d.** work for Miss Havisham

Drawing Conclusions

2. Pip acted coldly toward Biddy because she

    a. had not treated Mrs. Joe well   **b.** didn't believe he would visit Joe often   **c.** knew Orlick   **d.** asked him about Estella

3. Pip and Herbert joined a club that

    a. they couldn't afford   **b.** all their friends belonged to **c.** they enjoyed going to   **d.** they need for business

Understanding the Tone

4. Toward Orlick, Pip felt only

    a. hatred   **b.** indifference   **c.** friendship   **d.** sympathy

Logic and Deeper Meaning

5. Pip felt his expectations were

    a. just what he had always hoped for   **b.** better than he had wished   **c.** making his life miserable   **d.** getting him nowhere

THINKING IT OVER

Biddy seems to be wiser and more mature than Pip, even though they are the same age. Do you agree? Why or why not?

CHAPTER 22

Remembering Detail

1. Now that he was 21, Pip was to receive each year

    a. five hundred dollars   **b.** as much money as he wished **c.** five hundred pounds   **d.** five thousand pounds

2. Jaggers refused to give any information about
   a. how he knew Miss Havisham   **b.** his housekeeper   **c.** who his clients were   **d.** the identity of Pip's benefactor
3. Pip wanted to use some of his money to
   a. get Herbert established in business   **b.** buy a ring for Estella   **c.** hire a detective to find out the identity of his benefactor   **d.** open a business of his own

Drawing Conclusions

4. Pip hoped that on his 21st birthday he would
   a. find out the name of his benefactor   **b.** marry Estella   **c.** be taken out to dinner   **d.** receive a country estate
5. Pip told Jaggers he had no idea how much money he was spending because
   a. he was afraid Jaggers would tell Estella   **b.** he really didn't know   **c.** the truth would have been embarrassing   **d.** he was afraid Jaggers would blame Herbert

THINKING IT OVER

What new information does Jaggers give Pip about his benefactor? Does this add to the mysteriousness of that person? Does it add suspense to the story? Explain.

CHAPTER 23

Remembering Detail

1. Mrs. Brandley was
   a. Estella's aunt   **b.** an old friend of Miss Havisham's   **c.** Miss Havisham's former secretary   **d.** Mr. Jaggers's sister-in-law

Drawing Conclusions

2. Estella believed she couldn't love anybody because
   a. she would be hurt   **b.** Miss Havisham would disapprove   **c.** she had never been loved as a child   **d.** that would be giving in to Pip

3. Pip was upset because Estella
a. was in love with Bentley Drummle **b.** did not tell Bentley Drummle to leave her alone **c.** danced with Bentley Drummle **d.** left a party with Bentley Drummle

Understanding the Tone
4. At Miss Havisham's, Pip felt
a. sad **b.** at peace **c.** afraid **d.** full of courage

THINKING IT OVER
When he visited Miss Havisham with Estella, Pip thought that "the shadow of the dark and unhealthy house was on all of us." What do you think he meant?

CHAPTER 24

Finding the Main Idea
1. The chapter tells mostly
a. what Pip did during the storm **b.** how Pip learned the identity of his benefactor **c.** how Pip entertained his guest **d.** what Pip's new lodgings were like

Remembering Detail
2. Pip's guest had traveled from
a. Australia **b.** Marseilles **c.** Austria **d.** the north of England
3. When Pip gave the stranger the two one-pound notes, he
a. put them in his pocket **b.** returned them to Pip **c.** burned them **d.** threw them on the floor

Drawing Conclusions
4. When he learned the identity of his benefactor, Pip was
a. not surprised **b.** relieved **c.** shocked **d.** happy

Understanding the Tone
5. The feeling Pip had for his overnight guest was
a. admiration **b.** fear **c.** affection **d.** indifference
6. The feeling Pip's guest had for him was
a. pride **b.** hatred **c.** anger **d.** wonder

Logic and Deeper Meaning

7. When Pip "shuddered at the thought that . . . [his guest's hand] might be stained with blood," he meant that
   a. the hand might actually have blood on it   **b.** his guest was thinking of killing him   **c.** his guest might have killed someone   **d.** his guest was not clean

8. When Pip thinks of "the ship in which I sailed" going to pieces, he is referring to
   a. the little boat he owns   **b.** all his money being spent
   c. the ship his visitor arrived on   **d.** the expectations he had for his life

THINKING IT OVER

1. Why does Pip react so strongly to the news he receives about the identity of his benefactor? If you were he, how would you have reacted?

2. There have been many hints in the book so far about the identity of Pip's benefactor. Tell what some of them are.

Part 3

CHAPTER 25

Remembering Detail

1. What or whom did Pip stumble over on the stairs?
   a. the watchman   **b.** a broken bottle   **c.** a strange man
   d. a lantern
2. Mr. Provis was the
   a. stranger's real name   **b.** name the stranger had taken on his
   voyage   **c.** name Pip made up for the stranger   **d.** name of
   Pip's uncle who had died
3. Abel Magwitch was
   a. the stranger's real name   **b.** a friend of Mr. Jaggers's
   c. the name Pip gave the stranger   **d.** the name the stranger
   made up for himself

Drawing Conclusions

4. Pip was afraid that the stranger
   a. had been followed to his rooms   **b.** had brought someone
   with him   **c.** would kill him   **d.** would not like Herbert
5. The stranger tried to reassure Pip that
   a. he was wealthy   **b.** he could hide his real identity
   c. Mr. Jaggers would take care of everything   **d.** no one had
   followed him

Understanding the Tone

6. When he watched the stranger eat, Pip felt
   a. disgusted   **b.** like laughing   **c.** comfortable   **d.** sad

THINKING IT OVER

How does Pip feel about his uninvited guest? How would you feel?
Do you think Pip is being fair? What do his feelings tell you about
Pip's character?

CHAPTER 26

Finding the Main Idea

1. This chapter is mostly about
   a. Miss Havisham and her brother   **b.** the convict's past
   c. getting the convict out of England   **d.** Herbert's plan

Remembering Detail

2. Pip and Herbert decided that Mr. Provis must
   a. be given to the police   **b.** be taken out of England   **c.** see Mr. Jaggers   **d.** stay hidden in their rooms

Drawing Conclusions

3. The stranger was sent away from England for life because he was found guilty of
   a. trying to murder Compeyson   **b.** murdering Compeyson
   c. counterfeiting and stealing   **d.** escaping from a prison ship

Logic and Deeper Meaning

4. The stranger wanted to kill Compeyson because
   a. Compeyson had stolen everything from him
   b. Compeyson had made him his slave   **c.** he wouldn't help Arthur when he was sick   **d.** Compeyson and his lawyer had blamed him for Compeyson's crimes

THINKING IT OVER

1. How did it happen that Provis became a criminal? Do you think he is to blame for the life he led? Explain.
2. There is a connection between the convict's story and Miss Havisham. How do they relate?

CHAPTER 27

Finding the Main Idea

1. This chapter is mostly about
   a. Estella and Pip   **b.** Pip and Bentley Drummle   **c.** Pip and Herbert   **d.** Miss Havisham and Estella

Remembering Detail

2. Pip asked Miss Havisham to
   a. use some of her money to help Herbert   **b.** ask Estella to change her mind about her marriage   **c.** keep the secret of who his benefactor was   **d.** give him some money
3. The note the night watchman gave Pip told him
   a. to see Herbert as quickly as possible   **b.** to beware of a dangerous criminal   **c.** not to go home   **d.** to see Wemmick at once

Drawing Conclusions

4. Estella wouldn't marry Pip because she felt
   a. he didn't love her enough   b. she was not capable of love
   c. he wasn't good enough for her   d. Miss Havisham would
   not approve

Understanding the Tone

5. The feelings Pip and Miss Havisham understood but Estella did
   not were
   a. hatred and jealousy   b. friendship and loyalty   c. love and
   rejection   d. happiness and joy

THINKING IT OVER

Miss Havisham had let Pip think she was his benefactor. Do you
think she was wrong to lead him on? Explain.

CHAPTER 28

Finding the Main Idea

1. The chapter tells mostly why
   a. Wemmick lived at the castle   b. it was necessary to hide
   Mr. Provis   c. Pip liked Wemmick   d. Mr. Provis came to
   London

Remembering Detail

2. Herbert took Mr. Provis to stay with
   a. Mr. Wemmick   b. Mr. Jaggers   c. Clara and her
   father   d. Joe

Drawing Conclusions

3. Pip stayed overnight at an inn because
   a. he didn't want to go home   b. Herbert had warned him not
   to go home   c. Wemmick sent a note telling him not to go
   home   d. bad weather prevented him from getting home

Logic and Deeper Meaning

4. Pip went to Wemmick's castle instead of his office because
   a. the office was too far   b. he did not want to see Mr.
   Jaggers   c. Wemmick felt freer to talk at home   d. he hoped
   to stay with Wemmick

THINKING IT OVER

What was Herbert's plan for Mr. Provis's safety? What did Wemmick think of it? What advice did Wemmick give to Pip concerning the matter? What do you think of the plan?

CHAPTER 29

Remembering Detail

1. When Provis pulled down his shade, it was a signal that
   a. he needed to talk to Pip   **b.** everything was all right with him   **c.** there was danger   **d.** it was time to leave the country
2. Mr. Campbell was
   a. the name of Clara's father   **b.** the name of the landlady's husband   **c.** the name of Herbert's best friend   **d.** Mr. Provis's name in his new lodgings

Drawing Conclusions

3. Pip was afraid because he realized that
   a. Compeyson was following him   **b.** Mr. Provis was running out of money   **c.** he couldn't trust anyone   **d.** Mr. Provis had left his lodgings

Understanding the Tone

4. In his new lodgings, Mr. Provis was
   a. afraid   **b.** content   **c.** upset   **d.** nervous

THINKING IT OVER

1. How have Pip's feelings for Provis changed? How can you tell?
2. Pip was getting deeper into debt but did not want to ask for more money. Do you agree with him? Explain.

CHAPTER 30

Finding the Main Idea

1. This chapter is mostly about
   a. Molly's secret past   **b.** Mr. Jaggers's legal skill   **c.** Mr. Jaggers's home life   **d.** Molly's family

Remembering Detail

2. Pip realized that Mr. Jaggers's housekeeper, Molly, was
   a. Estella's mother **b.** Mr. Provis's wife **c.** Wemmick's sister **d.** Compeyson's wife

Drawing Conclusions

3. Molly worked for Mr. Jaggers because
   a. her mother had worked for his family **b.** she was in love with him **c.** he had defended her in a murder trial **d.** it was an easy job

Understanding the Tone

4. At Mr. Jaggers's house, Wemmick felt
   a. at home **b.** on edge **c.** comfortable **d.** sad

Logic and Deeper Meaning

5. When Jaggers says, "our friend the Spider had played his cards and won the prize," he means that
   a. Bentley Drummle received money from Miss Havisham
   b. Estella married Bentley Drummle **c.** Bentley Drummle won a boxing match **d.** Drummle would beat his wife

THINKING IT OVER

Why has Mr. Jaggers's handling of the trial of his housekeeper given him an outstanding reputation in his profession?

CHAPTER 31

Finding the Main Idea

1. This chapter is mostly about
   a. Miss Havisham and Herbert **b.** Estella and Miss Havisham **c.** Pip and Estella **d.** Pip and Miss Havisham

Remembering Detail

2. To help Herbert, Pip asked Miss Havisham
   a. to change her will **b.** for nine hundred pounds **c.** for nine hundred pounds a year **d.** to reopen the brewery

ving Conclusions

Miss Havisham was upset because
Pip had asked her to help Herbert **b.** Estella was married
she had raised Estella to be heartless **d.** Pip would not
anything for himself

Understanding the Tone

4. The feeling Miss Havisham had for Pip was
   a. distrust **b.** sympathy **c.** disgust **d.** love
5. The feeling Pip had for Miss Havisham was
   a. love **b.** admiration **c.** indifference **d.** pity

THINKING IT OVER

1. Do you think Pip was justified in asking Miss Havisham to help Herbert? Explain.
2. What made Miss Havisham change her mind about Pip? Do you think it is too late? Explain.

CHAPTER 32

Finding the Main Idea

1. This chapter is mainly about
   a. Herbert and Provis **b.** Provis and his wife **c.** Jaggers and Wemmick **d.** Compeyson and Provis

Remembering Detail

2. Provis told Herbert his wife had been tried for
   a. sending away her daughter **b.** murdering her daughter
   c. killing a man with her hands **d.** choking to death a stronger woman

Drawing Conclusions

3. Pip figured out that Provis's wife was
   a. Jaggers's housekeeper **b.** Miss Havisham's cousin
   c. Wemmick's friend **d.** Clara's mother
4. You can tell that Mr. Jaggers and Wemmick never discussed
   a. the cases they worked on **b.** Pip **c.** their home liv⌐
   d. world events

Logic and Deeper Meaning

5. Provis did not want to testify at his wife'⌐
   a. he thought she had killed their da⌐
   her kill someone **c.** she had thr⌐
   was afraid he would be tried ⌐

THINKING IT OVER

1. Provis told Herbert that when he s⌐

was reminded of his own lost child. How does this information help explain Provis's later dealings with Pip?

2. What information did Pip have that surprised Jaggers? Why did Jaggers try to hide his surprise?

CHAPTER 33

Remembering Detail

1. The unsigned letter asked Pip to
   a. leave by Wednesday **b.** send money for Herbert **c.** get a passport **d.** come to the old marshes
2. Orlick admitted that he had
   a. tried to kill Pip's sister **b.** killed Estella **c.** tried to turn Joe against Pip **d.** tried to kill Pip several times

Drawing Conclusions

3. Wemmick sent a note to Pip warning him to
   a. watch out for Herbert **b.** move Provis into his own rooms **c.** take Provis out of England **d.** visit Miss Havisham's by Wednesday
4. Pip went to the marshes because
   a. it was a chance to stop in to see Miss Havisham **b.** he was looking for adventure **c.** he was concerned about Provis's safety **d.** he thought Wemmick might be there

Understanding the Tone

5. Pip was ashamed of the way
   a. he treated Joe and Biddy **b.** Herbert treated Clara **c.** he treated Herbert **d.** he dressed

THINKING IT OVER

1. In this chapter there are more clues about the change in Pip's attitude toward Provis, Joe, and Biddy. How has he changed? What clues are there?
2. Were you surprised by who was waiting for Pip at the limekiln? If not, what clues did you have? If you were surprised, how do you think the author built the surprise?

CHAPTER 34

Remembering Detail

1. Pip planned to leave England with Provis
   a. in their own sailboat   **b.** by rowing across the English Channel   **c.** on a ferry boat   **d.** by rowing down the river to meet a steamer

Drawing Conclusions

2. At the inn Pip felt threatened because
   a. he did not trust the innkeeper   **b.** there were men on the river looking for someone   **c.** someone had been following them since they left London   **d.** there were two soldiers staying there

3. How was Provis injured?
   a. He was hit by the steamer while fighting with Compeyson.
   b. Compeyson stabbed him during a fight.   **c.** He was shot by a soldier while trying to escape.   **d.** He was thrown against rocks by the water current.

4. Pip realized that with Provis's arrest he
   a. would be free at last   **b.** would be wealthy   **c.** would get no more of Provis's money   **d.** would have to live in Australia

Understanding the Tone

5. On the river the least anxious of the four men was
   a. Provis   **b.** Herbert   **c.** Pip   **d.** Startop

6. Toward Provis, Pip felt
   a. affection   **b.** disgust   **c.** indifference   **d.** surprise

THINKING IT OVER

Provis told Pip that he had returned to England understanding the chance he was taking, in order to see Pip, a gentleman. Why do you think that Provis made that decision? What would you have done in his place?

CHAPTER 35

Finding the Main Idea

1. This chapter is mostly about
   a. Jaggers and Wemmick   **b.** Magwitch's money
   c. Wemmick's social side   **d.** Herbert's job

Remembering Detail

2. According to Jaggers, Magwitch's case was
   a. hopeless **b.** a good one **c.** strong **d.** uncertain
3. Herbert was going to work in
   a. Cairo **b.** India **c.** London **d.** the country

Drawing Conclusions

4. Wemmick wanted Pip to keep the wedding a secret because he
   a. wanted Jaggers to think he was tough **b.** had another girl-friend **c.** was embarrassed **d.** hadn't invited Jaggers to the wedding

THINKING IT OVER

1. Why do you think Wemmick didn't just tell Pip he was getting married instead of inventing excuses for taking a walk?
2. Do you agree with Jaggers and Wemmick that Pip had been foolish in not trying to secure Magwitch's money? Explain.

CHAPTER 36

Remembering Detail

1. Because he returned to England from exile, Magwitch
   a. was sentenced to death **b.** was considered a hero **c.** had no friends **d.** escaped justice

Drawing Conclusions

2. As a prisoner, Magwitch
   a. never complained **b.** acted violently **c.** never said a word **d.** asked a lot of questions

Understanding the Tone

3. When Pip told Magwitch about his daughter, Magwitch looked
   a. upset **b.** at peace **c.** surprised **d.** excited

THINKING IT OVER

1. Based on this story, what is your opinion of the criminal justice system in England in the middle of the nineteenth century? How is it like the justice system of the United States today? How is it different? Explain
2. Why, do you think, did Pip give Magwitch the news of his daughter just as he was dying? Why do you think he hadn't told him before?

CHAPTER 37

Finding the Main Idea

1. This chapter tells mostly about
   a. Miss Havisham's will   **b.** Pip's illness   **c.** Joe and Biddy
   d. Orlick's crime

Remembering Detail

2. When Pip was ill, the person who came to help him was
   a. Herbert   **b.** Joe   **c.** Biddy   **d.** Wemmick
3. In her will, Miss Havisham left four thousand pounds to
   a. Matthew Pocket   **b.** Pip   **c.** Joe   **d.** Herbert Pocket

Drawing Conclusions

4. Orlick was in jail because he
   a. tried to kill Pip   **b.** robbed Miss Havisham   **c.** broke into
   Pumblechook's   **d.** robbed Estella
5. Pip didn't want Joe to know how poor he was because
   a. he knew Joe had plans for spending the money   **b.** he was
   afraid Joe would tell Biddy   **c.** Joe might make fun of him
   d. he didn't want Joe to give him money

Understanding the Tone

6. Watching Joe write made Pip feel
   a. jealous   **b.** proud   **c.** happy   **d.** upset

THINKING IT OVER

Once when they were out walking, Joe called Pip "Sir," and Pip
said that he was hurt by it. Why do you think he was hurt by the
remark?

CHAPTER 38

Remembering Detail

1. When Pip arrived at Joe's house, he discovered that
   a. Joe had left **b.** Joe and Biddy had just gotten married
   c. Biddy had had an accident **d.** everything was just as he
   had left it
2. Pip asked Joe and Biddy for
   a. money to pay his debts **b.** understanding **c.** forgiveness
   d. some food

Drawing Conclusions

3. Pip was given a back room at the Blue Boar because
   a. the innkeeper had heard of his loss of fortune **b.** all the
   other rooms were full **c.** he looked tired **d.** he asked for it
   especially
4. Pumblechook still believed that he was responsible for
   a. Miss Havisham's being wealthy **b.** giving Orlick a job
   c. making Pip well **d.** Pip's good fortune

Understanding the Tone

5. When Pip saw Joe and Biddy, he was
   a. overjoyed **b.** angry **c.** surprised **d.** sad

THINKING IT OVER

Compare the times Pip left Joe to go to London for the first time with
his leaving Joe and Biddy to begin his new job in Egypt.

CHAPTER 39

Finding the Main Idea

1. This chapter is mostly about
   a. the feelings of Pip and Estella   **b.** Pips's business success
   c. Biddy and Joe's family life   **d.** Estella's marriage

Remembering Detail

2. How many children did Biddy and Joe have?
   a. a boy   **b.** a boy and a girl   **c.** two boys   **d.** a girl
3. Pip came back to visit Joe and Biddy
   a. after eleven years   **b.** every Christmas   **c.** twice a year
   d. after seven years

Drawing Conclusions

4. Estella's character had changed as a result of
   a. Miss Havisham's death   **b.** the terrible marriage she had
   had   **c.** her education   **d.** seeing Pip suffer

THINKING IT OVER

1. At the end of the book, the author describes the rising mists.
   What is the reason for this, do you think? What do they
   symbolize?
2. Were you surprised by the ending of the book? Explain.